COMPOSING WHILE
Dancing

COMPOSING WHILE
Dancing

An Improviser's Companion

MELINDA BUCKWALTER

THE UNIVERSITY OF WISCONSIN PRESS

Publication of this volume has been made possible, in part, through
support from the **Anonymous Fund of the College of Letters and Science**
at the University of Wisconsin–Madison.

The University of Wisconsin Press
1930 Monroe Street, 3rd Floor
Madison, Wisconsin 53711-2059
uwpress.wisc.edu

3 Henrietta Street
London WC2E 8LU, England
eurospanbookstore.com

5   4   3   2   1

Printed in the United States of America

Library of Congress Cataloging-in-Publication Data
Buckwalter, Melinda.
    Composing while dancing: an improviser's companion / Melinda Buckwalter.
        p.   cm.
Includes bibliographical references and index.
ISBN 978-0-299-24814-7 (pbk.: alk. paper) — ISBN 978-0-299-24813-0 (e-book)
1. Improvisation in dance. I. Title.
GV1781.2.B83   2010
792.8—dc22
2010011572

TO THE EDITORS WITH APPRECIATION:

Lisa Nelson and Nancy Stark Smith for providing thirty-five-plus years of *Contact Quarterly*, the dance and improvisation journal, and for the incredible education; Nancy Allison for her encouragement and enthusiasm; the University of Wisconsin Press editorial staff; John Selfridge for his unwavering support; and my mother, Renée Buckwalter, for pointing out that words were something that could be loved.

Something will shine through the body if you give it a chance.

—SUZANNE VEGA, "Priscilla"

Contents

Illustrations

Acknowledgments

I would like to acknowledge the artists, first, for their many years of dedicated work and for articulating such amazing ideas through the medium of the body and movement—and then, for their patience in conversing with me and redirecting me where I went astray in conveying that magic. The editing process has been a most educative one.

I would also like to acknowledge the photographers who have donated their work here, making the dance come to life: Bill Arnold, Stephen Aubuchon, Bob Braines, Nancy Campbell, Fred Covarrubias Jr., Carolyn DeMers, Rita Fazakas, Lona Foote, August Goulet, Malgorzata Haduch, Paul Kyle, Raymond Mallentjer, Dona Ann McAdams, Dominik Mentzos, Ilya Noé, Stephen Petegorsky, Theo Robinson, Ben Topf, and Carl Yamamoto.

I couldn't have completed the book without the help of many readers, proxies, and reporters: Peentz Dubble (Richard Bull); Bonnie Eldred (Katie Duck); Penny Campbell, Lisa Nelson, and Susan Sgorbati (Judith Dunn); Helen Pickett (William Forsythe); Pamela Matt (Ideokinesis and Anatomical Release Technique); John Solt (Kazuo Ohno); Stephanie Skura (Joan Skinner); Susan Bauer, Diane Butler, and Margit Galanter (Suprapto Suryodarmo); Dana Iova-Koga, Kazue Kobata, Melinda Ring, Roxanne Steinberg (Min Tanaka); and Jen Harmon (Nancy Topf).

Thanks to Nancy Stark Smith and *Contact Quarterly* for their help obtaining images, to Karen Schaffman for advice and encouragement, to Barbara Dilley and Miriam Zoll for an early draft read, and to Margit Galanter for an early draft read, consultation, and for sharing her vision, insight, and body knowledge on the topic over our years of friendship. Special thanks to Lisa Nelson for her draft reads, editorial feedback, advice, and inspiration during several stages of the book's creation. Thanks to Ann Cooper Albright for a critical read through as well as to Paul Langland, Andrea Olsen, and the other anonymous reviewers who gave constructive feedback on the project. Where would I be without my dance buddies, with whom I have danced, viewed, created, debated, and formulated—particularly my friend Jen Harmon, who read and indeed lived through many of the scenarios I mention in the field notes at the end of every chapter. Thanks to Loré Mitra, my godmother, who introduced me to the mysterious dualities of life and reviewed the enneagram in Living Backward. Also, many thanks to Pooh Kaye for consultation on the subject matter and for lending her design savvy eyes in the image selection process.

Thanks to Nancy Allison and Dance & Movement Press for initiating the project and for allowing me to improvise along the way. Without her foresight, encouragement, and support this book would not exist. Thanks for personal and editorial support to John Selfridge, who gave advice and editing help when dance jargon was gibberish and who puts up with being a "dance widower" more often than I might like to acknowledge. And finally, thanks to a loyal friend, my chocolate Labrador, Nellie, for accompanying me through grad school and patiently indulging my improvisational forays off the path during our walks through the woods.

COMPOSING WHILE
Dancing

Judith Dunn's The Dance Company performing during a residency in conjunction with the Smithsonian Institute at the American University in Washington, D.C. (1973 or 1974). *From left*: Barbara Ensley, Judith Dunn, Cheryl (Niederman) Lilienstein, Penny (Larrison) Campbell. Photo courtesy Penny Campbell

Introduction

There Is Room for You

A dance disappears as you see it. A movie of a dance is a dream. A description of a dance is just that. The nature of dance includes impermanence. This is both an opportunity and a problem.

—JUDITH DUNN, "We Don't Talk about It, We Engage in It"

I F A DANCE IS EPHEMERAL, at least it is repeatable, but an improvised dance has the possibility of changing from moment to moment and that makes it difficult to talk or write about. As a viewer, you can say what it is you just saw, but in improvisation it will be different the next time around. How will it be different, and what remains the same? Improvisation is more about the thrill that comes from *not knowing* what it will be in the next moment or the next time. That dare is its lure.

The danger of attempting to capture something of improvisation's essence and place it on the page is that to capture it is to stop it from being the thing that it is—changeable. And yet many artists have written specifically and inspiringly about how they use improvisation in their dance-making, about their improvisational process, methods, and works. (See the bibliography.) However, these artists' approaches are so varied that it is hard for an emerging dancemaker to get a feel for the field, to find a place in it. With limited exposure, it may even seem there is a *right* way to improvise. But that is ultimately absurd in an improvisation, where choice and possibility reign. Among so many individual ways, the questions become "What is my way? How do I find my place in a field where the only thing to hold onto is a process—a way of finding something?"

This book collects a range of practices, sorts approaches, and compares language, to shed light on the field of contemporary dance improvisation itself. For in comparing items of a collection, something of the nature of

3

those items as a group may be inferred, revealed; in a collection of shells, for example, something of shellness may be understood. Yet beware! They might just as easily remain dried calcium on the beach rather than breathing mollusks on the sea bottom. . . . Reading and imagining can lead to very different conclusions about a subject than holding it in your hands or doing it, trying it out, following a trail of trial and error to learn about it through experience. And improvisation is about just that, the experience of moving and not knowing, finding the next thing, and learning about what is becoming in the process. The shells in this book are there to lure you into practice. The purpose, dancing and finding your own way—improvising.

This book was researched with my body. As much as possible, I studied with the improvisers whose work (both performance works and methodologies or improvisation practices) I speak of. Otherwise, I studied with dancers who worked directly with them. If I couldn't get to a live performance, I watched it on video. Often my interest in a particular dancemaker was piqued through an article I read. Whatever writings, conversations, and email interactions I had access to, I considered. I incorporated the practices I studied into my own studio work, and while writing I refreshed my body memory of them through practice. When possible, the artists or their representatives reviewed my writing, contributing exercises or scores. My local dance culture (with whom my colleagues had studied and recommended), my particular interests, and the publications I read partly determined the people with whom I thought to study. The dancemakers included here are not an exhaustive list of those working in the field of improvisation by any means; the selection represents the web of my relatively local activities, mostly confined to the East coast of the United States. (See another non-exhaustive list of additional contributors to the field in the glossary.) My selections represent only specific cross-sections of the artists' work.

Body research takes lots of time. But I took the time because the idea that written or even video research of artists could replace physical experience seemed completely out of the question. Though my need to research with my body necessarily limited the scope of this book, in the end, I believe there is such diversity in the works—even amongst the small group of artists that I had access to—that there are plenty of examples to whet your appetite for working improvisationally.

For that is the idea of this book—to offer ideas to help you figure out how you might make your own improvised dances. If you aren't already, start improvising! As you begin to do so and discover what excites you—what questions, issues, and problems arise for you—you may see these examples of practices in a different light. Perhaps you will uncover more possibilities than you first suspected.

Let your own experience guide you. Use this book as a compass, as your companion. The information here can give you footholds in developing your own processes and practices. Follow your nose into whatever sparks your interest. Play with the materials presented here; make your own studies from them, because of them. Even if you react against a particular way of working, you can use *that* as a guide to make the work you *like*. The main objective here is to get to the dancing, not to find the best way to improvise. There is none, or—even better—there are too many!

THE GREAT BREAK INTO A MILLION PIECES

> Because this piece of John Jasperse and Juliette Mapp and a solo of mine are both improvised, the [viewers'] lens fogs over and the most significant identifying characteristics are ignored. I do not like it when someone quotes from a book on improvisation by Ruth Zaporah [creator of Action Theater] and feels they are talking about Contact Improvisation. The sense of ignorance [regarding improvisational dance performance] is overwhelming. I get a whiff of this in the article by Cyrus Khambatta—"The Great Divide." I would rather: "The Great Break into a Million Pieces."
>
> —DANIEL LEPKOFF, in an e-mail volley with Steve Paxton

Dancemaker Daniel Lepkoff's concern noted here is that the division of dance into two camps, improvisation on one hand and choreography on the other, is overly simplistic and, as a filter, puts a haze in front of the actual work that is being seen.[1] Lepkoff comments that Juliette Mapp and John Jasperse's movement language appears to arise from a distinctly different physical technique than his own. "A physical technique embodies a point of view, an aesthetic." His concern is that a truly significant and visible difference in two artists' way of moving might be overlooked if one's view is limited by the idea that all improvisers are doing the same thing—"just improvising."[2]

Lepkoff shifts the discussion from schism to prism with his "million pieces" metaphor. He continues, "Categorizing a festival as Improvisation rather than

Dance might distract people from seeing the actual dancing. The artists' work becomes less visible." Whatever the artist's choice of method in making a dance—improvisational process varies from artist to artist as does choreographic method—the metaphor of a million pieces encourages an appreciation of the multiplicity of the field of dance without losing individual detail. Whereas an improvisation versus choreography approach may narrow and polarize our view, Lepkoff says, "Rather than looking only in two directions, a million pieces causes a looking in all directions. The million pieces become integrated into a melting pot that is dance."[3]

Improvisation as a performance form surfaced in the contemporary Western dance dialogue in the works of individual artists such as Anna Halprin (in the late 1950s) and as a result of experimentation by groups such as the Judson Dance Theater in the United States (in the 1960s) and the performance collective X6 in the United Kingdom (in the 1970s). Other early experimenters in the United States include Richard Bull and his New York Chamber Dance Group (in the late 1960s); Daniel Nagrin and his Workgroup (1970s), who explored emotional and psychological motivation for movement to create social and political commentary; and Dianne McIntyre, whose troupe Sounds in Motion pushed the limits of improvised dance vocabulary to encompass the rhythms of free jazz (1970s and 1980s).[4]

Judith Dunn, Judson Dance Theater choreographer, said, "What made it so exciting was that our main concern was, ultimately, not methodology at all. . . . Our real purpose was to abandon old habits and find new ways of moving."[5] The chance operations of John Cage, composer/musician who collaborated with choreographer Merce Cunningham, informed the Judson Dance Theater, inspiring dancemakers to look outside current conventions in dance-making, or to look within them and see what was not being used. This climate of experimentalism fostered exploration and encouraged the development of individual approaches to making dances, resulting in the million pieces of Lepkoff's metaphor.

Though Cage himself did not recommend improvisation as a compositional tool, some in the next generation of dancemakers—exposed to his principles of indeterminacy through Robert Ellis Dunn's composition class—began experimenting with improvisation in performance. For example, in her work *Continuous Project Altered Daily*, Judson choreographer Yvonne Rainer juxtaposed movement material in different states of preparedness—

performance-ready, rehearsal mode, and improvised. The performers developed a taste for improvising together through the experience and the piece transformed into the acclaimed dance theater improvisation collective the Grand Union.[6]

Here, I will focus on dancemakers who work with improvisation—not to suggest it is *the* way to work, rather to propose another possibility among the many that may inform yours.

GAINING CULTURAL PERSPECTIVE

Improvising is a manner of expressing . . . of living. And I am skeptical about the current fashion that merely regards it as a mode or technical method of artistic expression.

—MIN TANAKA, "Quotations: Min Tanaka"

Everyone has some experience improvising. We improvise when we adapt our actions in the moment to meet changing circumstances. On a daily basis, the simplest things can require movement improvisation: navigating around a traffic jam on the way to school or work; changing a step mid-stride when the puddle on the path is deeper than first suspected, shifting seats to hear a hushed voice in a conversation; modifying the way a load is carried on realizing it is heavier than expected. These types of movement improvisation are basic to human experience.

As an art form, improvisation has throughout history developed in a variety of cultures and disciplines worldwide. Improvised movement or dance has been used by Siberian shamans and Chinese qigong masters; in traditional dances from India, West Africa, and Spain; and in contemporary American forms such as tap-dancing.[7] Here we will consider a particular development of improvisational dancing on Western history's stage: improvisation as a performance form of the late twentieth and early twenty-first centuries. Included are some influences from the East: Eiko and Koma, Min Tanaka, and Kazuo Ohno from Japan, and Prapto (Suprapto Suryodarmo) from Indonesia, who also perform and teach in the West.[8]

This current manifestation of improvisational dance is by no means mainstream in Western culture. Some speculate that its unpredictable nature and emphasis on process over product make it difficult for dance producers to sell in a market-driven arts world. And the heightened sense of presence considered by many a major charm of improvisation is not easily conveyed via video, which further limits its means of acceptance by a wider audience. Improvised dance-making in Western culture remains part of an alternative dance scene (with exceptions), shown mainly in venues such as artists' lofts and artist-founded performance spaces.

The improvisers in this book represent a small sampling of dancemakers in the field, yet many are major players in having helped define and spread the form through their performances and teaching. This group is not particularly diverse, arising mainly from the New York City experimental dance scene of the 1960s and 1970s. This urban demographic is understandable: concert dance demands a stage, a pool of dancers, and, in the case of alternative dance, an audience willing to try something out of the ordinary. Also, a dance culture can only grow between dialoguing members—a kinesthetic dialogue passed from body to body. As the discipline is somewhat limited by its medium and is still young, the early generations remain its major proponent.

However, the field is becoming more diverse—geographically and racially, across age and ability. The work first spread to the West Coast and Europe through teaching residencies and performance opportunities—at alternative venues in cities like San Francisco, places like Dartington College of the Arts in the United Kingdom, and the School for New Dance Development in Amsterdam. Today improvisational dance work can be found in Siberia, Australia, Taiwan, and Japan. It is safe to say that, while alternative, this improvisational dance scene is transglobal and has shown cross-cultural resonance especially with certain Eastern dance forms that value improvisation. Beyond this, its potential remains to be tested.

A Note on Applications for Dance Improvisation

There are many applications for dance improvisation in our culture, including therapeutic, self-expressive, social, artistic, and spiritual. Sometimes the differences among applications are clear-cut: dance therapists work with autistic children in a clinical setting while contact improvisation develops a sense of community through large gatherings called jams. On closer examination, the lines quickly blur. Self-expression through improvised movement can be therapeutic; at what point does it become material for dance-making?

Cross-pollination among applications can be fertile territory for art making. For example, Barbara Dilley and Prapto, both Buddhists, create dances for performance that are informed by Buddhist awareness practices. In this book we are focusing on the artistic application of dance improvisation, aiming to communicate aesthetics through movement to a broader public, while touching on the multiplicity of influences that inspire artists to create.

How to Use This Book

This book is meant to be a companion as you explore the field of improvisational dance-making in the context of contemporary dance. It suggests ways to engage the material as an artist; read it not just as a history or critique. It is arranged into chapters by issues that arise when making dances: Materia Prima, Form, Time Machines, Spatial Relations, The Dancing Image, The Possibilities of Music, The Eyes, Partnering Science, and The Magical Object. Each chapter starts with a short introduction defining the issue at hand and ends with field notes that compare practices from my perspective as a dance improviser. At the end of most chapters there are suggestions of ways to engage with the material for further research in your dance practice. Between chapters are short interludes, some thoughts from my personal practice and experience. These are meant to encourage and inspire you to start somewhere—to find your own interests and areas of research, develop your artistic practice, and engage in your own critical and physical thinking.

Twenty-six dancemakers and their approaches to making work are covered in this book. "Meet the Artists: Dancemakers' Biographies" gives some background information on each, including the context in which I encountered their work. You might use this section to familiarize yourself with each artist before venturing into the main text of the book, or as a home base for a more detailed investigation of a particular artist—following the chapter and page references for each entry on the artist's work.

The chapters are made up of a collection of entries focusing on certain of the artists included in the book. Each entry describes how a particular artist engages the subject in his or her practice. The artists whose practices I chose to represent each issue is based largely on my experience of their work, how central the issue appeared to be to that person's practice, but also on how different artists' perspective on the issue contrasts. A shorter entry reflects only my own limited exposure to their work; still, I included artists less familiar to me if their work suggested a substantially different approach to an issue or was important to me in my personal artistic development.

Composing as Companion?

The act of composing can be a kind of companion while improvising. You are not out there in the performance space all alone. You've got the space and your relationship to it and your relationships in it; you have time on your hands to shape like clay by marking it with activity or lack of it; and in many instances, you also have the other improvisers. You could say that composing with the materials of the moment (either as you perceive them or as they have been scored) is the activity of improvising.

Some dancemakers who work with improvised materials eschew composing. They consider composing planning ahead, and planning ahead takes the life out of improvisation, which they see as a purely intuitive or physical act. At the same time, some dancemakers working with improvised material are tired of people thinking that in improvisation you "just do anything," implying there is no study or skill behind it. These dancemakers often emphasize the composing component of their improvisation practice. There is thought, strategizing, and an implied study, as well as magical moments of chance happening and intuitive choice-making. These dancemakers might see composing as a combination of faculties—feeling, thinking, sensing, and intuiting through both mind and body—that inform the improvised moment. Intuition may or may not be featured as a guiding principle. Sensing is often highlighted. That they emphasize composing doesn't necessarily mean they plan ahead, although they might include planning or research as part of the activity of improvisation as they define it.

In other words, the differences may be semantic, residing in how individual dancemakers define composing and what activities they include in improvising. However, in a field like improvisation where process is key in defining the activity, semantics may be all there is. To compose or not to compose—the improviser's choice!

More Notes on Semantics

In this book we are looking at contemporary artists who use improvised material in the dances they make for performance. Some create improvised dances and also choreograph in the traditional sense. Certain artists refer to themselves as choreographers and their works as choreographies, though they use improvised materials. Some may not consider their dances improvised, even though by general standards/common usage they would appear to be. And there are even those who call their work improvisations though they may seem set for all intents and purposes. All these artists' works are included to delineate the boundaries and point out idiosyncrasies of the field.

You Say Impro, I Say Improv

In a similar semantic vein, some dancemakers prefer the full word "improvisation" over the slang term "improv"—as if the abbreviated word somehow implies a slapdash approach, a shortened or nonexistent study, whereas the longer, weightier "improvisation" carries the sense of extended study along with its extra letters. Maybe it is safer to say "impro" like the Europeans, who, to buttress their abbreviation, have an illustrious cultural history of dancing. We'll use "improvisation" here. Make your own choice!

1

Materia Prima

An important part of maturing as an improviser, indeed as an artist, is the process of choosing for oneself what to work with and how to work. Within what parameters, with what focus.

—SIMONE FORTI, "Animate Dancing"

A DANCE MAY HAVE COSTUMES, sets or sites, props, lights, music, and text as well, and these may have more or less importance, but (most would agree) a dance isn't a dance without a moving body. In improvised dances, the material is not limited to set sequences or patterns of movement but includes a means of finding or framing movement for viewers as the dance occurs. For some dancemakers who work with improvised material, it is the movement that although not set, defines the work—something inherent in it, something about its look or feel. For others, the interest in the movement material may be secondary to how it is found—as a trace of a process—or to how it may be juxtaposed or shaped with other movement or elements in a work.

In this chapter the issue at hand is the movement material and how it gets chosen in improvisational works. The content, or what gets communicated through the movement material, is a different, though somewhat related, topic. The content may simply be the movement itself. But content might also be communicated through metaphor or abstraction, narrative or commentary, et cetera.[1] Whatever the materials and whatever the content, there is also a context (cultural climate and physical setting, for example) for a work that shines light on what it is about and how it is to be understood, that gives it meaning. Here we'll look at the kinds of movement materials that improvisational dancemakers have chosen and leave the question of content (What are they communicating through the materials they have chosen?) up to you, as a viewer, to research when you see dance improvisation in performance.

Using What's Available

Simone Forti set very particular physical conditions for her early dance constructions, anything from negotiating moving around on a slanted board or twisting while suspended in ropes to climbing over people or jumping off an unseen height. The conditions of the dance limited the available movement choices as a result, and captured very particular palettes of movement. For example, *Huddle* (1961) is a structure in which six to nine people form a tight cluster and take turns climbing over and rejoining it without ever detaching from it. Because *Huddle* is self-perpetuating, Forti recommends that it be done for about ten minutes. Although unset, the movement is precisely defined by the physical task at hand. Another dance created for the same performance, *Slant Board* (1961), has three or four dancers climb on an eight-by-eight-foot board propped against a wall at a forty-five-degree angle by holding knotted ropes, with instructions to keep moving up and down, back and forth. The set-ups for these dances delimit the kind of motion available, putting a thin slice of human movement on display in performance.

Key to the design is that almost anyone can do it; the dance puts ordinary movement, not stylized or technical dancing, on display. When Forti made the dances, stylized movement defined mainstream dance. Today, because of dancemakers like her, audiences are not surprised to see some pedestrian movement in a dance concert; even in ballet it's not unheard of. But in the context of the early 1960s, Forti's choice of task-based movement material for a dance was radical.

Later on Forti gave up these controlled dance experiments. Her focus shifted to an open-ended, less controlled process of listening to body sensation and responding through movement that she had encountered in her early dance studies with Anna Halprin, a pioneer of contemporary improvisational dance-making based in San Francisco, California. Source material for dances came from wherever Forti found them in her environment and travels, for instance, balancing on the wobbling rocks of a crumbling wall, or observing animals in zoos, an area of research Forti continued for many years.[2]

Since the mid-1980s Forti has been developing an approach to movement she calls Logomotion, which she teaches and performs. The names of earlier phases, "animate dancing" and "moving the telling," catch the flavor of the developing work. Her breakthrough for this work came when she began to connect movement and speaking through the retelling of the news (*News Animations*, early 1980s). These pieces, often humorous, juxtapose serious world affairs with the intimacy of the human body in movement and gesture.

The material for these later dances arises from deep ties between speaking and movement—the kinesthetic imagery we often use in storytelling and its accompanying body language. In Forti's work, this body language is not a grace note added to a story as it is told but rather a preverbal embodiment that helps invoke language. To give an idea of the process, Forti uses the example of the "slippery slope," a metaphor with kinesthetic roots.[3] The phrase connotes a potentially escalating and dangerous situation; Forti reconnects the phrase to its physical roots by reliving the slippery slope in movement. Her work goes beyond figures of speech, developing a unique communication system using both words and movement sourced from the sensations and kinesthetic associations the words evoke. In the shifting back and forth of emphasis between verbal meaning and physical action during the dancing, the dances playfully expose a forgotten side of language.[4]

Sample Practice: Movement Memory Snapshots

We each tell about something that has stayed in our memory because of some aspect of movement. I ask people to go right for the image that comes up. The very moment of movement. The snapshot. And to forgo the lead-up or linear story. I don't say anything about moving, but it is hard not to get animated or even stand up when you are telling a movement story. So we do. . . . When we have gone around the circle and all have offered their snapshots, we try to play back some of the movements we saw each other do.

—SIMONE FORTI, in ALBRIGHT and GERE, *Taken by Surprise*

Barbara Dilley uses "everyday" movement as material for her dances. As a dancer for Merce Cunningham's company when she was in her twenties, Dilley was influenced by Cage's and Cunningham's ideas on art-making. John Cage, composer and Cunningham's artistic (as well as life) partner, had expanded his musical palette to include all possible sound, "even those ordinarily thought to be undesirable" as music, and visual artists in the Cage-Cunningham circles used ready-mades, found objects, as art.[5] Dilley was also part of the dance scene surrounding the Judson Dance Theater, which had started with composition classes taught by Robert Ellis Dunn, Cage's protégé, at the Cunningham studios just a few years before she joined the company. She saw and performed in the works of the Judson choreographers, who were experimenting with non-stylized and pedestrian—ordinary, everyday—movement as dance.

After leaving the Cunningham Company, Dilley continued to dance for Yvonne Rainer, a Judson choreographer based in New York City. Dilley became a member of the Grand Union, an improvisational dance theater collective that formed out of Rainer's *Continuous Project—Altered Daily*. In the later years of the Grand Union (1970–76) there was no preplanned material for performance, though ideas might be recycled from one performance to the next. Material was taken from whatever was at hand—sets, props, costumes, and music were improvised, as were movement and text—including any current emotional issues between collective members. Dilley found this blurring of boundaries between performance and everyday life exhilarating but often personally confusing. The mix of the two on stage left her feeling uneasy and raised many questions about the practice of improvisation.[6]

In the summer of 1974 Dilley heard Chögyam Trungpa Rinpoche, the founder of Shambhala Buddhism, speak at the Naropa Institute in Boulder, Colorado. Dilley was struck by Trungpa Rinpoche, who, in speaking of Buddhist practice, addressed many of her questions regarding her experience of dance improvisation.[7] She was especially taken with the concept of Dharma Art, an art that springs from the expression of "the appreciation of things as they are," the ordinary and everyday, rather than as an isolated act of creative genius. Dilley became a practicing Buddhist.[8]

In her own work, Dilley starts with pedestrian vocabulary. No fancy dance moves or personal vocabulary, no need for invention, cleverness, or originality. Simple everyday, pedestrian movement. Dilley will limit this vocabulary even further; for example, she will start off with "five basic moves": walking standing, turning, arm swinging, and crawling. She will use these in specific structures she has designed, like corridors, described below, or grids (see chapter 4). These limitations create simplicity, which informs the dancers about their movement habits, seeds awareness, and results in what Dilley refers to as "elegant pedestrian," everyday movement done with mindfulness.[9] Later on, Dilley opens up the limitations—all vocabulary of gesture is possible. Attention expands.

Add the study of influence: how we take on the movements of those around us in our own movement, copying bits and snatches, taking on timings, the impulse to move and change what we're doing when someone else initiates a change. Dilley uses her structures, for example, her corridors, as a laboratory to discover the many ways dancers are influenced—first of all, just noticing that we *are* influenced and then observing who and what influences us as we dance, and how and why they do so. Also up for study is our attitude toward being influenced. Dilley notes that imitating is often an uncomfortable practice for modern dancers, whose training is based on invention and originality. Yet we are imitating all the time. Dilley finds that speaking of influence rather than imitation helps open up the study and brings our natural tendency toward imitation to consciousness while widening the lens of imitation to include more subtle exchanges.

Another facet of working with influence: being able to accept influences, to pick them up and put them down; letting them arise, dwell, and fall away like they are thoughts in meditation. Dilley writes, "There is so much movement sourcing just by looking at ordinary movement. If you really pay attention to it, it's just endless."[10]

Sample Practice: Corridors

To start, three people travel back and forth in parallel (imagined and self-determined) corridors. Each must stay within the corridor that he or she starts in. At first the vocabulary is limited to five pedestrian movements: walking, standing, turning, arm swinging, and crawling. Notice the influence and exchange between dancers that takes place naturally. Next, the movers are allowed to switch corridors, but only at the ends, creating a new corridor between or alongside the original ones. This development creates a new flow pattern. Later, personal movement vocabulary may be introduced.

—BARBARA DILLEY, Fearless Dancing Project, summer 2004

Penny Campbell feels that dance improvisation starts with the basic skill of being aware of oneself in the moment. She starts beginners off with a body scan—a movement of the attention through the body looking for sensation and subtle movements already present. She instructs students: "Don't stop anything, don't exaggerate anything, Let the body be, let it express. Let it continue doing what it is doing." She encourages students to stick with these subtle movements, let them register in perception, and let the perceptions grow. In her master's thesis she writes, "Movement, any movement, is the raw material for dance, but we regularly ignore the ever-present activity that percolates through us. . . . A return to this rich resource of intrinsic motion is

crucial for the improvising dancer. . . . No matter how complex the movement eventually becomes, this is the basic underpinning: paying attention."[11]

It's this skill of being present and adaptable while dancing with a group that
can eventually lead to "ensemble awareness." According to Campbell, ensemble awareness is a sense of what's developing in the dance in a given moment
and how the individual's movement choices play into that development.

Sample Practice: Matching Practice

First students stand in a circle and scan their bodies. Next, they open up their
peripheral vision and other senses, especially hearing and the enveloping
sensations from the skin. Maintaining this listening to the inner and outer
worlds, they are ready to mirror each other, starting from a simple stand facing
one another in the circle. Students reflect everything as best as possible in their
bodies. I layer the directives: "Don't say 'no' to any movement seen," such as a
smile or scratch, and "If you see it, do it! And don't stop until you see something
else." Sometimes someone will think to introduce a movement, but this is a
different exercise (follow the leader). Subtle movement becomes amplified as
it ripples through the body of the ensemble.

—PENNY CAMPBELL, May 2008

DANCING WITH ALL YOU'VE GOT

Susan Sgorbati asks dancers to take all their influences from the various
movement studies in their lives (dance techniques, somatic studies, yoga,
martial arts, and other disciplines such as sports, competitive dance, et
cetera) and play with and investigate them in solo improvisation practice to
develop a "personal movement vocabulary." In this study, there is space for a
dancer to build his or her own techniques for sourcing movement, to develop
skills such as balancing and turning, as well as to integrate what he or she
has learned in technique class into movement made under the less prescribed
circumstances of improvisation. In Sgorbati's work, a personal movement
vocabulary is something an improvising dancer has at his or her fingertips to
use as an ingredient in solo or ensemble work. In her concept of building a
personal movement vocabulary, Sgorbati articulates what improvisers are constantly doing—integrating and assimilating influences through movement.

For Sgorbati's ensemble work, Emergent Improvisation, improvising skills
are more important than a particular method of sourcing material. A dancer

figures out how to source his or her own movement and brings this skill to the group. Another skill identified in Emergent Improvisation is recognizing a form as it emerges in the course of an improvisation and contributing to its development, which could be something as simple as joining a group moving in unison, choosing to "frame" a solo dance or a main group event, or something a bit more complex, like accumulating, shadowing, or paralleling the material in some way. As dancers contribute to the creation of the developing form, they use movement material that supports the form, accumulating more dance material. A self-sustaining dance evolves. New forms may emerge, adding to the complexity! Dancers learn to be on the lookout for unfamiliar patterns and develop a certain tolerance for ambiguity in the process, while the dancing takes shape.[12]

Sample Practice: Solo Practice for Emergent Improvisation: Physical Vocabulary

The practice of emergent improvisation focuses on the unexplored possibilities of organization and structure in the process of dance and music improvisation. The Solo Practice contains four elements: embodiment, physical vocabulary, spatial environment, and focus on the particular. Here is a sample of one of the practices for physical vocabulary.

Every dancer is capable of discovering a personal movement vocabulary. Create a series of movements that build a phrase. Repeat the phrase by altering it in as many ways as you can. Suggestions are to repeat certain movements in the phrase, retrograde the phrase, change the focus, the dynamics, the textures, and the speed. Practice the phrase with different spatial patterns and using different levels. Explore a part of the phrase that expands your technical ability (balance, turns, etc.) and deepens your physical sensations. Finish by performing a 2-minute improvisation using your phrase as a structure that includes a beginning, development, and conclusion, spontaneously selecting what interests you from the previous practice.

—SUSAN SGORBATI, July 2008

Regarding the kinds of movement dancers think to make while improvising, Katie Duck says, "You'll do what your teachers taught you."[13] For her, improvising isn't about generating new movement, nor is she concerned with the specifics of how a dancer arrives at his or her movement; rather, skills such as "remembering to exit," counterpointing, and using "biology" (i.e., playing with the rush a performer gets, for example, from being up close to an audience) are what makes the improvisation tick, not the particulars of the movements themselves. "Just don't work on it during the improvisation," she says about a dancer's movement.[14] Her concern is presence; you are "on" when you are on stage, not getting there, or preparing to dance.

Duck has an interesting perspective on technique. Rather than as the learning of a particular or preferred way to move, she sees technique as preparing a dancer to choose one thing over another by understanding what his or her body can and can't do—by knowing its limits. To that purpose, her dance technique class combines elements from ballet, modern dance, and Contact Improvisation and includes postmodern techniques. Duck values technical training, and her dancers are often highly trained. But in improvisation choosing and editing are also key skills, otherwise the number of available choices will quickly overwhelm a developing dance, no matter how great the dancer! Duck believes it is the knowing of his or her limitations that help a dancer to make the quick decisions—and exciting ones—in improvisation. Postmodern training, especially release technique, emphasizes freeing the body in order to have a wider range of possibility. But focusing on all the possibilities available in any moment may swamp an improviser in performance. Duck concentrates on skills of choice-making—culling movement rather than generating it.[15] And yet it's not enough to dance well and

---

Sample Practice: Looking into Biology

Take a pass across the studio floor so that you are forced to create movement that carries you forward in space—either with upright patterns or on the floor. While you are creating forward movement through the space, notice and play with the potential that the eyes contain to see in close, medium, and long ranges, exactly how a camera works when you change focuses.

Now cross the floor in the same manner with a partner, occasionally looking your partner in the eye. Try to not stare—or "over focus"—while playing with the different focuses of the eye. Using the eyes while creating movement and going forward in space may make you feel dizzy at first. Looking your partner in the eye needs to be a clear action—not passive—so that the "biological" impact is felt. Make it a clear interactive moment in time.

—KATIE DUCK, July 2008

---

make sound choices—it's the dynamics between improvisers that create excitement and interest in the dance. Duck suggests using what she refers to as "biology" to create and raise energy in a dance.

Going beyond What You Do

Nina Martin admonishes dance improvisers to "kill the choreographer" in themselves, that internal choreographer that likes to plan ahead, set something up, and consider what movement will work best next in an improvisation.[16] (She also choreographs and has quite a sense of humor.) When it comes to improvisation, she is interested in circumventing and subverting both the mind's (the choreographer) and the body's (sensory and kinetic) habits. She speaks of "dancing the brain," that is, at the speed of the neuronal activity— what she calls the "Neuro state"—and not from the planning mind or sensing body. The time it takes to deliberate over a movement slows dancers' reaction time, which Martin finds can make improvisation plodding for an audience.

The Neuro state practices are part of her ReWire/Dancing States, which also include Kinetic states—dancing the body (see practice below). In the Neuro state practices, Martin trains improvisers to work at a fast brain speed, gearing the dancer to enter an improvisation with no plan and fewer preconceived attitudes toward existing material. When you are "in," that is, onstage improvising, you react to what you find. Her practices aim at developing a

---

Sample Practice: The Fussy Baby: A ReWire Exercise in the Kinetic State from Articulating the Solo Body

The dancer lies on the floor and shifts from position to position as if trying to get comfortable like a fussy baby might. The idea is to make the shifts regularly like a metronome and at a speed that doesn't allow the mind to plan (or even care!) what the next move will be or the body to discover where it is comfortable. Move, pause, move, pause. If you find yourself able to think ahead, step your internal metronome up a notch. You may find this practice of quick shifts and "low ambition" movement opens up possibilities for movement invention as it releases you from your inner censor/judge/choreographer into spontaneous movement.

—NINA MARTIN, Ensemble Thinking, May 2006

---

speed-reading of the space and the ability to respond quickly and with clarity
to that read. Postmodern and new dance training often emphasizes sensory
awareness work, which requires, at least at first, a slower, more deliberate relationship to the body-mind—listening internally, tuning in to develop movement material. Although Martin's training may seem to come from a different
place, she feels her work also takes somatic approach. After all, she is working with the brain and nervous system to get at preconscious movement,
which "may be an impossible state to reach, but an informative research."[17]
Through her training, she offers options to the tendency to build material in

Dancing at "brain speed." *From left*: Mary Reich and Nina Martin doing a Neuro state
practice from the ReWire/Dancing States work. Photo © Carl Yamamoto

improvisation more deliberately. She calls the work Ensemble Thinking (group improvisation) and Articulating the Solo Body (solo improvisation).

Playing with What's Given

In Richard Bull's Choreographic Improvisation technique, choreographic skill is a partner in the improvised moment. Bull was interested in making the choreographic process and the collective negotiation of the choreography visible as an improvisation developed. He often used speaking in his dances, referencing the progress of the dance, to accomplish this transparency. For a dance improviser, being able to remember physically what has already happened in the dance and being able to reference those earlier choices are vital skills.

Dancers become aware of how the improvised material is taking shape by recognizing a formal structuring element underlying a developing dance. Take a simple spatial configuration like a diagonal. A dancer, noticing a diagonal forming in the space, might reference it by joining it or restating it later in the dance. Or he might catch on to an arising movement motif, and repeat or vary it or the quality of the movement or alter its relationship to the music.[18] Whatever the formal elements the dancers recognize, they reinforce them (both physically and verbally) by referencing previous material or introducing new material that bolsters the form. Because there are many levels of compositional structure to consider, the skill of developing the material of a dance lies in this recognition of formal elements and then in figuring out how to make them apparent in order to continue the danced dialogue. In this way, Bull and his dancers looked at how the dance was taking shape to create a basis for choosing and developing material.

To counteract a natural tendency to repeat familiar movement and to broaden their movement palette, Bull and collaborators Cynthia Novack and Peentz Dubble devoted days to research and development of movement material. They developed a practice they called "playpen." In playpen they pushed themselves to do awkward, physically challenging, or taxing movement, and learned movement from styles unfamiliar to them. To broaden their options in the choreographed-improvised moment, they also used movement quality descriptors in various combinations as another way to push themselves into unfamiliar physical territory.[19]

Dana Reitz refers to her work as the "radical middle," as it falls somewhere in between the worlds of choreography and improvisation. She works with

Sample Practice: Playpen

Create your own playpen. Choose a movement or movements from a dance style that you are unfamiliar with, or any move that you would like to learn. Try teaching it to yourself (and your "playpen playmates"). Or improvise movement combining one or two of these "effort actions" from Rudolf Laban's Movement Analysis: Float, Punch, Glide, Slash, Wring, Dab, Flick, Press. Finally, identify one or two edges for yourself, such as aerobic movement, continuous flow, balance, a less familiar Laban effort action, et cetera. Design an improvisation that pushes this edge by focusing on it in a timed improvisation. Adjust the parameters of your improvisation until you are satisfied that you have found and pushed your edge of comfort/endurance/familiarity.

—PEENTZ DUBBLE, on Richard Bull, June 2007

palettes of selected movement but doesn't set them in the traditional choreographic sense. She considers movement material, her choreography, to be materia prima, an entry point into the investigation of the dance.

According to Reitz, a dance must be lived through. In her solo performance work, she listens to her movement—both previously set choreography and movement chosen in the moment—and lets the listening inform what will come next. She gives herself the option to change the movement's timing or relation to space or to leave material out if it doesn't fit in the moment. Attending to the movement through the manipulation and placement of her material reveals even the simplest movement's richness and inherent potential. This treatment of material in performance—through phrasing and other choices regarding dynamics, spatial considerations, light, and costuming—brings life to the dance.[20]

Sample Practice: Adapting a Phrase

Create a short phrase of movement that you can repeat. Choose several new pathways through the space, and explore the phrase in each one. Adapt the movement to this path as you perform it, listening to how the path changes the movement—its timing and quality, as well as any other aspects that may arise for you.

—DANA REITZ, July 2008

In Nancy Topf's improvisation work a dancer looks to the body for material—using explorations of anatomy as a source for movement. These explorations are built around the study of anatomical imagery. The study starts with appreciation of anatomical form, cultivated by looking at the skeleton and anatomy books, and by holding bones and feeling their various shapes and weight. Topf's work, a variation of Anatomical Release Technique, which she pioneered along with Marsha Paludan, Mary Fulkerson, and John Rolland in the late 1960s and 1970s, mainly focuses on the bones, but includes certain muscles, especially the psoas, a muscle of deep spinal support, as well.

In Topf's work, which she called Topf Technique and Dynamic Anatomy, dancers study a specific image of a particular anatomical structure, both visually and through touch. For example, the sacrum's concave, scoop shape is compared to the soup ladle, and then felt with the hands on the skeleton and on the body, one's own as well as a partner's. The mechanics of the structure are also considered; for example, the sacrum is the keystone of the arch of the pelvis. As a bearer of weight and transmitter of force—from the spine through the pelvic halves to the legs and floor—it further develops the dynamics of an image. Drawing the structure and tracing these dynamics as cycles of support, often repetitively, on paper and above or on the body with the hands, reinforces the image and helps bring it into movement.

Once the specifics of the image are laid down, the dancer is invited to research the image through movement. In exploring it physically, the dancer follows internal kinesthetic sensation, investigating through movement what he or she had experienced through sight and touch. This research becomes

---

Sample Practice: Tai Chi Hands: The Gesture of Sacrum

I want to show you one more thing with the hands. It has to do with the sacrum and one of the first hand movements of Tai Chi. Place your hands with the palms facing down, arms straight out in front of you. This is the gesture: You draw your hands back toward you. Then let the heels of the hands feel heavy and draw them back and then drop down. The hand becomes the curve of sacrum. You have made the gesture of sacrum. When I do that movement with my hands I can think about my sacrum. I can imagine the form and then make contact with the bottom of spine in my mind while using my hands.

—NANCY TOPF, "The Anatomy of Center"

material for dances. Topf was intrigued by the recurring qualities of the dances created in this way: for example, a "sacrum dance," because of the sacrum's shape and function in the body as weight bearer, had a particular weighted and grounded dynamic. In contrast, a dance exploring the sternoclavicular joint (the shoulder girdle attachment to the sternum) is lighter, airier—because of its relation to the mobility and reach of the arms.[21]

Mary Overlie uses viewpoints—the elements of theater—as frames of reference to focus a dancer's or an actor's attention and perception in the task of making performance. Overlie's work is influential in both dance and theater—she is one of the founding members of and has taught for many years at New York University's Experimental Theater Wing. She created the Six Viewpoints, which have been adapted and widely used in the theater world.

In this work, Overlie identifies perspectives that directors, actors, choreographers, dancers, and audience use to create and read performance: space, shape, time, movement, emotion, and story. These have many applications; regarding dance improvisation, one possibility is to source movement from each of the Viewpoints individually, which develops versatility in performers who might be used to working primarily or habitually from just one or two perspectives.[22]

For example, to build material for a dance concerning the Viewpoint *space*, improvisers might focus primarily on the placement of their movements in the stage space or perhaps the relative space between elements, such as objects and people. A phrase done in a far upstage corner and then repeated down front is one simple way a performer might give the audience an experience of space (see also chapter 4). Focusing on *shape*, improvisers consider the design of the body as a shape in space. Overlie says, "When you isolate shape as a separate focus, you find that constant activity is not required onstage. Instead, like a vase in the window, the actor's visual presence interacts in the scene with a highly active language of its own."[23] For the Viewpoint *time*, improvisers might choose to work with rhythm, varying speed, duration, or a shift from habitual timing of their actions, what Overlie calls "unusual time" (see also chapter 4).

Rather than a specific emotion, the Viewpoint *emotion* focuses on the impact of the sheer presence of the performer detached from a specific storyline. Overlie's concept of emotion is inclusive: an emotion is not a single tone but a complex of them, like the bouquet of a wine that includes a variety of notes that may harmonize or clash with each other. To investigate the

emotional impact of presence, performers begin by sitting still and allowing
themselves to observe and be observed simultaneously, without suppressing
their own thoughts and feelings. Overlie says, "The basis of the language of
emotion in Viewpoints work is our ability to interact in the present from a
natural flow of being. . . . This focus demonstrates to actors that they are
interesting to watch and capable of being watched without a role to carry
them."[24] This includes, in the case of the improvising dancer, being interesting to watch without the need for continuous movement invention. With an
expanded experience of his or her own presence and its emotional impact,
the performer can include it as a conscious element in unspoken dialogue
with an audience.

Movement seems a strange category—isn't all dance movement? This
Viewpoint is concerned with shaping material from a focus on kinesthetics—
feeling momentum, movement pathways, and flow (a popular choice in contemporary modern dance), or stopping the flow, working with the muscles
in a manner beyond a common, utilitarian usage (see the sample exercise
below). Overlie describes the Viewpoint *story* as "narrative as flexible logic"

Mary Overlie, right window, dancing in her *Glassed Imagination II* at the Holly
Solomon Gallery in New York City, May 1977. Photo © Theo Robinson

or "an arrangement of information" without the usual standards for prioritizing that information. By treating it as a collection of data with its own implied logic, Overlie's concept of story embraces the linear and nonlinear narrative as well as the abstract. Stories are as easily told with inanimate objects or through movement as they are through spoken or written word. Overlie says, "People are natural sleuths—it is a necessity of life. We must find out what something means and where it fits into the structure that we know. Accepting this condition, the actor can play very complicated logics, because he or she knows the audience will be working to find out what is being said."[25] Likewise, this redefinition of story frees the improvising dancer to be in dialogue with the presenting logic of the movement material rather than imposing a conventional or preconceived one, such as a beginning-middle-end progression.

Sample Practice: Looking for the Voice of Movement,
One of the Six Viewpoints

Viewpoint—*movement* (Perceptual ability to experience and identify with kinetic sensation.)

As you begin to look for the "voice" of *movement*, be very cautious that you are not: adding exterior rhythm, or organizing or formalizing the movement into designed shapes.

Practice: Kinetic Feedback/Doing what the Body Wants, Solo work.

This practice derives movement from sensation.

Standing in a studio, bring your concentration to the level of sensation in your body. Allow your body to move from sensation and to move to create sensation. Allow the sensory dialogue to flow in a "logical" stream and observe how the kinetic logic is set up. What is the vocabulary of this sensation?

Benefit: This work will not create very beautiful movement. The practice is not designed to stimulate movement invention or creation. It is designed to strengthen the link between body, feeling and action.

—MARY OVERLIE, www.sixviewpoints.com

Dances sourced from a single Viewpoint have clarity of focus and develop their own particular character in dialogue with that Viewpoint. Of course there are infinite possible solutions, but a dance based on *time* could bring out a range of dynamics and use *space* (for example) in service of dynamics— rushing upstage, or a slow cross of the stage. Whereas a dance that focuses on

space highlights relationships in the space—the body standing in the far corner against the wall, crawling along a diagonal, running in a small circle downstage. These actions have different timings, but they primarily bring awareness to the stage space. The Matrix is a further development of work with the
Viewpoints, allowing a fluid shifting between them during performance.

Choreographer William Forsythe creates his unique vocabulary partly
through improvisational means and sometimes uses improvised movement
in his ballets. He thinks of movement as prescriptions. Movement is generated according to rules of operation, or algorithms, whose parameters can
be fiddled with, tweaked. What makes an arabesque recognizable as an
arabesque? What is its formula? How far can the envelope be pushed before
it becomes "not an arabesque"? By specifying a rigorous balletic lexicon without ballet's preferences for certain facings or traditional relationships of body
parts (e.g., épaulement: head tilted, shoulder forward against opposite hip)
he creates a variable vocabulary for his dances.[26] He works, for instance, with
set phrases of material that can be "operated on" by dancers improvisationally, or he gives them (or finds with them, as cocreators) algorithms with
which to make up their own movements.[27]

Forsythe uses these algorithms, which he also refers to as "technologies,"
to create a palette of interesting movement for composing his dances. His
CD-ROM, *Improvisation Technologies: A Tool for the Analytical Dance Eye*
(available to the public), is used as a training tool to familiarize dancers new
to his work with some of the more often used algorithms, for example, *universal writing*, using the body to inscribe the alphabet in space, or *fragmen-
tation*, deconstructing a specific phrase spatially (e.g., changing its facings,
stringing it out by making it travel, omitting parts, et cetera) to create an
improvised variation.[28] The algorithms are fairly specific in their instruction,
giving the dancer a focus yet allowing him or her choice. The algorithms
are designed to engage the entire body in unusual movement patterns, rather
than just the limbs or just the torso in isolation, for example. A noticeable
byproduct of their usage is the dancers' intense focus, which is necessary
in order to create the movement. Forsythe's ballets are remarkable for this
energy of focus as well as for their movement material that expands the ballet lexicon.

Sample Practice: U-ing, Rotating Inscription, and Tubing

Pick a point on or in your body and inscribe the letter *U* in space with this point. Be sure to include points on your torso and interior points like your organs; the idea is not to simply write from the extremities as in regular writing but to find unfamiliar ways of moving. In *rotating inscription* a dancer develops skill in writing with as many parts of the body as possible, shifting from one to the next. *Tubing*—now, instead of writing onto a "blackboard" in space, start writing on the inside of a long tube, so that the body moves through space. Get the feel for the kind of movement this exercise creates, then drop the detail of the task and follow the feel of the movement into dancing.

—WILLIAM FORSYTHE, February 2008

→¦ FIELD NOTES ¦←

My in-depth formal study of improvisation began with Nancy Topf, whose focus on anatomical imagery as a source for the generation of movement interested me with my background in science, athletics, and technical dancing. In fact, Topf saw her work, in part, as a way to improve technique. In it, the process of generating movement was primary; it was the movement that suggested the shape and structure of the dance. Later, I discovered qigong and encountered improvised forms within that discipline, studying with Professor Chen Hui-Xian at the Oregon College of Oriental Medicine in Portland and others. A similar principle was at work in these improvised exercises: in the exploration of energetic anatomy (e.g., the meridian pathways of flow), movement arose. These movements, I speculated, could have eventually developed into the multiple and various qigong forms that we know today, whether Soaring Crane, Jade Body, or Wild Goose qigong. I took with me to graduate school a curiosity in the forming of movement arising from these various kinds of anatomical investigations—which was immediately challenged.

I encountered in succession the work of Richard Bull (taught by George Russell through the Graduate Liberal Studies program at Wesleyan University), Susan Sgorbati, and Dana Reitz (both at Bennington College, where I did my MFA), all of whom had different approaches to treating the material of the improvised dance. In Choreographic Improvisation technique, we often started with a simple structure that generated movement material (for Bull's Palindrome, see chapter 4), or a short, repeatable improvised sequence. We played with it and developed facility with the manipulation of material. The process of sourcing movement wasn't belabored. Improvised movement became fodder for something else: a shape-shifting discourse. We weren't inventing a new language syllable by syllable; we were the debate club—and in any debate, you learn to make your point quickly and as eloquently as possible. It was a tough lesson for me, with my particular predilection toward a more deliberate process based in a slower felt-sense time, but I began to detach from that deep and slow sourcing and to be curious about shaping movement at higher speeds.

Susan Sgorbati's alternative was a happy compromise for me. Her work relied on the individual dancer in the ensemble having a "personal movement vocabulary"—his or her own method for sourcing movement—that was brought to the table in group improvisation. She deemphasized the importance of a particular sourcing process; rather she suggested many to her students, letting them choose. The dancers focused on the establishing of form arising in the ensemble work. In Sgorbati's work, I could add my previous technical training into the mix with my anatomical explorations. I began the work of integrating my past influences into a personal movement vocabulary.

I learned from Dana Reitz a performative aspect of improvised material: not to get hung up on sourcing (or re-sourcing) material during performance. That work has been done in the creating and rehearsal of the improvised dance and all the structuring and choice making that might entail: an a priori movement palette, a score or a system for keeping track of the progress of the dance, the lighting, the costuming. Trying to re-create and reconnect with what initially compelled me about a particular choice once onstage in front of an audience could be frustrating. Rather, I learned to refocus on the moment of the movement's unfolding, allowing myself to have a potentially new experience. The performance didn't have to be satisfying in the same way it had been the last time. This work deemphasized the preciousness of sourcing the material in order to discover various qualities that might lay dormant in any particular movement. This attitude allowed for fresh discovery in performance.

Keeping it fresh—at some point, sooner or later, the question of habitual movement arises. "I've done that movement a million times before." Do I get bored and want to change, expand, and develop new movement? How do I go about it? Some dancemakers address this issue by creating practices that push them into unfamiliar territory, such as Richard Bull's Play Pen or Nina Martin's ReWire/Dancing States. Others, like Katie Duck, accept habitual movement as a given limitation—as Duck says, "You'll do what your teachers taught you"—and focus on performance practices (using biology) to rejuvenate familiar material. Penny Campbell and the Architects' practice of getting to know and accept your "shtick," the movement material you fall back on when tired or nervous in performing improvisation, was very useful for me. Observing and acknowledging my habits helped me to be less critical of myself, stay present, and, in the end, expand my range.

In my encounter of many different teachers of improvised works, I began to question: "What is the purpose of the work they are sharing with me?" I started to classify each of them loosely as an artist who worked from a material base or one who worked from a form base. Was the artist offering a particular process of generating or sourcing material? I thought of this as material-based work. Or was he or she most interested in how I placed, re-stated, or integrated whatever movement I contributed to the class/ensemble/performance? I thought of this as form-based work. This understanding helped me navigate whatever skills I was learning and not reject them out of hand if they weren't familiar to the way I was used to working.

My favorite memory of the clash of cross-purposes was a workshop on the Forsythe Information Technologies taught at the Boston Ballet studios. Helen Picket, a former ballet dancer in Forsythe's company, had taught us, mostly modern/postmodern dancer/choreographers, a few days' worth of the technologies when a question arose: "So how do you compose with these methods?" We students for the most part had been introduced to improvisation as part of a dance composition class in college and were used to considering it in the context of making dances. The question confused Picket at first. The purpose of the Forsythe technologies she shared with us was to generate movement, which Forsythe arranged in his choreographies—material for his dances. Forsythe's technologies weren't compositional tools; they were colors in his palette. I found the collision of the two worlds most clarifying!

➤{ INTERLUDE }◄

So Many Influences, So Little Time . . .

There is so much movement influence in our lives that filters through us and becomes our dance "background": not just our various teachers but other movement in our lives, such as sports, social dancing, injuries and rehabilitations, exercises, bodywork. Add to this the performances we've seen, which influence what we think of as dance and define what dance is. And the culture we've grown up in and its relationship to dance and the body also affect our understandings. There are many more influences I am sure I am missing, but you get the point. Even if you don't think you have had much dance training, you could make a long list of movement influences.

Here are mine in roughly chronological order:

Doing yoga with Hittleman in front of the TV at age 3
Dancing at Miss Mimi's ballet school
Spraining ankle ice skating, getting thrown from horse at five years old
Growing up with dachshunds and ducks
Hanging out at community theater rehearsals and being dragged to
    the opera
Horseback riding, body surfing, and rock climbing
Mr. Richie's circus-influenced gymnastic team and Mr. Wilhelm's
    bareback riding acrobatics
Cheerleading in eighth grade
The movie *The Turning Point*
Diving
Bad back sprain from my own choreography in college
Peggy Lawler's one-woman barnstorm performances
Eiko and Koma, Oskar Schlemmer reconstructions, and Noh Dance
    come to Cornell
Losing a felt-sense of theoretical physics and finding my body through
    dance
Pina Bausch, Merce Cunningham, Ashton's Cinderella
Cecchetti Ballet and Miss Craske, the tendus and tales of Meher Baba
    on her back porch
New York Theater Ballet, meeting James Waring and Michel Fokine
    through their ballets

Working for next-generation modernists: Chris Gillis, Matthew Nash,
  Jumay Chu, Ellen Cornfield
Nancy Topf and Dynamic Anatomy
Qigong with Chen Hui Xian
The Lean Years: massage school and finding Contact Improvisation in
  Connecticut
Graduate School: Bennington College
Earthdance, more Contact Improvisation, Authentic Movement,
  improvisers from all over—the good, the bad, the ugly—all
  beautiful
Late nights at *Contact Quarterly*

Are we only born to be mime machines? To copy and pass on? To colonize? Is there more to it than that? How do we digest all this influence? How are we to be not simply carbon copies or flags in the wind. It takes time to take it on—the study part, the going to performances, and so forth. And it takes more time to take it in—digest or spit out, metabolize, detoxify our movement influences. How do we find our own movement interests amid the flotsam and jetsam, the swine and the pearls? And swim?

Here is my homemade digestive remedy: Take it on / Take it in: simile and metaphor practice.

First try an idea or an image on your body, in a representational mode, as best you can. Copy, mimic, take a shot at it (simile phase). Keep working with it—watch and wait for a transformation to occur. Let go. Suddenly you are in it, no longer acting it from the outside, but knowing it from the inside; you've made it your own through experience (metaphor phase). Watch for the transition!

2

Dancing Takes Shape

Remember the statement of Jean Cocteau: "We build traps for poetry," the kind of poetry inhabiting dance and the visual arts, as well as drama, verse, and fiction.

—ROBERT ELLIS DUNN, "Evaluating Choreography"

FORM IS THE SHAPE OF SOMETHING; recognition of form is a way we make sense of the world around us. There are many different ways to consider form in dance, for example, the shape of the body in movement, arrangement of bodies in space, or the shape a dance takes over time. Form is sometimes something we can name, like a twist or an arc, a diagonal or a trio, an ending or a rise to a climax. But form can also be the result of an organizing principle other than a spatial or temporal pattern, some activity that creates a functional relationship between parts that can be sensed through observation. The dance that results from Contact Improvisation's task of two moving bodies sharing weight while the dancers follow the point of contact between them is an example of form arising from a specific activity.

When choreographing, a dancemaker usually has an outside vantage point from which to arrange a dance. Since there often isn't the advantage of an outside eye in improvisation, alternative ways of organizing dance have arisen. In improvised dance, some aspect of form may be set—decided on before the dancing starts—as in structured, scored, or task-based improvisations. Sometimes the form is left open, to be discovered or revealed along the way. While some dancemakers enjoy the infinite variety in the invention and interplay of forms, others look on improvised dancing as the act of finding and articulating form; still others would rather not find it at all, preferring to remain in a perpetual state of questioning. Whatever the interest, there is plenty of room for surprise, as the way the dance unfolds or fulfills itself is left up to the dancers' spontaneous choices.

In the act of composing, material is arranged through form. While some dancemakers pre-compose a framework in which to improvise, others choose to compose the dance improvisationally. In this case, this arising form will depend on where, how, and on what the improvisers are choosing to focus their attention in any given moment. By specifying the aspects of materials and/or form they find interesting, dancemakers have created any number of variations for composing improvised dances.

The fourteen dancemakers covered in this chapter have specified these interests in different ways: through selective scores, structures, or tasks; by creating methodologies for choosing; by developing awareness practices; by suggesting a focus on a particular perceptual frame of reference; by posing a question to be asked or answered during the dance; or by proposing certain ideas to be researched and articulated through the dance itself. There are, it turns out, many different ways "to build traps for poetry."

To keep track of these dancemakers, we'll use the form of the spectrum. Our spectrum runs the gamut from highly structured or scored works at the beginning to investigations of free or open improvisation at the end. The spectrum metaphor will help us see the shades and variations among the choices of each dancemaker. As you read, given the descriptions of an individual dancemaker's investigations, you may be inspired to improvise with your own fine-tuning of their placement along the spectrum.

RITUAL: ANNA HALPRIN

Anna Halprin, currently dancing, teaching, and creating at ninety, has a long and groundbreaking dance career. She was an early proponent of improvisation as performance in contemporary Western concert dance. Through her early work, which investigated task and the kinesthetics of movement, she inspired a new generation of dancemakers, such as former students Simone Forti, Yvonne Rainer, Nancy Topf, and Trisha Brown.

Initially Halprin used the word "improvisation" to generally describe her work and distinguish it from the idiosyncratic modern dance vocabularies that had arisen and were dependent on individual artists like Martha Graham. Now Halprin distinguishes between the terms "improvisation" and "exploration." She uses exploration to describe a closed score study developed around a theme. By limiting the focus, an exploration generates movement in a specific range, potentially leading to a new movement experience. An example of an exploration is initiating a spiral from the ankle. Here, the mind focuses the body on the physical task. The body is imprinted by the work of the specific exploration. Once the explorative study has been exhausted, Halprin uses an open score improvisation to allow the body to play, leading the mind where it might not think to go and creating the opportunity for leaps in learning through the body's physical intuition. The exploration creates criteria for practice, providing a base, the groundwork in the improvisation for the intuition to spring from.[1]

A common thread throughout Halprin's work has been using dance and theater as a means to bring disparate elements of a community together. She works with the community at large, not necessarily with technically trained dancers. During a battle with cancer, her interest shifted to the creating of personalized rituals for individuals, and later, groups, as part of the healing process. Halprin uses ritual—an ancient form incorporating dance and movement—to promote the resolution of several contemporary issues: her own struggle with recurring cancer, HIV/AIDS patients coming to terms with their illness, race, or ethnicity relations and other community tensions, environmental issues, even the stress due to a serial killer at large in her community.

Halprin initially developed this work from investigations around her cancer. She had been experimenting with a method of drawing and dancing of self-portraits to investigate the mind/body connection. One portrait, she found, she just couldn't dance—she had drawn a round ball in her pelvis. At first she tried to explain it away, but her inability to dance the portrait nagged at her. Following the hunch, she went to the doctor who diagnosed a cancer right where she had drawn the ball! After surgical treatment, Halprin dived into an exploration of the drawings her students made for clues, thinking she might find some symbolic code to help her understand the images and how they worked to promote healing. Eventually she realized that it was precisely this process of moving back and forth between the drawing and the dancing that developed the images and their meanings. The drawings revealed their meanings through the dancing of them.[2]

A few years later after a recurrence, Halprin drew another picture she couldn't dance, one in which she was young and healthy. She immediately reacted to it by drawing another portrait, its inverse. She could dance this one: "I kept stabbing myself and howling like a wounded animal." After this release she was able to dance the first picture: "I had an image of water cascading over the mountains near my home, and that the water flowed through me and out to the endless vastness of the sea, taking with it my illness. . . . The movements of this dance started soft and small and as I continued to dance, I added sound . . . the movements grew and grew, until my whole body was engaged in the image of cascading water."[3] Family, friends, colleagues, and students supported the process as witnesses, responding with sounds and joining in a circle with Halprin at the end of the dance.

Her personal experience of healing through this method and many investigations with other individuals in her workshops led Halprin to create a five-part process, the Five Stages of Healing, to deal creatively with a variety of difficulties and contemporary issues, including individual health and personal growth, family, community, and the environment. The parts arose from the form of Halprin's healing dance: Identification of the issue at hand; Confrontation, which requires the facing of inner conflicts; Release, "a letting go in movement, feeling, and thought"; Change, the feeling of a new state of being; and Assimilation, integration into everyday life.[4] This process has been further developed by Halprin's daughter Daria Halprin-Khalighi in *Coming Alive! The Creative Expression Method* and is used at the Tamalpa Institute, in the Bay Area of California, in programs exploring dance as a healing art.

Over a ten-year period, Halprin evolved a ritual for the community she lived in using the Five Part Process as the underlying structure. *In and On the Mountain* (1981) addressed the stress in her community due to a serial killer terrorizing the mountain trails near where she lived. (A few days after the ritual was performed, a tip led to the killer's capture.)[5] From this ritual, *Circle the Earth* (1986) eventually evolved as the intention of the participants broadened to include a global community sharing a vision for peace. A shortened and adapted version of *Circle the Earth*, called *Planetary Dance* (1987), has been done in the spring around the world for twenty-plus years. This uses just one score, *Earth Run*, from *Circle the Earth*.

In *Earth Run*, participants start by kneeling in a large square, aligned to the four cardinal directions, facing its middle and contemplating the Earth and its inhabitants. The individual participants choose a loved one, community, animal, plant, environment, something that they will dedicate their participation to. As they begin running one by one on a circular path inside the square, they call out their dedications. Concentric circles of runners eventually develop, and they are allowed to rest in the interior of the square, facing one of the four directions. Drummers keep a pulse for the runners. As the running pattern takes hold, a narrator reads and repeats a text, such as Chief Seattle's statement of love and respect for the Earth. Finally, when the run has challenged the abilities of the participants, the drumming stops. Runners join those resting in the center of the circle. Once the narration is finished, participants touch a body part to the Earth. The score ends with three minutes of personal prayer, humming, or quiet.[6]

For *Planetary Dance*, participants are invited to create a preparation and closure for *Earth Run* that reflects their culture, such as a folk dance or blessing, and perhaps a substitution for Chief Seattle's text with an appropriate offering from their culture. For example, in 2007 *Planetary Dance* was done in conjunction with Al Gore's Live Earth Concert in San Francisco and dedicated to climate protection.

Halprin developed a method of scoring (written directions combining pictographs, symbols, and words) that gives participants an overview of the different types of activities they will encounter in a given ritual. Fairly simple to follow, the scores also enable the wide distribution of the ritual. An important aspect of ritual for Halprin is that the individual's needs be met as well as the community's. In a workshop setting, participants learn to creatively interact with the ritual's score rather than copy the actions or movements— part of the work of the ritual lies in the creative act of making a personal connection to it. Halprin believes that ritual promotes a possibility by seeding its suggestion in the imagination. She sees the ritual as a creative participatory act supporting and promoting peaceful actions in people's lives. "Some people do civil disobedience, protest marches, whatever—we dance!"[7]

Performance Practices: Deborah Hay

Deborah Hay is an experimental choreographer whose work, because it focuses on presence, also speaks to the performance of improvisation, although Hay's current work is choreographed. Over her years of dance-making, which began with the Judson Dance Theater, she has evolved a way of working with what she calls "performance practices" to focus the performer's attention on presence. Examples of performance practices include "What if where I am is what I need?" (1995–96) and "I imagine every cell in my body invites being seen perceiving no movement wrong, out of place, or out of character" (1985).[8] In her current work, Hay's dancers engage in a performance practice to navigate them through a given dance. The meditative performance practices are used simultaneously with the dancing of the score and affect the dancer's action and commitment to the movement.

One way Hay teaches her dance works is in Solo Performance Commissioning Projects. Participants learn the choreographic score and practices and sign a contract agreeing to practice the performance and perform the piece a specified number of times. Hay says "practice the performance" rather than "rehearse" to point out that the purpose of an ongoing performance practice is to unlearn the habit of learning a piece in one particular way.[9]

The choreography can range from a set combination of movements, to a spatial pathway, like an arc, for the dancer to fill with his or her own movement, to a direction to dance "office furniture," for example.[10] Some directions are practical, others impossible to achieve. The dancer is kept completely engaged by the score, multitasking to follow the layers of directions. Hay creates her multilayered scores to achieve the quality of performance she desires. Put into practice, her complex directions guide dancers to be rather than to perform.

ANCIENT MEMORIES: EIKO AND KOMA

When making a dance, Eiko and Koma usually start with a concept and, through improvising in rehearsal, develop a structure for it: a narrative built from multiple, concrete images, but not a typical "and then we did this" narrative. Eiko and Koma's narratives develop slowly; the audience might realize there was one only in retrospect. This narrative is open to interpretation.

Early on in their development of a piece, Eiko and Koma find a title that suggests the concept and catches the essence of what is drawing them to it. They choose simple titles that aspire to be cross-cultural so that an audience may have associations to them from their own experience (*Thirst*, 1985, or *Offering*, 2002).[11] They use visual components in the work that also evoke the central concept. Some are site-specific, unfolding in a landscape (a river in *River*, 1995); some take place on the stage with a set (*Grain*, 1983) or are installation pieces (*Breath*, 1998). *The Caravan Project*'s (1999) set was a trailer transformed into a people-sized "terrarium" just big enough for two. Ingeniously designed by Eiko and Koma, it could be towed to various sites for outdoor performances. The doors of the trailer opened on all sides, revealing a nest for the dancers, lit from within in hues of reds and blue-greens—a bit like a habitat for a pet lizard, a sunning slope with a hollow or cave underneath. The piece seemed to revolve around the idea of a small makeshift or portable home. In her *New York Times* review of the piece, titled "It's a Cave? A Temple? It's a Mystery," Jennifer Dunning says, "Is the set a cradle? A Japanese temple? A volcano? Womb? Eiko and Koma are not saying."[12]

Through improvised movement explorations within the narrative structure and based on the concept, Eiko and Koma choreograph movements and
create a space-time design for the performance. This serves as a base from
which they create a plan specific to each venue. Their choreography is flexible, allowing them to be spontaneous movers/performers. Their movement
is full of nuance and resides in a slowed-down dynamic range. Eiko points
out that the movement is ambiguous, not direct, and she feels that as a result
the audience reads the movement on an instinctual level. Perhaps this explains the mesmerizing effect of their work. In *The Caravan Project*, the two
dancers slowly crawl, twist, and nestle for thirty or forty minutes or more on
the slope or in the nest below, cohabiting but not comingling, as the audience
circles around them. The trailer is parked outside on a summer night; the
ambient sound becomes the accompaniment.

In Eiko and Koma's works, there are a few simple moments or movement
phrases that viewers may experience as climax points. These embody the initial concept, whether they are somehow elemental to it or evoke emotion for
the viewers. Well into *The Caravan Project*, the male (Koma) suddenly rises
up and "bites" the female (Eiko) on the neck. Two became one for an

Eiko in the caravan, with the Catskills in the background. *The Caravan Project* (1999).
Photo © Koma

instant—the nest has served its purpose. The bite, an action minimal in itself, stands out against the highly defined movement vocabulary, relieving tension. The story is told with the sparest action, leaving room for the individual imagination to fill in the narrative, conjuring archetypal (Eiko and Koma refer to them as "ancient memories") yet personal interpretations, such as my own above.[13]

In their Delicious Movement workshops, Eiko and Koma share their approach to improvising movement, an important aspect being that the movement generated is enjoyable, "delicious," to the individual mover. They use imagery as a source for movement. Eiko, a consummate storyteller, weaves the layering of images into stories as she talks the class through various phrases of the improvised vocabulary. For example, in "sleeping" I learned to move continuously yet gently as one might when asleep so as not to wake myself up. In "dreaming" I learned how to drift into a particular place of my imagination, but then to leave it just before it solidified, so as not to awaken.[14] Delicious Movement, while related to Eiko and Koma's own movement vocabulary, is open to adaptation by the individual, a resource people can take into their lives and use and develop on their own, which could be for, but not limited to, new movement patterns, relaxation or meditation, and personal growth as well as performance. Students are encouraged to create their own variations and find their own purposes for the practice.

In Delicious Movement workshops of a few weeks or more, Eiko and Koma offer a graduation ritual nicknamed "Crazy House," a celebration of the intensive work to aid in the digestion of the experience. They developed Crazy House from their memories of having been lost in improvisation classes taught by their teacher Kazuo Ohno.[15] In this ritual, participants are invited to get lost if they so choose. Not knowing what you are doing, or "where" you are—becoming lost—allows you the opportunity to find your way back to a known place *or* to find where you are now, in the new place. The process can help participants assimilate new material. Getting lost is a task, though an unusual one! It can also be a humbling experience. Eiko and Koma design their workshops to include a curious combination of both possibilities—the humbling as well as the delicious.

A New Form of Dance: Steve Paxton

Steve Paxton suggests considering the interplay of improvisation and set material as an ongoing dialogue. He says,

The relation between form and improvisation is intrinsic. In normal life, plans (envisioned forms of action) are the primary motivator of many tasks, interwoven with moments when unexpected events require intuitive or reflexive responses. Sports, for example, often have rigorous rules defining what is to be done and how it is to be accomplished, yet rely on improvisation to soar beyond definitions into the unforeseen, improbable moments which bring the crowds to their feet and a collective roar to their throats. Dance and music, in particular among the arts, have enshrined improvisation in their classical forms, and rely upon it as one means of creating new forms, styles, or modes of productions. In these arts, the form recedes into the background and the improvisations may acknowledge a relation to form by simply breaking the rules. Beyond this "negative" relation is the possibility of using improvisational methods to discover new forms, as in Contact Improvisation. . . . Improvisation arising from rules, or rules arising from improvisations; the relation between them is intrinsic.[16]

Many consider Contact Improvisation—which Paxton conceived for performance in 1972 and subsequently developed with founding collaborators such as Nancy Stark Smith, Daniel Lepkoff, and Nita Little—a new contemporary dance form. Contact is built around an initial investigation of the reflex reactions of two bodies sharing weight through a moving point of physical contact. The dance that results is whatever the body does to survive following this task. The form puts the reflex reactions on display for observation and study by dancers and viewers alike. However, Contact is unlike most dance forms in that the more the form becomes fixed in its vocabulary and techniques of execution, the less successful it is in fulfilling its initial task of putting the body off its guard. As dancers become familiar with the ins and outs of the basic movements that arise, they may create a flowing dance of negotiating how they will shift from one maneuver to another. To counteract this tendency, dancers challenge themselves to find the improvisation in Contact Improvisation in any moment, to look for unfamiliar territory within the familiar, to continue the investigation that is Contact's heart and soul. The dialogue that arises between form and improvisation becomes palpable, pushing dancers to new spine-tingling heights and interpolations of where the "rules" of Contact Improvisation might lead them.

Usually danced as a duet, Contact Improvisation has accumulated recognizable elements of movement—vocabulary, though based not on the aesthetics of shape or line as in ballet, for instance, but on the body's safely navigating its play with gravity and falling. For example, common shapings are surfing—one body taking a ride on top of another rolling body; counterbalances—one partner leaning away from the other while holding on with any limb to any limb; weight sharing head-to-head or back-to-back dances; pelvis-to-pelvis lifts; and spiraling circles around the shoulders and neck of the supporting dancer.

A physical training arises from Contact's practice, in which a dancer develops skills particular to the form.[17] Contact dancers practice a lower center of gravity than is usual in Western theatrical dance, develop a heightened ability to sense through their skin and enhanced peripheral vision. They hone their skill by attending workshops and classes and by jamming—open sessions that give Contacters the opportunity to interact with different partners. The jam offers interactions with partners of varying history and experience; it's an open source for technical development. And, through exposure to unfamiliar partners, jams offer Contacters a challenge to observe and hone their reflexes in the play.

STUDYING FORM: RICHARD BULL

Richard Bull, originally trained as a jazz musician, was interested in creating a dialogue of form in dance improvisation much like there exists in jazz music, where a familiar theme might be stated and varied, turned upside down or passed from one player to another. Bull became interested in looking at other arts and their use of forms as well. He experimented with scavenging forms from literature to use as structures for improvisational dances. Instead of the literal storytelling often used in traditional dance, he translated forms he found in works such as Italo Calvino's *Invisible Cities* and James Joyce's *Ulysses* into danced analogues—"storytelling" with a modernist twist.

For his piece *The Joyce of Choreography*, made with his students at Wesleyan University, Bull developed danced counterparts to literary devices that Joyce used, such as allusion, interpolation, and interior monologue. A danced *allusion* was a movement reference from *Swan Lake* or the tango; *interpolation* was a short, unrelated dance inserted into a larger dance. The use of *interior monologue* in rehearsal (the dancers' thought aloud) led to the development of dance steps colored by adjectives from the text—"displeased and sleepy turns, spouting and hobbling entrechat quatres, stale smoky modern dance triplets."[18] These devices used within the text shaped the movement vocabulary, and the structure of specific chapters based on these devices lent shape to sections of the dance.

Bull often used spoken improvised text as an element in dance improvisation. In *The Dance that Describes Itself* (1977) dancers gave live commentary on their actions in performance, creating a meta-narrative to the typical narrative reading of a dance that an audience might make. This action-based commentary emphasized the dancers' formal concerns in the shaping of the dance, providing the audience an alternative way to look at the dance.[19]

Bull's fascination with improvised text as a companion for improvised dancing continued throughout his career. He, and his dancers, including his long-term collaborators Cynthia Novack and Peentz Dubble, developed many different ways to deconstruct and reconstruct the narrative of their dances for audiences—by establishing then relayering text and movement

While Richard Bull's *The Dance that Describes Itself* (1977) included verbal commentary from the dancers regarding their formal concerns in shaping the arising dance, his *Camera Mobilia* (1989) offered the audience an alternative visual perspective. During the dance, the dancers passed around a video camera and later showed the footage to the audience. *From left*: George Russell, Peentz Dubble, Millen Mahaffey, Cynthia Novack, and Richard Bull. Photo © Dona Ann McAdams

relationships, by providing multiple narrative viewpoints to the dance action, as well as through live action commentary on the shaping of the dance. The premise of *My Story* (1981) was that each dancer tell a previously agreed upon story using both words and movement. As the performance materialized, dancers began to appropriate one another's lines and moves to express their version, visually revealing the multiple reads inherent in any story. In Novack and Bull's duet *Ithaca* (1989), the premise was for the dancers to comment on their actions in the past tense and third person: "Was there any significance in the fact that she had backed into the space?" "Hadn't he noticed her upstage actions?"[20] The performance pointed out, often humorously, the leeway in interpretation among words, movement, and motivation. For Bull it was this play with the structural elements within a dance—a good-natured questioning of the activity of forming and composing—that ultimately gave the dance its shape.

FROM CHAOS TO FORM THROUGH PLAY: KEITH HENNESSY

Keith Hennessy thrives on multiple influences in his working process. His sources range from visual arts, theater, dance and somatic techniques, queer performance, performance art, performance and gender studies, popular and scholarly culture, shamanism, the circus, politics, camp, drag, and cabaret. Hennessy doesn't just mine these disciplines for material—topics or themes—for dances; he appropriates their means and methodologies for making and discovering movement as well. One of Hennessy's favorite influences is Josef Beuys (1921–86), a German conceptual artist and sculptor, an engager of public and social spaces—a "social sculptor." Beuys considered art a vehicle for political and social change and, among many interests, experimented with play as process.

Hennessy might approach the topic by asking his students, while improvising movement, to observe and explore the transitions from chaos (a lack of structure) to play to form, a theme that Beuys used in his seminal work, *Fat Corner* (1963). Chaos/play/form may be a familiar structure for dancemakers or artists of any sort who go into the studio with no initial idea, or, as the case may be, many ideas, then "noodle" or "fool around," that is, play, and come up with something that intrigues them—a form that is repeatable or engage-able. Recognizing that chaos can lead to form through play helps improvisers develop a tolerance for chaotic situations and disparate energies that a group might normally work to avoid. Hennessy points out that for the sake of group cohesion, dynamics often get watered down in an attempt to avoid conflict. This can flatten the work by leaving out a vital piece of the equation—chaos. Hennessy encourages dancers to consciously include physically as well as socially dangerous elements, allow sparks to fly in the service of creating tension, energy, and excitement in the work.[21]

In a solo improvisation, *Laugh Scream*, performed at CI36 (Contact Improvisation's thirty-sixth birthday celebration), in Huntingdon, Pennsylvania, in June 2008, Hennessy created an edge for the audience by giving *us* a score. In a pre-performance talk, Hennessy told us that we were probably going to want to laugh during the performance due to his costume and movement. Our instructions were to examine the motivation for our laughter. Hennessy returned, his bare, hairy masculine legs showing under a black, cross-strapped-back, sleeveless leotard and wearing sequined cuffs on his wrists and a copy of the mask made for the horror movie *Scream* (1996) by Wes Craven. Chuckles arose immediately. Was it the gender-bending or the odd juxtaposition of sequins and iconically "scary" mask that evokes this laughter? Hennessy began moving: lopes; leaps; and long, athletic, sideways dives onto the floor. His score for his movement included not doing anything intentional for laughs, following impulses connected to sensation, and to dance—not speak, sing, or mime.[22]

Straightforward movement followed, and several in the audience laughed openly and wholeheartedly. The laughing continued; Hennessy stopped and reminded us to follow the score, then resumed his athletic dance movement circuits of the stage space. At one point, he stood as a curtain on the backstage wall rose to reveal a window at the back of the stage space, reflecting us. The laughter that had continued since our reminder to follow the score gained a hysterical quality, uncontrollable, with a certain high pitch— a soundtrack for the piece. An edginess arose in examination of our laughter. Questions came up: can you tell that I am following the rules if I *choose* to laugh? Issues were revealed: the depersonalization that occurs through masking the face, the hyper-physicalization of the body that occurs through masking the face, attitudes toward socially acceptable audience behavior or the cross-dressing transgression of the performer, and perhaps a stirring of collective cultural guilt on the association of the masking of torture victims at the Abu Ghraib prison during the Iraq War. On which side of the line did I fall as audience member? Hennessy's audience score cleverly ramped up the tension and made at least some think twice about how we see and interpret dance performance.

Keith Hennessy in his scored improvisation *Laugh Scream* at the University of California, Davis, 2007. Photo © Ilya Noé

ARTICULATING FORMS: NINA MARTIN

Performance of open improvisation is Nina Martin's goal, though she is quick to point out that nothing is truly open, that there is always some structure or pattern involved in how we engage in dancing. Her work, Ensemble Thinking, is a group of training structures designed to help improvisers read what is going on in the dance space and to make choices based on that read. Martin feels that when improvisers focus on their personal movement vocabularies, their attention inevitably draws inward and they lose awareness of what is forming in the space around them—where other dancers are in space, what is being offered by other dancers, and how they are relating to one another. Awareness to the group composition is overwhelmed by concentration on articulating the detail of the solo material.

Her training structures focus dancers' attention on various aspects of form as it relates to the ensemble: spatial arrangement, functional groupings (e.g., solo, duet, trio), where the viewers' attention is being drawn in the space at any given moment, and the shifting dynamics of the developing dance. To do this, Martin uses what she refers to as the "straitjacket" technique, or a limitation of personal vocabulary. That is, in many of the exercises only simple movements like walking or running, standing, lying down, or sitting are allowed as movement options. Often the initial stages of the training structure will start with an arrangement of bodies in space in stillness. Once the compositional principle is mastered, locomotion is added in. Martin characterizes this straitjacket work as tedious but necessary. After familiarity is gained in reading the space for formal elements, the straitjacket comes off and improvisers begin to work with more complex movement material as part of the mix.

In her training structure One Idea, dancers practice recognizing a simple stationary spatial idea that a solo dancer puts forward. For example, a dancer might come to stand facing a corner of the stage space. This represents the dancer's simple spatial idea. The group acknowledges it by making a group tableau based on the initial idea—without making it more complex. If the first dancer has stood facing the diagonal, then a second dancer joining the idea by lying down along the diagonal is not allowed—it is not the same idea, but a complication of it. The exercise creates an ensemble skill of recognizing and making a simple—and quick—group choice.[23]

Martin and half the group sit out to coach, honing the working groups' response to the single idea. Clarity of design and speed of recognition are developed by moving quickly from one formation into the next. One Idea and other training structures that comprise Martin's Ensemble Thinking create a laboratory to focus dancers' attention on specific forms and to develop skill in realizing them. Later, in open improvisation these skills are available as a toolbox of possibilities for composing the dance.[24]

FOSTERING FORM: PENNY CAMPBELL

Penny Campbell finds that "form is always present—it's just a matter of perceiving it from inside the dancing" if you're an improviser.[25] To develop this ability, Campbell starts with the present moment. She encourages students in her improvisation classes at Middlebury College to include more and more of the present into their dancing—by paying attention to sensation as a basis for movement vocabulary and by learning to notice and accept local conditions, whatever they are.

Campbell builds attention to the moment and to the group—ensemble awareness—through a series of specific practices such as the matching practice (see chapter 1) to clarify her students' notions of how her approach differs from other experiences of improvisation they might have had. As they begin improvising dances together, Campbell remains flexible in response to what she sees the students are able to handle, introducing a particular practice as it seems appropriate. Campbell calls the work Performance Improvisation. Her aim is for the ensemble to perform open improvisation and create pieces of dance art collaboratively.

As a guide, she creates opportunities for dancers to discover the working principles of improvisation for themselves. Temporarily acting as an outside eye for the group, Campbell establishes what she refers to as an "art culture" by making aesthetic choices about, for instance, what a beginning is, when an end comes, what constitutes a development of dance movement, and what dance material is developing in the space. Then she stirs up discussion over these choices that she has initially made for the group.[26]

Case in point: a practice called Beginnings. Campbell asks the ensemble to do a series of just the beginnings of dances. Campbell calls "end" when she thinks the initial movement material has been stated. She also calls end, stopping the action, if she senses that a development of the material takes place. Students start on or off stage and enter to take places in "black out"; Campbell calls "lights up," and the action begins. (These are fictitious cues— by the time the group is in theatrical light they don't need to call them.)

When end is called, the dancers clear the space, ready to start again. Sometimes the dancers take issue with the end that Campbell calls, as in this example of a controversial beginning call:

> Nothing happens. No sound. No dancers. Just waiting. That's good. It's important that dancers not feel they must be out there moving all the time. We are uncomfortable with silences, with stillness, but it is another element of our material. I'm glad to see the dancers taking their time. Of course, it could go on forever. That might be too long. We'll see.
>
> The waiting continues. And continues. Helen steps out, very close to the downstage edge.
>
> "End!"
>
> "What?" she barks in surprise. "I just got here."
>
> "Yes you did," I toss back. "And that long, wonderful stillness was the beginning. You were the development."[27]

These experiences become fodder for discussions of "beginning-ness," and the group amasses examples of beginnings through practice. A "felt" group consensus process takes shape with less and less need for discussion and direction. Eventually, the ensemble takes over this role of negotiating the aesthetic—how it forms beginnings, what constitutes a development, when to come to a conclusion—in the dancing itself. Once this art culture is functioning, an ensemble is born.

EMERGING FORMS: SUSAN SGORBATI

Susan Sgorbati has been following form since the mid-1980s in her work with improvisation ensembles of dancers and musicians at Bennington College. She started to make lists of forms that repeatedly appeared in her observations of improvisation and to name them—forms such as unison, accumulation, shadowing, washes (a group of dancers crossing the stage together in a wave), solo with a chorus, and main event with a chorus, to name a few. (The forms for the musicians in the ensemble are generally analogous to the dancers'.) Sgorbati observed these forms consistently emerging during dance improvisations and noticed that dancers would also recognize, play into, and develop them. She wondered what clues dancers picked up to help them recognize developing forms. How did improvisers cue one another in these situations and agree to collaborate to develop a particular form? To help dancers become skillful in this process, Sgorbati asks dancers to practice the forms, deciding beforehand to work with just one form, such as unison or flocking (a following form with changing leaders), for example. These forms are the "musical scales" of her ensemble improvisation work. Dancers familiarize themselves with the forms and learn to negotiate clear developments of them as an ensemble.[28]

Bruce Weber, an evolutionary biologist colleague of Sgorbati's at Bennington, introduced her to complexity theory—a scientific theory that considers complex systems, their properties, and the emergent phenomenon that may arise from them. For example, color, surface tension, and temperature are emergent phenomena that groups of atoms and molecules may exhibit, while flocking behavior is an emergent phenomenon of herds of animals, swarms of insects, or schools of fish. Sgorbati was fascinated by complexity theory's resonance with her own observations in improvisation. She noticed that sometimes a particular structure for an improvisation leads to a dance that will feed and reinvent itself in endless variation—whereas others seem to fizzle out. She was curious: what is it about a form, what properties must it have, to lead to a self-sustaining dance?

Sgorbati found that complexity theory considers similar questions. How do the initial interacting systems—whether groups of molecules, insects, or dancers—give rise to the generation of distinct yet infinite possible outcomes, thus an emergent phenomenon? To this end she appropriated the language of complexity theory to research self-sustaining structures for dance improvisation. She is enthusiastic that she is onto something big yet basic: deep underlying structuring principles that cross disciplines.[29]

FRAMES AS FORMS: MARY OVERLIE

Mary Overlie considers the audience's point of view and asks what it is that we look for when we watch dance or theater. She finds six elements of theater, or Viewpoints, through which we make sense of what we see on the stage—space, time, shape, movement, emotion, and story. Overlie uses the Viewpoints to make work that is nontraditional, for example, has a nonlinear storyline, but they may also be used as critical tools to examine any type of work, traditional or otherwise.

Overlie finds the Viewpoints are interwoven in traditional theater or dance; in classical and modern performance they build on one another in a particular hierarchical order. For example, from a Viewpoints perspective, in a classical ballet the space is generally arranged symmetrically. Movement ("kinesthetics") is subsidiary to line (shape), as well as rhythm and phrasing (time). Emotions are portrayed through shapes and movement, and a story unfolds that has well-known subjects such as love, death, or madness. Whatever the particular tradition of an era or style, directors, choreographers, and audience become so familiar with the six elements in a particular hierarchical pattern of usage that they forget that at one point it was a choice to pattern them in that way.[30]

Work with the Six Viewpoints examines that hierarchical order. Overlie introduces students to each particular element of the Viewpoints and leads them to develop the skill of shifting rapidly between them. This shifting and reshuffling creates performances that often confound our expectations as viewers and causes us to reflect on the mechanics of how we build meaning. For example, Overlie enters the stage space and picks up an orange electrical extension cord. She unravels it in a determined, workmanlike fashion. From the audience, I see the plug in the wall. As I watch her actions, I build a story around them. However, as she comes to the end of the cord, instead of plugging the cord into the wall, she holds the end out in the stage space toward a ladder. My mind jolts! I quickly drop the storyline and notice that she has created a beautiful arcing Day-Glo orange line across the stage, complementing the framework of the ladder. My attention shifts from story to space and shape. The surprise of suddenly being shown the space is delightful, and I see the space with fresh eyes for a moment, until another story takes over and I am pulled in, bumping along a nonlinear pathway awaiting another surprising development.[31]

As a dancemaker, discovering your predilections for working (Do you mostly work from your emotions? Are shape and space the guiding elements of your dances?) may open you up to other creative possibilities or strengthen the choices you already make.

The Senses as Composers: Lisa Nelson

Lisa Nelson observes that our bodies compose themselves to focus our attention on the task at hand. These "compositions" are automatic responses (both genetic and learned) to circumstances and have simultaneous functions: like tilting your head toward a speaker to hear better, focusing your eyes on his or her face to read its expression, and composing your expression to show your interest. We are experts at composing our bodies in this way and also at reading the intentions of these compositions in others—body language, which happens mostly subliminally. Nelson takes this kind of composition into consideration in her performance works and teaching.

One way she investigates how the body composes itself for action is to work with closed eyes. Instead of navigating with the usually dominant sense of vision, dancers respond to circumstances—compose themselves—by relying on other senses. In a practice she calls the Blind Unison Trio, three dancers are asked to dance in unison with their eyes closed. Often stymied at first as to how to accomplish the task without looking, they soon develop strategies to create an unsighted version of unison. Sound, touch, smell, the kinesthetic sense, and memory all come into play. The activity of composing the body from sensory information usually happens so reflexively that it goes unnoticed. But with less familiar senses involved in this practice, this level of composing is brought to awareness. By working with eyes sometimes open and sometimes closed, the dancers gather further information about how they make choices via the interplay of the senses.[32]

Forming a Dialogue of Spirit, Nature, and Culture: Prapto (Suprapto Suryodarmo)

Prapto is a Javanese dancer who as a young man loved to move but found the traditional dances of his culture weren't the right form of expression for him. Instead he started doing "free movement" in the 1970s. He experienced that these improvisations could sometimes go on for hours, even days; with no frame for his movement, he found that he had no way to relate to others and felt disconnected. Prapto refers to this phase of his early improvising as "flying."[33] He was drawn to study Vipassana and Javanese Sumarah meditation, and found that through these practices, which develop awareness while attending to simple actions, he could do free improvisation and "if feeling flying, be embodied."[34]

With this discovery, Prapto created *Wayang Buddha* (Buddha's Shadow-puppet, 1975) and other new ritual artworks that combine elements of religiosity and art. He then developed an improvisational movement practice that he calls Joged Amerta, which is influenced by his meditation studies. Prapto sees this approach as more than an improvisation technique; rather, it cultivates an attitude toward life. He places the practice in a context of nature, sacred space, and cultural exchange. Dance and movement artists, musicians, installation artists, architects, sculptors, painters, poets, filmmakers, teachers, social workers, art therapists—students and professionals alike, from many different cultures around the world—attend his workshops. The workshops are held both internationally and at his school, Padepokan Lemah Putih, in Mojosongo just north of Solo, Central Java, where he works site-specifically. He leads the workshops in his garden and in temples, beaches, and other historical and cultural areas in Java, Sumatra, Bali, and Sulawesi.

For example, he practices in Samuan Tiga-Bedulu, Central Bali, particularly because, he says, in the eleventh century a dialogue among three religions (Bali Aga, Hinduism, and Buddhism) occurred there, resulting in the creation of three village temples representing each. Three temples can still be found in the villages of Bali today. The concept of diversity in unity (*bhinneka tunggal ika*) grew out of this dialogue. Prapto also chooses Tejakula in North Bali to practice, as a place where cultures were in dialogue. He explains that in the seventeenth century Bali Mula aborigines met with migrating peoples from other regions of Bali and maritime cultures of the Nusantara Archipelago, Southeast Asia, and Asia, including China, Indi-Persia, and the Middle East. By agreeing to lay aside their social castes, they resided together as an intercultural society.[35] These special contexts are integral to Prapto's practice of Joged Amerta.

Prapto might begin a dance by handing a leaf to someone as an invitation to dance. He dances with the person; the leaf is passed back and forth; he proceeds to dance with others, again exchanging the leaf. His students remark on how the simple exchange of a leaf or a stick or stone structures and vitalizes the dance, creating relationship among the dancers.[36] In subsequent dances, he might offer guidance, often in metaphorical language. Susan Bauer, a workshop participant, offers these quotes from Prapto from her memory and class notes: "The wind has emotion, the water has emotion, not just the fire. Can you find the emotion of the wind and the water, too?" "I see the space and the air, now can you find the bone in the wind of your dancing?" Or more simply, "Your skin is late."[37] Students express amazement both at the practicality and the depths of Prapto's insights into their personalities and attitudes, which he has observed through their movement or through moving with them.[38]

According to Prapto, improvisation begins with everyday movement, "the cycles of life," including resting, sitting, crawling, and walking with variations: "How to find there something not yet awake but something potential. And then finding the key—click—vrrrmmm. . . . Then how to put in the communication."[39] He moves, sings, and prays, or speaks to give guidance for participants. A particular style of dancing or moving isn't expected, rather, one is trying to cultivate "how movement has quality as 'a dance,' and dance has quality of movement." His statements become points of inquiry. For example, when does movement become dance? And how is dance like an ordinary movement? He offers reflections to each participant "to support their growing for discovering their own way and their own form."[40]

From rock gardens to English country gardens to elaborate formal gardens with topiary, each garden has a certain form—we may all recognize its beauty and delight. Prapto uses the "realm of the garden" as a source for creativity in art-making. In "Web Art Garden—An Idea" (1997), he writes that a garden has qualities such as "freshness, joy, healing, and an opportunity for social gathering." The idea of a garden is transnational, multicultural, and inter-generational and as such allows for people from diverse cultural backgrounds to come together within it. He asks, "How can we have sharing, gathering, and dialogue without fanaticism between the modern and the traditional cultures? We need a realm that can accept all human, nature, and religiosity resources."[41] Since 1999, Web Art Garden, a worldwide network of artists and presenting organizations, has initiated annual cultural events around the world to celebrate the June 5th World Environment Day.

Prapto has created other international intercultural art events as well. For instance, Sharing Time, first held in Köln, Germany, in 1993, happens every other year in different places throughout the world. Each locale creates its own theme and approach for sharing art and the cultural environment. The event is held in town or out in nature—perhaps at a site of religious or cultural importance. These events allow participants of Prapto's workshops to share their experience of his Joged Amerta within their own communities.

INVESTIGATING OPEN SPACE IMPROVISATION: BARBARA DILLEY

In the mid-1970s Chögyam Trungpa Rinpoche, the founder of Shambhala Buddhism, invited Barbara Dilley to develop a dance program at the Naropa Institute (now University) in Boulder, Colorado. During this same period, she had begun her own journey into Buddhist meditation practice. She started to ask how improvisational dance practice and meditation inter-related and complemented one another—for it was clear to her that they did.[42] Earlier in her career with the Grand Union, an improvisational dance-theater company, Dilley had found that in following impulses in the heat of the improvised moment onstage, her private feelings became public material.

Though that had been disconcerting for her, she still longed to re-create the deep sense of play she had experienced in improvised performance with the Grand Union. Eventually, she found that Buddhist meditation and philosophy helped her gain the perspective she had been searching for.

Dilley finds that "open space" improvisation—improvisation with no predetermined rules—is demanding of dancers no matter how experienced they may be. Dancers are often used to having a teacher or choreographer tell them what to do. With no limits and no authoritative voice in an open space improvisation, the responsibility of what to do and how is left to the individual, which can leave a dancer not knowing either what to do at all or how to choose from an overwhelming number of possibilities.[43] As an experimental dancemaker and improviser Dilley didn't believe she needed to directly explain how dance practice and meditation related. Instead, she created the Contemplative Dance Practice as a physical investigation of that query.[44]

In Contemplative Dance Practice, Dilley creates an opportunity for intentional study of open space, not to avoid its difficulties but to meet them prepared with tools of meditation and a variety of body-mind awareness practices. Its structure combines aspects of sitting meditation and dance improvisation. To cultivate an attitude of attention and awareness to the thought process and a relaxed presence in the body and mind, it starts with sitting meditation. Personal warm-up follows, to investigate movement patterns and pursue individual needs, interests, or studies such as Authentic Movement, Body-Mind Centering, or any variety of somatic, release, or alignment techniques. This time is for practice of whatever current work a dancer might be involved in. Last, there is an open space improvisation, in which people sit around the edges of the space and enter, move, and exit as they wish. A short final sitting meditation and time for group discussion end the practice, which is designed to take about three hours. The time frames for each of the three main sections—which, in practice, may be varied according to necessity—are marked with the ring of a bell.[45] In some contexts, a ceremonial bow to the space on entering and exiting is made "to acknowledge the atmosphere and the environment that's been created for its opportunity to wake you up," according to Dilley.[46]

⤬ FIELD NOTES ⤬

From my general schooling and a few dance composition classes in college, I understood that form was the arrangement of material and there were rules and principles to be followed. As a dancer in a ballet company, I was generally happy to leave the arranging of material up to the choreographers. However, early on I became intrigued by Eiko and Koma's ability to tell a story in a nonlinear fashion with surprising emotional impact. When I first began improvising, it was for pure kinetic enjoyment, but gradually I became curious about how to present that delight to others.

Initially, the premise of generating movement material from a researched source made sense to me: Simone Forti's portraits of animals or exposés of crawling, Nancy Topf's anatomical dances. Starting with compositional concerns, from scores or structures, often seemed superficial to me. I suppose I enjoyed the security of knowing how I would be creating my movement; without a defined process, it seemed arbitrary and disconnected.

Ensemble work with Susan Sgorbati changed that. I became caught up in the excitement of contributing to and bolstering the emerging forms of the ensemble as we co-recognized them. The movement I chose and how and where I placed it could add to or contrast, solidify or destabilize the arising dance. I learned to develop my own at-my-fingertips movement sourcing to keep up with the ever-shifting terrain of the improvisation.

Further work with Penny Campbell and the Architects helped me to hone my interests and taught me to hold my own ground in their lively mix of movement, spoken word, music, and theater. The survival of the fittest atmosphere in the performance space was a rigorous test of mettle, a battle of improvisational wits. I learned to stake my claim in the dialogue and give it weight to be considered (even noticed!) by the group. (If I repeat this long enough . . . or if I place this right smack in the middle of the stage space . . . or if I wait until there's a lull . . .) I learned how to give value to my own contributions. It was exciting to have something I proposed picked up on, restated, transformed. Everyone learned to sink or swim by sinking and swimming and getting over it, then going back out in the performance space yet again.

By the time I studied with Nina Martin, I had several years of improvisation study under my belt. Her work distilled into basic exercises, and qualified and quantified principles I had discovered through trial and error. With some patience, because it is tough work to go back to basics and tease away the unnecessary, I learned to reverse-engineer my improvisation knowledge into the many building blocks of ensemble work that Martin calls Ensemble Thinking. Then, putting those sharpened skills back together in open improvisation with the ensemble had the magical effect of an improvisation that feels effortless—as if circumstance presented itself ripe for the plucking.

This could have been enough! But there were other unusual and compelling perspectives to be considered. For example, how did a body compose itself in a particular social situation? Lisa Nelson's work suggested another layer of consideration to the composition question, a subliminal habitual world that required close observation and nondominant senses to be brought to the forefront. How might an improvised dance be composed when the dancers can't see?

Suprapto Suryodarmo offered me the compositions of a completely "other" culture. There were only a few intuitive handholds to grasp in his teaching, and those were slippery—Indonesian doesn't translate easily into English. Fortunately, dance is a universal language, and dancing with Prapto turned out to be his preferred method of communicating. He danced with us in duets and in groups, and when he didn't dance with us, he sang or drummed for our dances. I learned from Prapto that the dancer didn't always have to be the subject of attention in the dance. Prapto could remove himself from a scene through his dance movement—even though he was right in front of me—in a way that would make him not stand out. He could dance what was unseen in my culture: the context, the backdrop rather than a foreground. I remain intrigued to discover what the rules and regulations of composition might look like in this inverse world.

PRACTICES FOR FURTHER RESEARCH

1. How comfortable are you with chaos? Set up a dance situation, whether viewing or dancing, that investigates and tests your "chaos comfort zone." When you don't know what is going on or can't make sense of it, do you get edgy? How, as a dancer, do you respond to chaos? Do you feel the need to drop out? Do you look for structure? Move more or become still? Become dictatorial or go with the flow?

2. Some people think limits spark their creativity; others are thwarted by too many rules. How comfortable are you with limitations? Create an improvisation with strict limitations of your choosing to test your tolerance.

3. After an open improvisation with a group of people, review and write down the formal structures you remember arising (solos, canons,

chorus with main event, or make up your own names for the forms).
Did they just seem to happen, or did you help create them by some
action you took?

4. Review the dances you've made from the perspective of the Six
Viewpoints. Do you "stack" the Viewpoints in a particular order when
you choreograph, for example, first creating dynamic movement and
then placing it in the space? After identifying your comfortable
ordering, try rearranging that order and use it as a structure for
improvising a dance.

5. When does movement become dance? And how is dance like an
ordinary movement? Use these questions as research for an
improvisation. Try working with and without music.

⇥ INTERLUDE ⇤

Notes to Myself: Wait!

> No room for form with love this strong.
>   —RUMI, "No Room for Form"

The poet trawls the depths for material, not knowing what, just being magnetically attracted to the hunt. . . . Pulling stuff up in the net. That whole
process of trawling, pulling in, collecting can be so juicy and thrilling. Being
in love with the material and surfing that love crest. Not caring, just blending.

Then the naming phase kicks in. What have I got in my net? And how do
I justify this luscious activity to others? It has to be something recognizable,
be "for some reason," or be usable. Then the collectors ask: well, can you
bring me back more just like that? And the pressure is on. Who knows if there
is more like that down there? Cleverness was invented to fool the collectors.
But I can end up fooling myself.

Naming, framing, forming. If it happens too soon on the hunt, I end up
with house sparrows for lunch. Leave a little more time, create that space,
MA, that the Japanese speak of, before calling it a dance, before knowing just
what it is. In that space, that's when it tells ME what it is. A satisfying dinner,
a delicacy, a glass of port before bed. Lingonberry jam on toast at breakfast!

3

Time Machines

I am estimating here, but I would guess the history and the future of "from the moment" dance improvisation, when added together, is about 30 milliseconds. Perhaps less, when things are going well.

—STEVE PAXTON, "The History and Future of Dance Improvisation"

TIME SLIPS THROUGH OUR FINGERS like sand through an hourglass. Pendulums swing, the earth turns. We measure time through movement. It's not surprising that time shows many faces in dance improvisation. For example, rather than measuring the length of a dance by a clock, some dancemakers use cues from the body or the improvised material as the timekeeper for their dances, finding a felt ending as signaled by the body or an organic ending that comes out of the material. Body time is measured from the internal sensing of time as opposed to the time on a clock; it can be much slower or pass more quickly than clock time—time may drag or fly. In work that examines habitual responses or engages the reflexes to a high degree, we can experience the body as much quicker than the conscious mind. On the other hand, movement that focuses deeply on sensation can expand and fill our sense of the moment, making one minute feel like ten.

Movement may be used in a more objective way as well, for instance, to mark time—a sudden shift into a fast section of dance movement creates a reference point from which to measure. Clock time is often used to section and end works. Time spans are set and signaled by lighting or music shifts, for example—some kind of arbitrary cue based on actual time passed. Time— it's no longer the simple choice between a waltz and the tango; it's a whole other dimension to be explored.

A CHANCE ENCOUNTER: KATIE DUCK

Katie Duck points out that because dance is a "time art" (i.e., a performing art, or an art form that unfolds in time), duration is of major concern, but that the dancer's relationship to time is very different when improvising than when dancing set choreography. In improvisation, dancers choose not only what movements to make but when to make them. Because choice is available to the improvising dancer, time becomes a tool. That is, the improviser measures time through movement choices—when to enter, move, pause, or exit. Because of this, the improviser learns to juggle a whole other set of time-based skills, whereas in dancing set choreography, keeping time—often in regard to being in sync with other dancers or the music—is the dominant relationship. Duck talks to dancers about "remembering to exit" and "remembering to pause," for example. These are choices of the improvising dancer—ways that a dancer has to create duration and to place, mark, or locate a dance in time.

These choices of the improvisers drive the dance initially. Once an improvisation starts, the choices begin multiplying exponentially. "There are more choices available than the space can contain," Duck says.[1] In other words, a dancer, in the instant that exists after finishing a movement, could probably come up with two or three different choices to follow it but of course can only pick one. Very quickly, if you do the math, there are thousands of potential dances that didn't happen!

The choices made create a context to be considered, and so, as the dance progresses, there is less freedom for individual choice—suddenly a dancer can't do just anything. Perhaps a certain mood is developed or a relationship established, which needs to be accounted for. Sometimes a dancer finds him- or herself literally stuck with a choice, for example, sitting facing upstage and not being able to see what is happening in the rest of the space. At that point choices are few, and chance—the way one dancer's choices and another's choices intersect—becomes an operating factor in shaping the improvisation. By chance, another dancer's path comes into the view of the one facing upstage, giving him or her options to respond to. As the dance progresses, it becomes more and more reliant on chance happenings.

It is not choice that interests Duck so much as chance—she is interested in the aesthetics of chance. As she sees it, choice (when as well as what) and chance (the intersection of events) are the composers in improvisation. The dancers don't compose, that is, make something happen directly through their choices—at least she is not interested in this type of choice, which is basically choreography in her book. Rather she asks that her dancers make choices that "create space" (or possibilities) for the dance to happen amid.[2] After all, the excitement of improvisation is in chance happenings; what need to be created are the conditions for those chance encounters to occur. Dancers don't time an encounter in improvisation as they do in choreography. Through their choices they can only create the conditions for the possibility of coincidence to happen, placing themselves in a very different relationship to time than the usual being "in time."

Options to Glacial Time: Nina Martin

Nina Martin notes that while improvising, dancers tend to default to a "glacial timing," by which she means a rhythm marked by cautious dynamics and "creeping" entrances as dancers assess how material is building, their personal interest in it, and how they will fit in. To give an ensemble options other than glacial time in performance, for example a "jump cut" or a dynamic shift, she has developed practices such as "number scores." In one of these, the score is just a predetermined sequence of numbers representing the number of dancers in the performance space. Dancers enter an improvisation arbitrarily to fulfill a quota. For example, five, three, two would be a quintet, then a trio, then a duet. Dancers don't choose to enter the dance based on an intuitive sense of the building dance material, but simply to fulfill the score. In this way the score creates dynamic shifts and eventually a flow, as dancers welcome the fast-paced, sudden shifts in numbers of performers. The exercise suggests another option for entering an improvisation and forces development of a "quick thinking on your feet" kind of skill, based not on the developing of movement material but in the service of dynamics and timing.

Martin reckons that the average attention span of the improviser in any given material is often about three minutes. Because of this, improvisations develop predictable rhythms that lull the dancers and audience alike. To keep the dancers' attention, Martin encourages them to stay with something longer than might be habitually comfortable and to practice making extreme timing choices.[3]

Time Warp: Mary Overlie

On the issue of timing in improvisation, Mary Overlie takes a different tack. She warps space and time into an "egg-shaped pool table" to combat improvisation entropy—that tendency of improvisers to wind up doing similar things at the same energy level as they play off one another's material.[4] Balls don't end up predictably in their pockets on an egg-shaped pool table; to establish this table, Overlie asks that the dancers don't fuel their improvisations off one another but politely (or not) agree to improvise in the same space together. (They focus on their own material but still remain aware of what is occurring in the room.) The energy level, rather than winding down predictably, stays high, like the ball that reaches the middle of the table, curves unexpectedly, and accelerates down the gravity well. This model for improvisation allows for chance interaction rather than the propensity toward habitual imitation to drive the shaping of the improvisation. Improvising in this practice produces quirky shifts of energy and direction as dancers focus on their own agendas and relate to each other only through proximity.

Another exercise Overlie uses to counteract improvisation entropy is to ask that dancers not do something as long as they might want to, that is, not develop the material to their liking but cut it off arbitrarily and start something new. The practice develops an acute sense of time regarding duration of improvised material: How long do the life spans of my improvisations tend to be? How do I react to their interruption? Can I let go of my material? Is it possible to redirect the energy I was building and put it somewhere new? The practice is an exercise in shifting dynamics while tracking the material that is forming. It shifts the predictable development of material from a "beginning, middle, end" arc to something interrupted and unexpected and, as a practice, makes a dancer aware of his or her use of time.

SURPRISE: MIN TANAKA

A concern in Noh, a traditional form of Japanese theater, is that the interior and exterior worlds of an actor should not necessarily match.[5] This runs counter to the popular idea of the actor as striving to create a truthful rendition of an interior world, his motives, to match his exterior actions, his deeds.

Min Tanaka considers this disparity between interior and exterior in terms of dancing. His preference is that the speeds or timings of the inner and outer world of the dancer be different, creating interest in the movement.[6] Somehow an inertia or lethargy sets in if the two worlds match. Perhaps it is that the audience can predict too easily what will come next; there is no element of surprise in the movement. When the worlds don't match, the audience somehow senses something unusual, that more attention needs to be paid to the action—interest picks up. Tanaka says, "When we move, we may be telling a lie. Choreography is fundamentally deceptive. I am concerned with how a dancer fills the gap between what he/she feels in a given moment and how he/she is moving."[7]

In Tanaka's work, he uses imagery to generate movement in the body. The imagery might be very complex but the movement small or slow in comparison to the intensity of the dancer's interior world. For example, in *Locus Focus* (2007), his improvised solo performed at P.S. 1 in Brooklyn, New York, Tanaka leans against a concrete wall almost still, yet his quivering body suggests a tremendous internal struggle. There is more going on here than a body taking a rest. Who is he, how has he come to be here, and for how long? From the way he softly paws the wall out of all proportion to its mass, it seems that he knows he is powerless to affect it. Or perhaps he is the spirit of the wall, released but hovering close, unused to this freedom. As a member of the audience, I try out any number of stories to fit the situation, paying close attention to the nuance of his movement for clues. At the same time, I realize there isn't just one interpretation. The open quality of the narrative invites my engagement in the action. Viewing the piece, I may never suspect the imagery underlying the dancer's movement—that there could be an image

Min Tanaka in his improvised solo *Locus Focus* in the courtyard of P.S. 1, Long Island City, Queens, New York, December 2007. Tanaka says, "I dance not in the place; I dance the place." Photo © August Goulet

such as "hands climbing a waterfall" imbuing the movement with its tenuous quality.[8] What I do see is the effect that image has in the dancer's body.

An example of the opposite situation—where the speed of the movement outside is faster than that of the inner world—is the martial artist who performs quick, action-packed movements with a calm mind, or the calligrapher who makes a swift mark on the page with no apparent thought. The two situations might be contrasted in a dance, creating tension and allowing for a dramatic as well as physical release, perhaps in the form of a surprise, at some point during the performance. In *Locus Focus*, suddenly, startlingly, Tanaka walks away from the wall. After his struggle there, it seems a shocking, incongruous act. If he can walk away from the wall just like that—now, who is he? My mind is busy reformulating past actions and correlating current information to create a new accounting to fit the scene.

SHAPING TIME: DANA REITZ

Phrasing, how a particular movement or movement series fills a span of time, is one of those magical attributes that extraordinary dancers seem to possess, a kinesthetic musicality. Dancers of set choreography do not choose their movement in a dance, and the phrasing is often set and coached as well. For a dancer, the attribute of "good phrasing" is akin to having a beautiful singing voice, a naturalness and fluidity that isn't forced or imitated.

Dana Reitz expands the idea of phrasing of set material. Set choreography exists in unalterable sequences, but improvised phrasing of set movement allows the dancer to be very much in dialogue with the dynamics of the movement in the moment. Usually with set movement, the choreographer demonstrates (or otherwise relays) how he or she wants a movement to be executed, including its timing. The dancer's job is to reproduce these dynamics. Reitz asks her students to set a sequence of movements, but to improvise with its phrasing. The arc of a movement might be drawn out or contracted, depending on how a dancer feels the movement's musicality as he or she is performing. Reitz allows for the option of repeating or letting material go in the moment of dancing as well.

To keep track of material and its placement within the larger dance in improvised work, Reitz suggests creating predetermined markers within the dance. A buoy of spatial and/or temporal clarity, the marker helps improvisers keep their bearings as they navigate through an improvisation.[9] It could be any kind of cue: lighting, a stillness, an action like sitting in a chair or facing

upstage, a momentary resting place to settle and regroup before the next outing into the improvisation wilderness.

Time to Digest: Nancy Topf

Nancy Topf found that the body usually needs more time to pick up information than we give it. While we might be exposed to hundreds of facts in a
two-hour anatomy lecture, the body needs ample practice time to absorb and
integrate that new information, such as an anatomical image or mechanical
principle on which she based her improvisations. In her work it isn't enough
to get an idea conceptually; the body needs to be included. Maybe only one
or two images can be grasped physically in a two-hour practice period. These
improvised explorations lasted as long as it took to chew, swallow, and digest
an image.

Through the Looking Glass: Steve Paxton

Steve Paxton's suggestion for Contact Improvisation, that two moving bodies follow the point of contact between them, creates a dance of shifting
weights, sometimes unexpected, between bodies. This element of surprise
engages the reflexes, often as survival mechanisms that protect the body in
falling. The reflexes, mediated subconsciously, occur in milliseconds. We
experience the reflexes as fast because they come into conscious awareness
after their initiation. In trying to observe them at all, we can usually only
catch a glimpse of their passing after the fact.

Paxton's early investigation and safety training in Contact Improvisation
focused participants on becoming better witnesses to their own reflexive
actions. Contact improvisers develop sensory awareness through prelimi-
nary exercises like the "small dance," in which they observe minute weight
shifts of postural sway while standing. This practice expands their ability
to stay present to sensation even when they experience fear during a fall in a
Contact duet, for example. Highly developed sensory awareness offers the
body more options during a fall—more time—to adjust the weight and shift
the outcome from something injurious to something workable. This "extra"
time creates magical moments in a Contact duet when time almost seems to
stand still for the dancer. Suddenly, as if on the other side of the looking glass,
a Contacter may observe his or her own freefall tumble in slow motion, with
precision, decision, and clarity.

Epic: Nancy Stark Smith

Nancy Stark Smith developed the Underscore over a twenty-year span. As a teacher of Contact Improvisation, she had observed that particular warm-up exercises and movement activities were helpful in bringing dancers to a state of body-mind preparedness for engaging in a Contact duet. The Underscore is a scored collection of those exercises and activities, complete with pictographs that represent each phase and subphase of its progression. Stark Smith gives a talk to prepare dancers for practicing the Underscore, drawing the pictographs and explaining what each entails. This score is then hung on the walls of the studio space for handy reference during the dance.

The Underscore charts the development of the dance from the moment of arrival in the practice space through warm-up to full-out dancing, then a cool down and a time for reflection on, or "harvesting" of, the event. Within this larger arc are phases and subphases. Optional or potential interactions are listed in detail for some of the subphases. For example, at some point after warming up on the floor for a while, some dancers feel ready to move through the space. The *Connection* phase begins when chance interactions or more deliberate ones occur between dancers. These brief associations and short dances will eventually lead into the longer Contact duets of the full-out dancing phase.

Stark Smith has detailed many different ways of connecting, both physical and perceptual, that might transpire within Connection. She suggests noticing and enjoying *coincidences* of various kinds, such as an unplanned unison movement or two dancers arriving at the same corner of the studio at the same time or wearing color-coordinated clothing, for example. A *confluence* occurs when the paths of two dancers navigating through the space come together to form a duet. A dancer might experience an *attraction* to some event happening in the space or come to *touch* another dancer, whether it is a casual brush or purposeful action on a dancer's part. And why not take advantage of a *collision* to start a dance? During Connection dancers are invited to notice and catalogue the interactions along the way that warm them up to connecting with others, ultimately leading them into Contact dances, however brief. *Aversion* is also a possibility in Connection, conveying "Nothing personal, but not for me right now," according to Stark Smith.[10]

A series of short connections, also known in the Underscore as "grazing," is a time to enjoy little tastes of interaction before committing to a longer, fully engaged Contact dance. Participants may easily recognize when Connection has begun. It is a signal that full-out dancing is just around the corner.

Although the phases are generally sequential, there is the possibility to skip, repeat, or return to a previous phase. As a dancer develops his or her own path in the course of an Underscore, the dancer might find that he or she lags behind or pushes the overall timing of the group, creating a measure of time between individual progress and the group's. It's acceptable to be slightly off or even further off; the Underscore's progression supports individual excursions to a degree. How far off an individual might wander becomes part of the improviser's dialogue with the group as well as with the form itself. In this way, the score doesn't dictate but supports navigation; it's a four-dimensional (space and time) map of territory, the improviser's almanac.

In addition to the phases that mark time, there are wild-card states of awareness—identified by Stark Smith as "nonsequential anytime all-the-time aspects"[11]—that can happen at any time in the Underscore, and in a sense, these are out of time. One of these, called "Gap," describes what happens when a dancer loses his or her place in an improvisation and suddenly doesn't have any idea of what is going on. Recognizing a gap helps an improviser to ride it out rather than panic, and even learn to enjoy a gap, study it, and develop different strategies to deal with gaps when they arise.

Open Score, part of the full-out dancing near the end of the Underscore, is also an open time for dancers to experiment with material from any of the phases and to explore different methods of composing with the group, as well as a time for longer Contact Improvisation duets (see chapter 4).

The Underscore is an arc that usually takes from three to four hours to complete, though it has been abbreviated to a thirty-minute score or extended over a whole day. Dancers create their own time sense—from the milliseconds of the reflexes, to a person-to-person timing as a duet engages in Contact, to the "geologic" timing of the group as it recognizes and develops its own sense of composition. Time is mutable—minutes may take hours, and hours may take minutes, depending on which phase or state a dancer chooses to engage with at any given moment.

COMPRESSING TIME: WILLIAM FORSYTHE

In *Eidos:Telos*, William Forsythe's partially improvised ballet made in 1994, clocks in the wings triggered entrances, exits, and pauses, while onstage clocks, with letters instead of numbers, suggested movement vocabulary. Forsythe often sets phrases of movement that the dancers then operate on using various algorithms. Mostly these algorithms focus on spatial variation,

Christine Bürkle, dancer, in "Part 1: Self Meant to Govern," of William Forsythe's ballet *Eidos: Telos* (1994) with Maxim Franke, violin. Clocks in the wings triggered entrances, exits, and pauses, while onstage clocks, with letters instead of numbers, suggested movement vocabulary. Photo © Dominik Mentzos

but some work specifically with time, like *reverse temporal order*. Using reverse temporal order, a dancer runs a select piece of the phrase backwards. If the initial phrase expanded in space, reversing the temporal order might change the variation's overall dynamic drastically, in this example making it contract. In *time compression* a dancer shortens the length of time it takes to dance the phrase by abbreviating it. The dancer, while guided by the algorithm, is ultimately choosing how to operate on the set phrase, thus improvising. Though the phrase and the algorithm are specified, there is potentially infinite variation available to the dancer.[12]

A Sense of Time: Barbara Dilley

Barbara Dilley uses the familiar "beginning, middle, end" arc to mark time in an improvisation, inspired by meditation practices that observe thoughts as they arise, dwell, and fall away. In Dilley's variation for improvised dances, the dancers call out the beginning, middle, and end of the dance as they feel them arise as the piece unfolds. Making the calls strengthens awareness of what is happening now, as well as sharpens intuitive perceptions. At other times, the call (perhaps from a viewer or based on clock time) may come arbitrarily to create a reference point or to shift the intention of the dancers. Rather than come to some communal agreement about when the beginning, middle, and end have actually occurred, Dilley uses the practice in the spirit of questioning and investigating a sense of time, and to create an awareness of its nature and effect.

BACK IN TIME: LISA NELSON

Lisa Nelson has a movement practice that investigates the felt sense of time by looking at the nature of beginnings and endings. The practice has a twist: an end might come before the beginning. In one version, an improviser moves and the viewers can continually call "begin" or "end" when they see a flow of movement that reads to them as either a beginning or ending of a dance. (The mover takes no action in relation to the calls, continuing to move or be still as desired.) To give a straightforward example, the first movement could appear to be a bow and exit, followed by a splashy entrance from the wings—an ending followed by a beginning. Research lies in the gray area between these two culturally iconic extremes. Viewers might agree or disagree with one another and with the mover, for that matter. But in practice, the viewers' calls of "begin" or "end" create a kind of conversation about what, when, and how movement and stillness signal a beginning or an ending, tuning participants in to each other's take on the matter.[13] The curious ways we read movement in a sequence in time become visible through the dialogue.

In Nelson's Tuning Score, players who act as both movers and viewers use a set of verbal calls, simple dance editing directions such as "pause," "replace," "reverse," "repeat," "sustain," to tune the dance according to their interests and tastes as the dance is created. The movers accept the calls as support for their action rather than as commands, doing the best they can within their skills or circumstances. Thus, the calls are a means of investigating desires in the viewing and the dancing of the dance. Through observation of the impact of the calls on the developing dance, the players (movers and viewers) refine the timing and choice of calls they make, honing a particular taste, for instance, for seeing a particular movement go on for a longer amount of time. In the process, they begin to articulate and educate themselves about their tastes.

In the Tuning Score, a nonlinear relation to time is developed through a call in which a player reverses movement in time as far as the body remembers—like rewinding a videotape. Nelson is not looking for an exact movement-by-movement "reverse." When "reverse" is called, a dancer reverses from memory as far back as desired, the movements just made, perhaps revealing and reminding him- or herself of the subliminal feeling states, choices, and chance happenings that come packaged in the physicality of movement. Clock time is still moving forward, but the body has gone through a kind of wormhole, reliving in sensory Technicolor its recent past. This call (among others) creates a way to examine how we construct our sense of causality, giving an impression of time as malleable rather than as an irretrievable sequence of frozen movement moments. With this new ability to manipulate time and relive past choices, players become explorers of choice and the multiple options available in any given moment.

⊁ FIELD NOTES ⊀

An extraordinary aspect of working with improvised movement has been noticing how its practice shifts my perception of time. I had experienced the grounding effect of a dance technique class—focusing with concentration on my body for an hour and a half made me feel more present throughout the rest of my day. However, Nancy Topf's three-hour improvisation class felt like a week-long Caribbean holiday, restful and rejuvenating. Time stretched out in her class as my body-mind stretched, tracing sensation and imagery.

Initially, I was less attracted to improvisation techniques that required quick frontal lobe decision-making and left me feeling like I had drunk a double espresso. I gravitated toward the techniques that came from the inner experience, often working with the senses, taking time to let movement unfold at its own luxurious pace. In fact, I had an aversion to quicker-paced work. And I found that the inverse was true; people who liked quick-paced work shied away from an inwardly directed movement sourcing. One dancer reported to me that this type of work made her feel sick!

These preferences became clearer to me from an experience I had in Nina Martin's Ensemble Thinking workshop. Martin, looking to simulate "choreographic time" and the ability to jump-cut in improvisation, prohibits a slower, organic development of movement in her training exercises, referring to it aptly (and wryly) as "glacial timing." This approach worked well for those who wanted to get on with the compositional dialogue of the shifting elements in the stage space; they happily accepted Martin's toolkit for ensemble work. However, a few dancers from somatic studies backgrounds (like myself) had trouble separating the compositional dialogue from the developing of movement material; the two were entwined in our training. We weren't so easily or quickly (and perhaps this was typical!) persuaded to adopt Martin's exclusive edict. I was reserved but willing to go for the ride, and though I found it difficult at times, I was curious about how the other side of the coin liked to work.

And it did end up working for me. I found that I had to let go of my comfort zone at first, but what I knew deeply still served me. Martin's work offered me a way of getting up to speed—if reluctantly—and taught me, most importantly, how to shift gears.

Katie Duck's work was another challenge. Sensory-based movement sourcing was a fine practice in her book—as long as you didn't work on it onstage, where you were supposed to be "on." This spotlight of "on" gave her work an intensity and quickness, but of a different sort than Martin's. While I found Martin's studies formal—arranging bodies in space and time—Duck's were social. She spoke of crowd dynamics, interpersonal chemistry, eye contact, and getting in too close. The chance encounters in her work were not the cool cerebral ones of Merce Cunningham but those of star-crossed lovers, vengeful enemies, long-lost friends. It was just this hormonal response—which Duck looked to engage in dancers and audience alike—that actually made it possible to achieve the kind of presence, alertness, and speed of reaction required in her work. In giving myself over to the human interaction, I received the juice I needed to be "on."

It turned out there were more options than just fast or slow. In Nelson's work, there was the ability to move backward in time by retracing a pathway. With the possibility of reversing time came the ability to take back and redo a movement. Then there was the warping of space and time by Overlie (accelerating) and Forsythe (compressing), and the timelessness of the eternal present, a result of Dilley's meditative explorations. As Duck points out, once the Pandora's box of choice is opened, dancers become artists in the manipulation of duration, weavers of multicolored time in their improvisations.

PRACTICES FOR FURTHER RESEARCH

1. Move for what feels like one minute. Time yourself with a stopwatch. Was your body sense of a minute shorter or longer than clock time?

Try again or with longer time spans to see how your time sense shifts (not necessarily to get better at guessing!).

2. How is time passing for you right now? Think up a movement practice for yourself that might shift the way you feel time. See if it works. For example, if you are feeling rushed, try a doing a minute of slow-motion movement. If time is dragging for you, start improvising, see what tempo you are tending toward, and speed that up. Or try making highly specific and detailed movements for a minute.

3. Dancemakers talk about how they are good at making dances of certain lengths, like a seven-minute solo or a twelve-minute solo, but not a ten-minute solo. What's your comfort zone? Improvise a series of dances, calling "beginning," "middle," and "end" to see what time span arises most frequently and naturally for you. What time spans never happen for you? What happens when you push yourself to work with a less comfortable duration?

4. Set up a sequence of arbitrary movement cues to signal the beginning, middle, and end of an improvisation. (Maybe use a timer or internal cues, like "after we cross the room twice we'll start the middle section.") See how these synchronize with your *felt* sense of the beginning, middle, and end.

5. Try reversing your movements during your daily chores like folding laundry, dressing, washing dishes, or brushing your teeth. How do you remember what you just did? Do you figure it out abstractly or through your body memory, or a combination? Expand this practice to your dancing. Work with a partner and use a call as a signal to reverse.

⇥ INTERLUDE ⇤

Notes to Myself: Living Backward

In T. H. White's *The Once and Future King*, Merlin the magician lives backward—growing younger with the years to his infanthood.[14] Yoshi Oida in his book *The Invisible Actor* remarks that finding a good ending to a piece curiously creates a good beginning.[15] He must have figured out how to live backward! It would be incredibly helpful in improvisation if while dancing I could flip back and forth—living forward sometimes and then living backward at others.

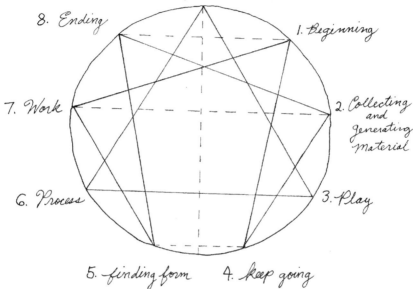

9.
Making
an improvised dance
8. Ending   1. Beginning
7. Work   2. Collecting
                                and
                                generating
                                material
6. Process   3. Play

5. finding form   4. keep going

the Living Backward chart

© MB

Drawing and Enneagram. © Melinda Buckwalter

In improvisation, many different phases of making a dance are interwoven. The Living Backward chart, an enneagram, may shed some light on the process.[16] The secret to living backward may lie in making connections between each of the phases of the dance—recognizing them as I go.

For example, if I am stuck in a workaholic attitude, I might completely miss Beginning (phase 1) by jumping right to Work (phase 7). It is a great feeling to have something to work on. But the addiction can swamp the developmental phase (the right half of the chart). It can be scary to go all the way back to square one (Beginning) to start an improvisation with "nothing"—the clean slate of open space. However, reentering the Beginner's Mind can be also be freeing.

Also, notice how Work and Collecting (phase 2) are directly across from one another on the Living Backward chart. Collecting materials can be fun work and this relationship reminds me that I don't have to wait till phase 7 to get to work. Play (phase 3) is magical, but it can be a place to get stuck in Never Never Land: to circle without moving ahead, to go off in multiple directions and not settle down, or to eventually get bored and drop out. Here commitment enters—commitment to keep going (phase 4), to find out what is developing from a broader perspective (finding form, phase 5) and to articulate that. Once a process (phase 6) is established, work can begin (phase 7), the goal becomes clear, the dance is over in a way—but not until the Ending (phase 8) presents itself.

Maybe it's possible to jump to any element on the chart to start and then live backward. Why not? Anything goes; artists' processes are so individual. For instance, if I like to begin with a form or score in order to generate my material, I will enter at phase 5 (finding form) and then live backward to collect my material (phase 2). These phases are mysteriously related on the chart through Ending (phase 8)—there is something complete about a form once I have collected enough material to fulfill it.

In fact, why not enter the circle at any point, not just at Beginning. The beginning can always be found later; that's the key to living in the nonsequential reality of improvisation.

4

Spatial Relations

Margot [Fonteyn] broke the rules and made her own path. She even broke a rule of geography, for wherever she danced, she was the center of the stage.

—MARTHA GRAHAM, *Blood Memory*

RRANGING MOVEMENT IN SPATIAL PATTERNS is perhaps the most familiar form of dance composition. Shaping the dance in space through floor patterns (lines, diagonals, circles, and so forth) and groupings (solos, duets, trios, quartets, or solos with choruses, for example) is what we have come to expect in Western concert dancing. Although improvisers use these patterns to organize dancing as well, some have investigated alternative ways of relating to space.

The relatively new field of psychogeography, developed in the 1950s, considers how human beings map the space around us subjectively (through perception and memory) as well as objectively (e.g., simple two- or three-dimensional "to scale" paper maps) and the corresponding impact of these maps on our behavior. Improvisational dancemakers might create alternative mappings for their dances by using less familiar senses or by recombining and reordering the familiar ones and by taking into consideration the psychological importance we associate with certain placements or configurations in space: no need to chart a new frontier, just reformulate the existing territory.

THE PALINDROME: RICHARD BULL

Richard Bull used the Palindrome, his simple mirroring exercise, to introduce students of Choreographic Improvisation to the realities of working with space from a vantage point inside the dancing—that of the improviser. The exercise involves a trick of attention and learning to multitask. At first, in following the instruction to mirror a partner, the beginner is so focused on the detail and nuance of mirroring another moving body that all his or her attention goes into replicating gesture and body position. Partners stay close, as if each is working in front of a changing-room mirror. It may take some prompting before the duet discovers there is a studio full of space to explore—depth and width as well as the flat screen of body shape. The experience is a bit like finding you can fly in a dream! And just as suddenly, the dancer finds he or she is not alone in the mirror—other dancers and multiple relationships become available for play.[1]

Bull was able to introduce in one simple exercise the potentials of composing in an ensemble. This gives many fledgling choreographic improvisers a first taste of the multidimensional thinking needed to negotiate the complexities of the interrelating levels operating in improvisation.

THE GRID: BARBARA DILLEY

In the early 1970s Barbara Dilley started working with "the grid," a maplike graph of space, as a structure for performance with her group the Natural History of the American Dancer. She developed the grid as a teaching tool for dance improvisation classes at New York University and later for the dance program at Naropa University. The structure has proven durable; Dilley still uses it as a basis for performance work and teaching.

The grid is a two-dimensional graph of imaginary perpendicular lines superimposed on the space. Dancers use this map to image the space around them and inform their movements and movement pathways. For the dancers' initial experiments, Dilley often limits the movement choices to basic pedestrian vocabulary.

At first, the grid may feel confining, an orthogonal prison of left and right, instigating robotic or martial-style movement. But after a bit of work, it magically opens up—dancers find that they no longer have to follow it, that it has been following them all along, describing with coordinate precision every movement made—it is just a matter of the scale chosen. The smaller the grid squares, the more precisely the grid details a movement. And, just as suddenly, a dancer is no longer isolated in space but connected by the weblike grid to all the dancers in the space, close and far away. This ability of the grid to connect dancers across space opens the possibility of being influenced by another's movements. Individual movement options multiply exponentially.

A development of Barbara Dilley's grid work in performance. The Fearless Dancing Project, directed by Dilley at the historic alternative dance venue the Judson Church, New York City, 2000. *From left*: Wendell Beavers, Barbara Dilley, Steve Clorfeine, Cara Reeser, and Steve Featherhuff. Photo © Carolyn DeMers

A dynamic shift of space occurs when the grid is placed on the diagonals. Diagonal energy is lively, especially in a rectangular room. Circles are also an option. As they get good at using the grid, dancers may choose to switch among these various grid configurations.

Dilley finds several qualities she likes in the movement that arises from working on the grid. For one thing, the grid produces movement that is equally weighted throughout space, as opposed to being frontally oriented, as is the Western cultural habit that arises from performing in the proscenium. Also, rather than fostering "solo" dancing (even if in an ensemble), where the dancer is mainly focused on the audience connection, the grid encourages interconnection among dancers across space. Another quality Dilley finds is that because the dancers' attention on the body is as an object in space rather than one focused on interpersonal interaction, the grid fosters genderless interactions between dancers.[2] These qualities produce a movement aesthetic that is abstract yet has an element of connection that continues to intrigue Dilley, causing her to return again and again to the grid in her dance-making.

SPHERICAL SPACE: STEVE PAXTON

By following the point of contact with a moving partner, the practice of Contact Improvisation develops its own sense of space. The sharing and bearing of weight that results to keep contact between the two moving bodies creates a dance in which a Contacter is as likely to have feet in the air as on the ground. Familiar reference frames—the pedestrian "head up-feet down" and the performative "face the audience"—are superseded as a dancer's attention is drawn to the dialogue of weight shift and the play of reflexes activated in the constantly changing body orientation and falling that create the dance. Alternative reference points prove more useful—the point of contact is a felt reference for the duet and the center of weight of an individual dancer's body, a functional focus.

With no space between dancers to consider, attention is instead tuned to listening to the nuance of the shifting touch and weight of the partner. The space around the duet is backgrounded in consciousness—to be called on when necessary—less vital information than the immediate dialogue of the touch and kinesthetic receptors taking place through the enveloping skin and soft tissues. Peripheral vision takes over. Having redefined gravity by including another body in the equation, Contacters build a sense of space from a focus on the center of gravity to the outer reach of the limbs, a sphere of potential movement, and gather information about the surrounding space by peripherally using the senses.

"The result of so many changes in spatial and kinesthetic orientation in a short time has caused me to perceive space as spherical," Steve Paxton says in the soundtrack for the video *Chute* (1979). "The sphere is an accumulated image gathered from several senses—vision being one. As if quickly looking in all directions gives me an image of what it might be like to have a visual surface all over my body, instead of skin. The skin is the best source for the image, because it works in all directions at once. . . . In Contact Improvisation I find I am hanging by my skin. And relying on its information to protect me, to warn me, to feed back to me the data to which I am responding."[3]

With their attention drawn to organizing their bodies in a spherical space, Contacters need to make a conscious effort if they choose to compose the space around the duet more traditionally. Contact was initially shown in gallery spaces as an ongoing event for as long as interest held; viewers could walk around and see it in the round, with an air of a demonstration rather than formal performance; an early performance tour was called "You Come. We'll Show You What We Do." The gallery showings let Contact's spherical nature be the defining principle of how the dance was viewed. Watching an early performance, Simone Forti coined the term "art sport," catching the genre's unique blend of paradigms for interactivity.

Over more than thirty-five years of Contact's existence, many groups have brought it into traditional performance settings as well. Some have put Contact Improvisation's sphericality aside, using it as a source for generating movement and placing it more deliberately in the stage space. Some questions arise: Is Contact still Contact without its spherical space? Is it possible to become skilled enough to work from two different spatial models (spherical and proscenial) simultaneously? Or to be able to switch between them fluidly on demand? Can room be made for a "flatlander's" spatial perspective in Contact Improvisation? The experimenting continues.

The Global Underscore: Nancy Stark Smith

Nancy Stark Smith's Underscore is a vehicle for exploring Contact Improvisation simultaneously with other elements such as music, composition, and other dance improvisation practices—for instance, Barbara Dilley's grid (in this chapter). This integrative work occurs mainly in the Open Score phase of the Underscore (see chapter 3) toward the end of its arc. Suggestions of potential investigations for the Open Score might be loosely seeded in the *powwow*, an early phase in which participants gather in a circle to discuss the practice and particulars of the day. For example, a simple compositional device such as looking for a group stillness or some kind of group unison moment within the Open Score phase might be agreed on in the powwow. The Underscore invites dancers to place Contact Improvisation within a larger framework of dance and composition practice.

Due to the international popularity of Contact Improvisation, it has been possible for a French group of Underscore practitioners to organize a Global Underscore, which happens once a year near the northern hemisphere's summer solstice. This version of the Underscore includes a group "small dance" (in which dancers observe minute weight shifts while standing), synchronized in time and space with the other groups around the world. In a predetermined order, one group faces in the direction of another, creating a chain of dances that span the globe—for instance, from Paris, France, to Helsinki, Finland, to Sydney, Australia, to Los Angeles, California, to London, England, and back to Paris, with other groups and satellite individuals in between. Each year the sites vary. Because of the differences in time zones and the

Contact Improvisation performed in a gallery space of the Provincetown Art Association in Provincetown, Massachusetts, 1977. Steve Paxton and Nancy Stark Smith. Photo © Stephen Petegorsky

length of the Underscore, some Contacters dance from night into morning. (See Suprapto Suryodarmo and Anna Halprin in chapter 2 for other types of global dance practices.)

THE HOT SPOT: NINA MARTIN

Nina Martin's Ensemble Thinking training structures developed out of her experience teaching and performing dance improvisation and Contact Improvisation. For instance, she was a member of Channel Z (1982–90)—a performance improvisation ensemble that used Contact Improvisation as a common movement vocabulary—with collaborators Daniel Lepkoff, Dianne Madden, Steve Petronio, Randy Warshaw, Robin Feld, and Paul Langland.

Martin's experience is that improvisers either get so absorbed in composing their own movements or so focused in a Contact duet that they have little attention for compositional concerns of the group at large. To remedy this, she separated movement-making and composing into practices she calls Articulating the Solo Body and Ensemble Thinking, which complement the practice of Contact Improvisation (and other improvisation practices) in performance.

In Ensemble Thinking, dancers are limited to simple pedestrian movements until they master basic composing skills. They are also restricted to working in a proscenium reference frame; Martin finds that learning to spontaneously compose the space in an ensemble is difficult enough, even with a defined front. She is clear that she wants dancers to make spatial choices and not leave framing up to serendipity or the audience, as may be the choice in some improvisation works, such as the early showings of Contact Improvisation.

Martin designed some of the Ensemble Thinking training structures to address particular issues of composing the group in space. For example, in one structure the ensemble practices recognizing and forming regular shapes like lines, circles, diagonals (see chapter 2). In another, which she calls "Complete the Form," the ensemble practices creating a unified tableau in the dance space so that no matter how complex it is, it can still be read as a unified whole (see chapter 5). Martin identifies these as basic skills that require practice because she has observed that this kind of clarity rarely happens on its own in a group improvisation.

A structure Martin calls "status work" (adapted from Keith Johnstone's status work for actors) reveals an unusual quality of space—its relative value, a shifting ability to draw attention, sometimes referred to as the "hot spot."[4] Center stage is usually thought of as the main hot spot, but its value, according to Martin, is actually quite dependent on what other activities are occurring simultaneously onstage. As with most Ensemble Thinking training structures, half the group and Martin sit out in the position of the audience to coach, giving feedback on the success of each trial. First the working group practices "giving status." With the dancers in the space, a dancer's name is called out and the rest of the ensemble arrange themselves one by one, giving focus to each person in turn. In the early stages of this exercise, personal vocabulary is not allowed; the only tool dancers may use to give focus is their position in the space relative to the dancer of highest status.

This is not as easy as it may sound! Martin points out that dancers are more often concerned with taking focus. This exercise shifts the tables by making dancers practice a generally less developed skill. With coaching by the group, all master the skill, and Martin moves on to the exercise of taking focus. Now a dancer must position him- or herself in the space according to where he or she will best draw the audience's focus. Dancers are coached; this time the shy dancers are challenged to be bold in the space.[5] All acquire speed and skill until coaching is no longer necessary.

In these Ensemble Thinking training structures and others, Martin trains improvisers to consider and compose the dance space first—ahead of developing movement vocabulary. As a dancer learns to make a quick read of the space, he or she begins to use movement vocabulary in the service of composing the space. This is a huge shift for many dancers, as their training has often exclusively emphasized composing movements and personal space. Ensemble Thinking's focus on the composition of space is an antidote to solo or material-based improvisation practices, but not an end in itself. Martin says, "In performance, of course, there are times when one can dive into a Contact duet and to hell with the space!"[6] In this instance, the ensemble, with the tools of Ensemble Thinking, can pick up the slack and compose more broadly.

LISTENING TO THE SPACE: DANA REITZ

In high school, Dana Reitz traveled in Japan, where she studied calligraphy. In the practice, a calligrapher prepares his or her materials—good light, clean table, fresh paper and brushes, and the ink, which he or she grinds and mixes. The calligraphy itself is the result of all these preparations purposefully coming together in the moment of making the mark on the paper.

In Reitz's solo dance work, she reframes her experience as dancer-choreographer in a similar way—she is accountable for the preparation of the dance by defining the range of materials to be used, developing the score for both movement and light, and knowing the space well. She spends a few days or more becoming familiar with the stage space—by photographing or drawing it—before a performance. From Reitz's point of view, the dancer-choreographer is not in charge of what actually happens in the space but is responsible for being attentive. Relieved of having to be the "boss of the space," she is free to feel the dance as it happens in the moment of performance and to respond accordingly, which could mean shifting the phrasing, editing, or repeating material.[7] Her choreography is plastic, improvised, as she gives herself the freedom to play with a base of choreographed material.

To Reitz, space isn't generic or empty. Each space has character. She speaks of the pushes and pulls of a particular space. Like Einstein's "space/time," this space can warp; it isn't consistent but relative, and it demands the attention of the dancer. This means that a soloist is never alone in a space; the space is a partner to listen to and work with.

Dana Reitz in her *Sea Walk* at Summer Stages Dance at Concord Academy, Concord, Massachusetts, July 2005. Photo © Nancy Campbell

Listening to a space may seem like a strange idea, but we do it all the time. For example, when we restrain our movement in a cluttered room or when we move in a carefree manner in a wide-open space, we are listening and responding to the space. The character of a space tells how small or large, how quick or slow to make our movements. We may also read a person's relative comfort in a room by the way he or she might spread out (arms and legs akimbo and propped on furniture), or contain him- or herself within it (legs folded demurely and hands clasped in lap).

In her dances, Reitz works extensively with full-body gesture, which she uses as a means of listening to a space. People often equate gesture with the hands, but Reitz considers gestures of the entire body—a raised shoulder, a hip shift, a slight twist of the torso, and a movement of the eyes are all gestures in her dance lexicon. Reitz says, "It takes the full body in rooted space to understand the gesture of one finger."[8] For her, making a gesture is something akin to making a sound to locate the body in space, like a blind man taps his cane. By waiting for the reverberation of the gesture to bounce off a far wall or a person nearby, Reitz creates movement that reflects the space as she feels it around her.

ARCHITECTURE: MARY OVERLIE

Space is one of Mary Overlie's Six Viewpoints. Overlie suggests that once traditional theater is deconstructed into its elements, a dancer or actor could take any one of these elements singly and study it for years. With this Viewpoint, for example, she asks that improvisers learn to let the space talk to them, to learn its language, rather than to fill it with movement ideas, as dancers are often used to doing.

A practice she calls "architecture" invites improvisers to physically explore in detail the architecture of the room they are working in, to acknowledge its structure and quirks, brick by brick, floorboard by floorboard. Props and loose structures are fair game as well. The practice focuses dancers on looking to external information for the impulse to move, rather than to the kinesthetic sense. Overlie invites dancers to turn the room into an instrument and play it by listening to it. The body may be used as a measuring device, for instance, of just how long a wall is or how high a window is as compared with a door. Taking the time to simply look and investigate a familiar place such as the studio, which is usually valued more for the space it provides than its structure, reveals a logic or language of space as negotiated by the body.

Using the familiar in an unfamiliar way (in this case, focusing on, observing, and responding to space rather than dancing in it) is part of Overlie's deconstruction process. In a practice like architecture, she might overlay some of her other practice principles like "not staying with something until you are finished" (see chapter 3) or "doing the unnecessary," where a performer does everything but the task at hand. For example, if opening the door is the task, the dancer does everything but that. The fun is in how close you can come without doing it, or how far afield you might stray and still keep the connection to the task.

Through these practices, expectations are confounded for both the movers and the viewers, and this keeps the attention high. Overlie quotes John Cage: "You can have art, all you have to do is change your mind," to which she adds, "All you have to do is change what you expect."[9] She likes to take something out of context or suggest a different context for it, so that it is given attention and seen in a different light. She sees art as a perceptual event—you can't *make* art, you can only observe something become art and "participate in the magical transformation that it is."[10] In this case, by interacting with space in unexpected ways, she makes the hidden visible.

ROOM WRITING: WILLIAM FORSYTHE

William Forsythe has the dancers of his ballet company practice describing a room and its furniture from memory using specific points on (or in) their bodies. In this practice Forsythe calls "room writing," they must describe or "rewrite" imaginary sofas and armchairs while keeping track of the furnishings' positions in space, creating an imaginary room that the dancers navigate as they are dancing or describing it. Here, the dancer has more leeway than in the real world—he or she might break a coffee table into pieces and put it back together again (describing all this in movement). A dancer might use a foot or a shin to describe the edge of the coffee table, meanwhile leaning so that the head can get to a corner of the sofa while an elbow spans the armrest. The dancer falls off balance from here, slipping between the sofa and a standing lamp. Sometimes ballet vocabulary comes in handy, a rond de jambe en l'aire conveniently describes the circular top of the footstool by the easy chair.

The practice builds imaginative dancing—a clear imaginary picture creates precision in improvised movement. However, the practice is not only about generating new and unusual combinations. Forsythe also challenges his dancers to make these combinations travel through space by having them switch from writing a room in three dimensions to two, and to switch fluidly from writing the furniture with one part of the body to another. For Forsythe, what is important is not the original source of the movement but that the dancer's vision is so intense in performance that he or she seems to be interacting with something "hyper-real."[11]

EXIT AND DANCE: KATIE DUCK

Katie Duck has created a "Copernican Revolution" of the performance space. Rather than centering the dancing universe around the choreographer's eye, she places it in the individual improviser's body and describes the world from this new vantage point. This improviser-friendly description speaks to the experience of the dancer but sounds rather strange, as dancers are accustomed to the language of a choreographic perspective.

For example, Duck says that dancers are trained to enter and execute but that she wants them to remember to exit and dance. She asks that dancers lose the option of entering. Sounds impossible! But from a dancer's perspective, you are always *somewhere*. To create a change, you need to choose to exit to be somewhere else. This is semantics, perhaps, but many improvisers struggle with the habit of dropping attention when they come offstage, a habit developed from dancing prelearned movements or working in the proscenium. If a dance is set, one needn't pay attention to the action onstage to know what is happening—keeping time is enough. "Off" is a resting state of attention; invisible from the audience or choreographer perspective, it is "nowhere." This state of attention creates the need to enter, which becomes problematic in improvisation. What brings an improviser back onstage? Is entering somehow different than dancing? Duck points out that improvisers need to pay attention to the action onstage no matter whether they are on or off. In this sense, they are always on—always leaving where they *are* to be somewhere else—rather than entering from a fictitious, invisible land of off. By recontextualizing the stage space and getting rid of off, Duck solves the problem of entering for improvisers.

From her perspective, by exiting the performance space a dancer is creating empty space, for the dance to happen in. It's another choice the improviser has—to leave, as well as to make movement—and one that she points out needs to be remembered and practiced. Dancers new to improvisation often get stuck spinning out more and more movement with little discrimination and need to learn to choose *when* to move. "Flow/pause/exit" is an exercise Duck uses with a group to practice remembering to pause or exit. Dancers move (flow) and are allowed the options of pausing in the space (not moving, but remaining alive and attentive) or exiting to shift the attention of the viewer onto the performance space and what might happen there next.

As far as Duck is concerned, it is not the job of the improvising dancer to make the composition happen, that is, fill the space with interesting movement, but instead to allow the chance for something to happen by exiting. Exiting creates empty space, potential, for something to occur by chance. In other words, an improviser doesn't decide to take a solo but may find him- or herself left dancing one. This may seem theoretical, but in improvisation the most exciting moments often happen by chance—the skill of improvisation frequently lies in creating opportunities for happenstance rather than in inventing movement.[12]

⤜ FIELD NOTES ⤚

The practice of improvisational dance demanded new kinds of awareness from me with my technical dance background. For example, I had to be aware of my timing and my movement choices. But the use of space seemed very similar to what I experienced as a dancer of set work: bodies arranged in a stage space. True, I had to remember to position myself consciously upstage or downstage, in a group or solo, enter and exit, and yes, my experience of internal space shifted dramatically through using Topf's practice of anatomical imagery. But otherwise it was "space as usual." Placing, positioning.

Or so I thought. If it hadn't been for Contact Improvisation and its insistence on the reconsideration of conventional spatial values, I might have missed the opportunity to expand my own. In some ways, it remains an awkward child of the stage in my experience. Dance companies have successfully brought Contact Improvisation into performance for decades, but it demands accommodation: in-the-round viewing; ongoing, come-and-go-as-you-please showings; contextualizing within a larger made-for-stage work; lecture-demonstrations; the jam itself. It was these accommodations and a few of my own attempts at performing CI that gradually made me take notice: Not all dance forms conceptualize space in the same way. They may prescribe their own. Contact's was different enough that it behaved like a grain of sand in the oyster of my topographical awareness.

Alternative cartographies emerged: Dilley's grid creates the equally weighted use of space and gender-neutral relationships. Nelson's sightless space of the Blind Unison Trio demands a revising of the notion of unison and creates a vaporous spatial quality equally dependent for drama on near misses as on chance convergings. Reitz's solo dance of rhythm and gesture weaves a web of palpable surroundings in an empty stage space. Tanaka creates and breaks his own laws of physics: his movements, governed in one moment by an overwhelming sense of gravity and attraction, are suddenly freed from these laws as if he had stepped onto another planet.

My body, too, radiates how I am conceiving the space around me through my movements. This can shift! I needn't live by the same set of spatial concepts in every dance.

PRACTICES FOR FURTHER RESEARCH

1. Imagine yourself in an overstuffed china shop and then in an empty parking lot. What feelings do these images bring into your body? Move as if as if you were in the china shop and then in the parking lot.
2. Play "space charades" with a partner—have your partner describe the space as you move in it. First describe the space you are in and its contents with your movement. Next simply let the character of the space you imagine affect your movement. How close does your partner come to guessing where you have imagined yourself?
3. Practice Katie Duck's "flow/pause/exit" structure with a group of improvisers. Which of the actions is most difficult to "remember" to do? Easiest?

⊁ INTERLUDE ⊁

Ma

In Japanese *ma* refers to the space between, an interval, spatial or temporal. People wonder, "What is this ma trying to ask? What is it trying to do?" It is here in this space between that spirits and gods dwell.

—AKAJI MARO, in Michael Blackwood, *Butoh: Body on the Edge of Crisis*

I first encountered ma while in college in the works of Eiko and Koma, in reconstructions of Oskar Schlemmer's architectural ballets, and in the Japanese Noh troupe that came to campus. It would be years before I heard of ma, but at the time I was taken with what I described as an openness of interpretation that these works offered me, an audience member. There was space left for my imagination and personal experience to enter, to play and live in the watching. Yet the works themselves were quite specific and developed; they wouldn't be described as open-ended or unfinished in any way. So how did they create this openness of interpretation? I wanted to understand that and be able to make works of my own that had this quality.

In a 2005 interview with Simone Forti, Daniel Lepkoff talks about the lack of "empty space"—breathing space—in the atmosphere of some contemporary performances that uses "a rhythm similar to television" with no gaps between images. Typical American TV programming aims to hold viewers' attention and direct it. Space, in the sense of ma, is not useful in this paradigm.[13]

In works that use ma, we are invited to look rather than shown what to look at. These works are vehicles for imagination; they don't tell viewers everything, but allow them to fill in details (a bit like when reading a book or listening to a story on the radio). It's a different paradigm than our current cultural norm. Leaving breathing space between images acknowledges an unknown element between performer and viewer. There is no way to know what associations or previous experience the viewer brings to the performance. Making space allows for the uniqueness of each viewer to engage the work—the viewer is invited to take part in the drive rather than to just go along for the ride.

Lepkoff explains that he identified "being present" as a fundamental aspect of dancing that creates this space. He says,

> I have realized that "being present" is actually a movement and I have identi-
> fied what is moving. "Being present" is the movement of my attention . . .
> taking a second, third, fourth, or fifth look. . . . When a performer is engaged
> in this activity of "moving their attention"—unhinging themselves from the
> inevitable and taking a moment to alter their view, shifting their intention and
> playing physically in this way—as an audience we may not immediately under-
> stand what we are looking at. The behavior doesn't read in the usual way. This
> creates a space for us, the audience, to move our own attention to compose
> what it is we are seeing.[14]

Improvisation practices that shift frames of reference, like Overlie's Viewpoints, or that switch the mode of perception and sensory engagement, like Lisa Nelson's Tuning Scores, provided me with a starting point for the study of ma.

5

The Dancing Image

People tend to think that visualization will be visual, but in fact visualization can involve different senses than just seeing.

—BARBARA DILLEY, "Two Streams: Many Ways"

THE DANCING IMAGE CAN BE CONSIDERED from the outside or from the inside: as an exterior image, what is seen from the audience's perspective, or as an interior image, what a dancer works from to motivate movement. While there is one image, there are two different perspectives. In this chapter we'll progress from the outside in. Note: Practices that begin with an external perspective often lead to investigation of the internal and vice versa, making for messy categorization. Use this classification merely as a starting point for investigation.

THE EXTERIOR PERSPECTIVE

When we view dance, we take in the images mainly through the eyes but often through the ears as well. There is an orchestra of senses, including the kinesthetic, involved in the perception, making the watching of a dance a full-bodied experience. Whether we read ease or effort, softness, sharpness, or weight, grace or awkwardness, movement communicates from body to body. The dance may be perceived mainly through the eyes, but rhythm and tactile and kinesthetic memory may also be paramount. The dancing image is not just a visual picture—bodies in particular shapes grouped in space. There is context to it as well, a body-mind that experiences the world through multiple senses and correlates and prioritizes those perceptions according to personal habit as well as to the aesthetics of the time. Dancemakers take advantage of this sensorial multiplicity and organize movement making by considering various aspects of the dancing image.

Daniel Lepkoff performing in his *Time, Space, & Sound* at the Bakelit Theater, Budapest, Hungary, March 2007. In his works, Lepkoff examines the body's relationship to its environment through all of the physical senses. This viewpoint has led him to a variety of mediums that address both sound and visual space. Here he works with a video composition that is a photographic chronology of the building of his house, which he built completely by himself. Photo © Rita Fazakas

The Red Square: Barbara Dilley

The Red Square is a structure based on creating an image that Barbara Dilley evolved out of Dharma Art workshops that she participated in with Buddhist teacher Chögyam Trungpa Rinpoche. According to Trungpa Rinpoche, Dharma Art looks for "art which springs from a certain state of mind on the part of the artist. We can call this the meditative state: an attitude of directness and unself-consciousness in one's creative work."[1] Ikebana (the Japanese art of flower arranging) for instance, is a Dharma Art study. Dilley has used the Red Square in performance and now uses it mainly as a training tool for her students in performance programs at Naropa University or in Shambhala Buddhist workshops. It leads to open improvisation but starts with basic work with an image.

To begin, the square is made out of a thick red cord laid on the ground to delimit the space (twelve- or fifteen-foot sides can accommodate several dancers). Actually the "square" can be any straight-sided shape that makes sense in the room being used. The players sit outside around the empty square and quiet the mind. First, they take in the presence of the empty square. Then they are invited to visualize themselves in that space and to go, one at a time, and inhabit their visualization, taking care to find the image physically and adjust as necessary. Once there, they allow themselves to be seen—staying present in their bodies and with the images as they have chosen to inhabit them—until attention wavers and the images begin to dissolve. Then they return to their seats. Dilley notes that visualizing is often a difficult skill to learn because people expect it to be purely visual like a photograph. But in her experience people "visualize" differently, combining different senses. She suggests giving people time to relax if they struggle with the process.

Next, one dancer inhabits his or her visualization in the square and another enters in response to the image the first has created. That is, the second "sees" him- or herself in relation to the first and takes that position, and now the two dancers inhabit the image together. Once the image fades, they leave. The energy of the practice begins to build at this point because of the excitement at the possibilities of engagement with the image offered. Trios are practiced. Larger constellations of people are also possible.

The next step is to move to a round robin. One dancer enters, a second, then a third, as before, responding to the image created. Then the first one leaves, and a fourth enters. Attention to sequence becomes an issue. An interest here is in the play of relationships created in the image: whether the image is formal—calling attention to the spatial relationship—or develops a narrative or emotional context. The exit of one of the dancers can shift the reading of the image entirely; how the image shifts is one of the delights of the practice. The process reveals something of the impermanent nature of the dancing image itself.

In further development of the Red Square, props and costumes are included. Some players are designated dancers who create the image, and others are designated to add elements to the image as they visualize it. Simple movements like walking or circling are introduced as well. Eventually this play leads to a fluid entering and exiting of the space. (Dilley calls this incarnation of the Red Square "the River.") Ultimately the Red Square becomes an open space improvisation, the red square often reverting to a red cord, just another prop in the play of images.[2]

The Single Image Score: Lisa Nelson

The Single Image Score is a basic practice of Lisa Nelson's Tuning Score. For this score there are a group of dancers or players on the edge of an image space they define for themselves—part of the studio or a space outdoors where the images are played. It begins as a duet form. A player imagines him- or herself in the space in stillness according to his or her desire, then closes his or her eyes and enters the space to realize this imagining as closely as possible. The rest of the players watch as the whole space comes into focus for them, taking time to absorb the image fully with their senses and in their imaginations.

When another player imagines him- or herself in the space completing this image, he or she enters with eyes closed and fulfills it. The duet maintains this stillness while gauging when it is time to begin a simple action culminating in a second stillness. The two dancers maintain the new image, sensing it as it resonates between them and with the viewers. Any player from the outside may call "end." The dancers exit the image space, and the play starts over.[3]

The very first placement of the body in the image space reveals aspects of what a player is tuning into in his or her read of the space, choices that often surprise the other players. And from there, the ensuing dialogue of images responds and reacts to, reconsiders, and refines these choices, educating players about their personal habits, styles, and strategies while expanding on them, introducing new options through the play.

For example, a player might find that he or she habitually completes the image by being close to the other player or by relating the image to the architecture of the surrounding room. Some players tend to look to formal elements of shapes in space, perhaps through imitation or repetition, while others become engrossed in developing the narrative, whether as antecedent or consequence of the first player's action.

Players get to experience the image from both outside (eyes open and viewing) and inside (eyes closed and embodying the image) perspectives, comparing the seen and the felt worlds. What is it like to "read" an image from differing sensory perspectives? For example, with eyes closed, reading the image space and sensing when an action will occur entails a sending of the senses out to feel for the other, to get instruction for what is coming. In working with the visual and other senses in the Single Image Score, the anatomy of the image gets teased apart, uncovering a physical dimension of seeing that may feel familiar but forgotten, like a long-lost friend.

Complete the Form: Nina Martin

One of Nina Martin's Ensemble Thinking training structures, Complete the Form, challenges improvisers to present a unified idea as an ensemble. Martin also uses the example of Ikebana, in which flowers are arranged, blended to create a harmonious whole. Though the floral grouping is perceived as one by the viewer, it is made up of distinct elements. Martin suggests, "First you see the arrangement and then the details."[4] The objective is similar in this exercise—dancers contribute individually to the grouping without disturbing the overall form or sticking out. To avoid endless symmetrical groupings, Martin finds it optimal to do this work with five people.

At first, the group works with creating a still-life tableau, which they make one dancer at a time but swiftly, so that the skill of speedily reading the overarching image is developed. The tableaux are built one after the other, and the order of dancers building each is switched so that each dancer gets a turn at decision-making in every spot, first through last. Initially, movement vocabulary is limited to a mixture of levels—lying, sitting, and standing.

The Lower Left "completes the form" in *Suitcase*, Marfa, Texas, 2006. *From left*: Nina Martin, Kelly Dalrymple-Wass, Margaret Paek, and Andrew Wass. Photo © Fred Covarrubias Jr.

Martin and the rest of the ensemble stand out to coach the working group toward success. After sufficiently satisfying the coaches, the group flies on its own wings. Movement may be added into the mix in a variety of ways between tableaux, and eventually the group is moving constantly—continuously reading the space to clarify the form that is always present though shifting.

One of Martin's Neuro state exercises uses the image as a motivating source for movement. In the exercise, a dancer visualizes his or her next move in as much detail as possible and then realizes it as quickly as he or she can, creating a series of stop-action dance images. In this practice, the dancer works at "brain speed"—as quickly as the next visualization materializes in the mind's eye, rather than from a place of choreographic design or physical interest. (Martin finds these take too much time in a performance situation.) Speed at physicalizing a visual impulse is emphasized and developed. Because this exercise short-circuits physical habits through imagery and speed, it serves to repattern movement. Martin refers to it as ReWiring work.

Martin finds that doing this exercise with a partner is a great preparation for learning Contact Improvisation. Dancers working in duos imagine the next position of their Contact duet and spring to realize it. There is some inevitable compromise in the resulting position, as each dancer doesn't know what the other will have visualized. Both may have imagined being on top of the other, so partners have to adjust quickly in the moment and then move on to keep up with the speed of visualization. Martin finds that, counterintuitively, the stop-action exercise helps beginners find flow by forcing them to work with their reflexes rather than through imitation of more advanced Contact Improvisation dancers.

THE INTERIOR PERSPECTIVE

There are many different methods of creating or sourcing movement from imagery. For instance, heightened sensory awareness and an accompanying sense of connectivity can translate imagery into movement. Total immersion in a specific environment—as if learning a foreign language but in a visual or tactile form—is one means by which artists achieve this connectivity. Poetic language that makes use of the multisensory can be used to evoke movement, as can physical exploration of anatomical principles and imagery. Making or looking at drawings or other visual art can also suggest movement and its various qualities With so many possibilities at play in building and sourcing imagery, there are many options for dancemakers to choose from.

Poetic and Anatomical Imagery: Joan Skinner and Marsha Paludan,
Mary O'Donnell Fulkerson, John Rolland, and Nancy Topf

Two movement education techniques, Skinner Releasing and Anatomical Release Technique, were among those that arose in the United States in the 1960s and 1970s during the shift in the contemporary dance aesthetic from highly stylized techniques of movement to include pedestrian and other "natural" movements. These movement education techniques, developed by dancers interested in creating ease in movement, use imagery to suggest alternate and more functional pathways of movement in order to release excess effort. Joan Skinner (Skinner Releasing) and Marsha Paludan (one of the founders of Anatomical Release Technique) had met as dance teacher and teaching assistant at the University of Illinois, Urbana-Champaign, in Skinner's experimental, groundbreaking class. Paludan, who had studied with Anna Halprin, gave invaluable input, according to Skinner: "It was the students who coined the name 'releasing technique' since they told me I was constantly referring to releasing this and releasing that."[5] Paludan and Skinner's paths separated when Skinner moved to Seattle, and their methods developed into separate techniques that use imagery in distinct ways.

Skinner Releasing works with poetic images. Through a series of exercises with specific image *clusters*, the participant practices letting go of conscious control and allowing the image to take on its own life as guided by his or her imagination. As the process takes hold, the participant experiences becoming the image, at times allowing the image to move him or her, creating an improvised dance. The dance is a direct experiencing of the image rather than its imitation through movement. From Skinner's viewpoint, this provides the possibility for new patterns of movement and, with them, a new feeling of an integrated self rather than a self in relation to a body.[6]

Anatomical Release Technique works with images based on human anatomy—particularly the shapes of the bones and the mechanics of their articulations and weight bearing. (Some deep support muscles such as the psoas are considered as well.) The movement education technique developed by Marsha Paludan along with colleagues Mary O'Donnell Fulkerson, John Rolland, and Nancy Topf, was greatly influenced by their studies (independently) with Barbara Clark (1889–1982), who in turn had studied with Mabel Elsworth Todd (1880–1956), movement educator at Columbia University and author of *The Thinking Body* (1937).

While Todd's method uses both anatomically based imagery and other images to repattern movement through neuromuscular means, it did not involve moving during the imaging process; the therapeutic image work was done while relaxing in a still, "constructive rest" position. "The student was encouraged only to think the image and told not to make even the smallest voluntary adjustment through the musculature," according to Pamela Matt, Clark's student and biographer.[7] The imagery alone would affect change in movement patterns. Once they gained familiarity with the new pathway through imagery, students used their new kinesthesia in simple active movement like rolling or crawling. Inspired by their work with Clark, the Anatomical Release Technique pioneers introduced movement investigation, often based on the developmental path (the stages through which the baby learns to locomote, including rolling, creeping, crawling, sitting, standing, and walking) and incorporated dance improvisation into the movement repatterning process.

Dynamic Anatomy: Nancy Topf

Over a period of thirty years Nancy Topf developed her own approach to Anatomical Release Technique (as her colleagues refined theirs), which she later distinguished as Topf Technique and Dynamic Anatomy. This work involved study of anatomical form, mostly skeletal but also key support muscles, especially the psoas. Some images of organs were also included, for example, the lungs and their multi-branching bronchi, which Topf would liken to the negative space of a potted succulent plant she had growing in her studio.

The study involved lecture but with an invitation to visually and tactilely appreciate the forms themselves. Steeped in this information, the movement work would begin with a simple theme, such as connecting the arms into the sternum or feeling the depth of the lumbar spine in the body. While the mind enjoys complex thinking, Topf found that the body liked to keep it simple, a principle that she had learned from Clark. Yawning was encouraged as an entry point into a dynamic dialogue with the sensation and space of the interior body. The still, listening hand was incorporated as an information giving and receiving tool, which brought focus to the location of the image and enhanced the kinesthetic experience.

Topf's work consisted of a variable series of stretches, done not in the usual sense of a purposeful, often forceful, lengthening of muscle but instead following sensation and image. The stretches flowed from one to the next in an improvised timing based on individual need. The class might start with students sitting in a cross-legged position, hands on the skull bringing sensation to various bony landmarks to key interior sensory exploration, like the bridge of the nose, cheek bones, and ear opening (auditory meatus) keying the location of the top of the spine. A student would be cued to nod the head gently to feel the height and depth of the spine. From the ears the finger-tips might smooth down the jaw line to the chin and "drip" on to the ster-num, feeling the weight of the sternum acting as an anchor for the head. (The sternum is the attachment point for muscles that move the head, such as the sternocleidomastoid.)

This action would begin a series of circles of the spine (circumductions), first, the cervical spine (the neck), next, the thoracic spine (the rib spine), and then the lumbar spine (low back). This portion of the class might take a half hour or more, as students were talked through the sequence and prompted to connect sensation with image in their own time.

The class continued, perhaps to lie on the belly on the floor, experiencing the developmental path—lifting the head and reaching, creeping, and crawl-ing. Depending on the day's focus, arm or leg stretches and explorations might be emphasized. The class would be guided back to the original seated position to start again with the emphasis on the opposite side of the body. The stretch portion could take one and a half to two hours or more to com-plete. The pacing was luxurious.

The stretches were designed to elucidate the anatomical images offered in the lecture. If the theme was the connection of the arms to the sternum (breastbone), the image would be reinforced tactilely, for example, by wiping up the arm with the opposite hand, from the thumb along the inner arm and clavicle (collar bone) to the sternoclavicular joint, the bump at the end of the clavicle on top of the sternum. An arm reach would be added into the open-ing spine circles, integrating the arm into the spine through image and sensa-tion. Topf would verbally coach the class with images, such as the "brooch" of the sternoclavicular joint holding together the "cape" of the arms. Topf would ask students to place their fingertips on the sternoclavicular joint and roll forward, pulling the cape (scapulae and shoulder girdle) forward, then roll up the spine and feel the cape of the arms hang easily down the back. The "anatomically correct" imagery based on the structure and mechanics of the body promoted efficient pathways of movement, according to Topf—for example, the image of the brooch helped release neck and shoulder muscle tension and freed the arms.

Afterward, guided improvisations on the anatomical theme of the day further supported the imaging process. These allowed the individual time to integrate and experiment physically with the anatomical imagery gathered visually in lecture and through kinesthetic sensation in the stretches. Crossing the floor individually on a diagonal or perhaps in groups of twos and threes, students might be instructed to play with the brooch image, now incorporating it while moving through space. When the new imagery and movement pattern was integrated with existing patterns, a dance would emerge.[8]

Becoming Butoh: Kazuo Ohno

In Butoh, an image—often from the natural world—is used to elicit movement. The image in Butoh is not used as imitation or representation where, for example, a dancer makes swanlike movements with her arms, representing the swan on the stage. In Butoh, the image, of a swanlike neck, for instance, is internalized, and movement comes (with practice over time) from focusing on the image to the point that the dancer's movement, as well as his or her whole deportment, is affected, as if the neck had actually become the swan's neck. Note that unlike with representational imagery, where the point is for the dancer to portray an identifiable image, the viewer of Butoh may never guess that the dancer is imagining his neck is a swan's. The motivating image isn't what's important generally—it's the quality of the resulting movement, the dancer's presence to it and physical transmission of it that make the dance.

Kazuo Ohno, cofounder of Butoh, made a solo signature piece in which he re-creates La Argentina, a beautiful female tango dancer he saw as a young man. He doesn't impersonate La Argentina, that is, mimic her movements and mannerisms. Rather he becomes her, through an intense Proust-like remembrance: absorbing, revitalizing, and spreading his memory of her in performance, a physicalized imagination.[9]

Progressions are another kind of image used in Butoh, from baby to adult, from seed to tree. For both workshops and in performance, Ohno has used the image of "the walk between life and death." The image work is further complicated—for instance, Tatsumi Hijikata, Ohno's cofounder, made a solo for Min Tanaka in which he whispered contradictory images in Tanaka's ear.[10]

Finding an edge is a recurring theme in Butoh. Hijikata, who was attracted to and lived on the fringes of society in the turmoil of post–World War II Tokyo, explored cultural taboos such as pornography, prostitution, and homosexuality in his works. An image that pushes the body to the edge of its capacity might be chosen—the body must continuously adjust to fit a situation that it can barely tolerate or cope with or that is paradoxical or impossible, like becoming invisible or being headless. Edges of the body's tolerance

are explored—working under extreme conditions of cold or heat or of physical endurance; pushing boundaries of fear, disgust, and other emotions;
or sensory deprivation (working blindfolded, or naked in cold weather).
These edges create an immediacy—an intimate dialogue with the body.[11]
The movement speaks directly of the limits of the human condition and
human endurance.

Body Weather: Min Tanaka

In his training called Body Weather, Min Tanaka asks dancers to work with
several different images (or stories) at once, each located in a different part
of the body. In a 1993 course at Bennington College, according to student
Kristin Kantner, Tanaka asked them to work with "sixty-five movement
images for isolated parts of the body, such as fish swim in your stomach; your
face becomes your mother's or father's face; your hands climb a waterfall;
your legs become a cow's legs."[12] As words on a page, these are poetic or
fanciful images. As the dancers work with them, they come to life, they
become *more*—lived experiences, body memories. There is no "how" to
dance with the images, no special process of paying attention to them—they
come to life by being "danced with," concentrated on while performing specific tasks or movements. This image work, when done with skill and artistry,
transcends (or goes beneath) the personality of the individual dancer and
speaks from a visceral level of body experience, from a place of our shared
humanity.[13]

For his company Tokason, Tanaka created group performance pieces by
working with images. In *Los Caprichos: Goya's Guests from the Dark* (2001),
based on *Los Caprichos*, an eighty-etching series by Francisco Goya, Tanaka's
dancers worked intensively with the images over a period of years, creating a
deep pool of source material to be drawn on in performance. The images
came from several sources: directly from the characters in Goya's work and
from more general dance exercises Tanaka gave, as well as from communal
life on his farm.[14] Goya's fanciful and satiric caricatures are given body in the
dance. The movement is imbued with the quality or character of the images,
rather than portraying the people pictured in them. One dancer's character is
a hunched-over groveler who miraculously stands up straight for a glorious
instant. Another has a wobbly head that tips dangerously and erratically, giving the impression that it could fall off at any moment, but he smiles all the
while—not someone to be trusted. The characters enter and exit, sometimes
interacting with each other or dancing to music.

For this piece, Tanaka would set elements such as a stage set, music, light-ing, and lengths of sections for each new performance space. Because their pool of source material was so developed, the dancers could quickly adapt to these new configurations. In a post-show talk at Bennington College, where I saw it, Tanaka insisted that the piece is improvised, though he generally encouraged his dancers to set what would happen when. He believed that having this structure allowed them to find freedom in the movement; with-out it, the dancing couldn't deepen or grow.

The intensive image work created movement of consistency and speci-ficity; the dance and its images evolved and became clearer with repetition over time.[15] In performance, the dancers listened to the "weather," the ever-changing relationship of body-mind, and filled the framework they had built with movement, bringing it to life. Any changes that came up in structuring would be discussed with Tanaka as director and perhaps incorporated.[16] The audience sees Goya's etchings embodied and the humanity latent in those caricatures revealed.

Disappearing: Mary Overlie

All of the preceding practices, while considering both perspectives of the image, seem to emphasize either external or internal imagery. Where would you place this next one?

Martha Graham said, "Movement never lies," but only because we are so adept at reading body language that it is difficult to hide our intent, however hard we might try.[17] And we do try—Lisa Nelson points out that we compose our bodies in various situations, such as listening to a speaker, by facing them to show our interest while orienting toward incoming sensory information. She notes that sometimes we even compose our bodies "not to be seen." For instance, imagine you are at a party and someone whom you wish to avoid walks in. In order not to be seen, you might avert your eyes, turn your back, and try to blend in so as not to call attention to yourself.[18]

In his introduction to *The Invisible Actor* by Yoshi Oida, the director Peter Brook tells the story of Oida's command of this ability—Oida, seated onstage with the rest of the cast, disappeared from a jazz concert in full view of a packed house. Nobody remembered seeing him leave, even though they were in close quarters on the tiny stage with the jazz musicians.[19]

In her Invisible Theater Dance, Mary Overlie explores the edge of what makes a dance be seen as dance. Out of this research, she has found that there are a variety of invisible dances that can be played with in public spaces. One possibility is a bit of dance so out of place and unexpected that it isn't recognized as dance. Overlie gives the example of how once, in a bodega, she heard a bit of Shakespeare recited in substitution for the decision to buy a loaf of bread. She didn't recognize the text because it was so completely out of context. In her Invisible Theater Dance workshop, Overlie asks dancers to translate this experience into their medium. What would be the equivalent of reciting a well-recognized text? A popular dance movement, perhaps. Instead of stepping out of someone's way in the dairy section, try a shuffle step or a samba. How does your "audience" react?

Another variety of invisibility is a dance, for instance, some choreography, that pops up out of nowhere in a public space and then quickly dissolves—that is, the dancers return to pedestrian behavior, "disappearing" into their surroundings, before the dance really can register with onlookers as being organized. With either variety of invisible dancing, dancers investigate the edge of pedestrian versus dance movement. When does an arm swing cross the line and become performative? How does a movement call attention to itself as art? When does stillness become more than just waiting for a bus, rather a movement choice in a dance?[20] Depending on the variety of "invisibility" being practiced, dancers step mightily or minutely over the edge, creating an image of dance that appears as a flash or a whisper.

⊰ FIELD NOTES ⊱

I found myself mesmerized by the images of Butoh; something familiar and personal in them spoke to me. This sense of familiarity excited me because the form was from another part of the world. I was curious to know more about how the dances were made. I saw that imitating the movement style alone didn't do it; I could tell when dancers were copying versus doing whatever it was that made the imagery of the dance come to life. What was it about those physical images that made them speak? I was baffled by the minimal answers or non-answers that seemed to pervade the genre as well as its impenetrable mystique. But I accepted this all as part of the mysterious package.

Meanwhile, I was introduced to Western-based artists' use of imagery in improvisation practice. Through Nancy Topf's work, I learned to bring the anatomical image into movement. Barbara Dilley taught me an important distinction: visualization isn't necessarily solely visual; other senses may be involved. Each person's process of visualizing may be different. And I learned to listen in on this dialogue of senses—visual, kinetic, sound, pressure, temperature, smell—when I entered into an image in Lisa Nelson's Single Image Score. Movement was the senses' common language.

My own experience finally began to seep in and correlate with my curiosity around Butoh's imagery. In my quest to understand something of this process for my writings here, I failed over and over to alight on the authentic process—banging my head against the proverbial wall of the Eastern enigma. Then, a statement from Roxanne Steinberg, a dancer in Tanaka's company Maijuku, stood out: "It's not a question of how." That suddenly made sense. There isn't a how! It happens in the doing and that informs the movement, the dancing. Finally, I had found some peace, if not an answer— a place to begin.

PRACTICES FOR FURTHER RESEARCH

1. Work with image by creating a score from an object in the room around you. Your score might take into consideration your spatial relationship to it, an abstracted quality of its form, or an approach to embodying the object. Do you find anything unexpected from this study?

2. Get together with another dancer or two and do some improvised solos for each other. As the audience, allow yourselves to move your viewing positions as you watch the dancer, reframing the action according to your visual interests. Take note of your tastes. Do you enjoy framing the dancer against a particular background? Do you like to view certain movements from odd angles? Up close or further away? Do you enjoy having a choice in your viewing, or do you prefer being still and having your view decided for you? In either case, let the exercise inform you about what you like about watching movement. Let your visual desires be met, even if it means planting yourself in the middle of the action!

3. Go for a walk alone or with some dancers. Pick an image space, a defined area within which to move, and imagine what movement you would like to see in the space, then try it out in the space. Take turns realizing your movement imaginations in the image space. How did your imagination of the movement compare with the actual doing of it? How did others' movement choices inform you about the space and their tastes for movement in it? Try a variety of image spaces.

⊁ INTERLUDE ⊱

Invisible Dances with Mary Overlie at the Open Source Movement
Research Festival, December 2005

The invisible dance workshop started with some promising workmanlike methodologies, practices, doings, and demos—astonishing demos. Here is truly an edge, the boundary between dance and the pedestrian. Coming and going between the two, practicing dancing and disappearing back into the ordinary. It was slipping back into the ordinary that made you invisible. And the questions: What makes walking or standing suddenly a dance? How close could you ride that edge? You knew you were effective when fellow pedestrians double-checked to see if you were just another one of them or a potential crazy person—and when you began to wonder about your sanity yourself.

Our last night of invisible dancing—well I really wasn't sure about it. Over the previous two nights, the workshop had seemed to devolve into coffee talk, which was an uncomfortable edge for me: too much talk not enough doing, but then . . .

So the workshop *appeared* to devolve into coffee talk—or did it? Maybe it wasn't devolving but disappearing, a disappearing act; who could say? Certain principles of invisibility were laid out and then—just wait. Just wait and see how they play out. And they did indeed; the workshop and the workmanlike methodologies disappeared. We couldn't see them anymore because we were *in* them. I definitely didn't see it at first, only later, afterward. But then it was an invisible workshop, so it makes sense that I would only apprehend later how it disappeared. I swear! We really disappeared. The very last act of the workshop Mary, Milka, and I jumped on the train and left the others waving kind of stunned on the platform. Mary turned to us and said, "That was incredible how that happened, we just disappeared!" So I think she knew all along, she was just waiting and watching for something to happen, for it all to play out.[21] A little methodology, a little coffee, a little weirdness and confusion, KABLAM! Invisibility powder. It might have happened that way.

6

The Possibilities of Music

Some music invites dialogue and other music says, "I will speak" and then you shut up.

—WILLIAM FORSYTHE, "I Think the Body Likes to Move"

W HEN MANY PEOPLE THINK OF DANCE, they think of music. And if they enjoy dancing, they probably remember the marriage of music and dance that occurs—the feeling of being magically moved by the music's rhythms, that place of not knowing whether it is the body moving or the music moving the body.

The postmodern dance aesthetic questions this relationship, as it questioned many of the conventions of dancing before it. People often wonder why in postmodern dance music isn't used in the traditional fashion—that is, to support the dancers' movement in timing and quality—or why it isn't used at all. A more relevant question from a postmodern perspective would be: Why use music in the investigation of movement? Music influences the body's natural rhythms and phrasing by suggesting (some might say imposing) an external rhythmic score.

To the initial dismay of the modern dance establishment, John Cage (composer) and collaborator Merce Cunningham (choreographer) made famous the "separate but equal partners" relationship of music and dance. In Cage and Cunningham's work, dance and music are treated as coexistent, independent events rather than supportive or imitative of one another. This experiment resulted, for one thing, in dance movement made and rehearsed independently of the music and put together for the first time in performance.

Cage's student and protégé Robert Ellis Dunn taught composition classes to a generation of what were to become postmodern dancemakers in the United States in the early 1960s. These classes introduced dancemakers to

Cage's methods of structuring music and eventually led to the formation of the Judson Dance Theater. Cage was interested in indeterminacy, in making something outside of his own experience. He explored this through disciplined use of chance operations, creating scored events that give players particular degrees of freedom so that he could not foresee the specificities or the relationships that would arise in a composition. Cage's chance operations suggested a reframing of the field of inquiry in music and, through Dunn's composition classes, renewed experimentation in dance.

In this climate of experimentation, the relationship of music and movement was also up for negotiation, but not everyone decided on such a radical separation as Cage and Cunningham.

EQUALS IN PROCESS: JUDITH DUNN AND BILL DIXON

Judith Dunn was a dancer in Merce Cunningham's company from 1958 through 1963. During this time she was married to Robert Ellis Dunn. She assisted him and was an influence on the composition classes he presented at the Cunningham Studio from 1960 through 1962, participating in the Judson Dance Theater as well. In 1965 Dunn heard Bill Dixon's music at a friend's house and asked Dixon, an African American musician (trumpet, piano) and composer, if he would collaborate with her on a project.[1] Dixon, influential in the experimental music scene, called his work Advanced Black Music.

Dunn and Dixon began a fruitful collaboration that opened up new territory in Dunn's performance work. At the time of their meeting, Dunn's works were highly scored, but under Dixon's influence she moved to a more open way of working with improvisation. Dunn and Dixon believed music and dance could be equals in process and still influence and support one another without giving up creative independence. They made this relationship visible at the Newport Jazz festival in 1966. Dixon describes: "Much like the musicians, when she wasn't performing in the 'ensemble' or solo form, she 'laid out,' and in her case simply laid down on the floor full length on her side with her head resting in one of her hands."[2]

In 1968 Dunn began teaching dance and dance improvisation at Bennington College, and Dixon started laying the foundations for what would become the Black Music division there in the early 1970s. They cotaught composition classes for musicians and dancers. The mixing of disciplines was met with some skepticism at the time, even at Bennington, which had a progressive reputation.

Dunn referred to her method of working with dance improvisation as "compositional improvisation" or sometimes improvisation/composition. "Improvisation as I see it means composing and performing simultaneously. . . . One considers structure, order, space, time, materials and 'tone,' and one practices daily to make these decisions quickly, consciously and with control. . . . What provided me with encouragement and material for study was the example of the improvisational tradition of Black Music, particularly in its most contemporary aspects as demonstrated by Bill Dixon and others."[3]

Later, Dunn combined Compositional Improvisation with improvised text in collaboration with her second husband, linguist-activist Peter Lackowski, in work with her company The Dance Company (Dunn, Penny Campbell, Barbara Ensley, Cheryl Lilienstein, Erika Bro, and Robert Kovich). Sadly, in her last years, Dunn became wheelchair bound, and died in 1983, at fifty, of brain cancer. Her work in compositional improvisation has influenced generations of dance improvisers and has been passed on and developed individually by her students at Bennington, particularly Penny Campbell, Cheryl Lilienstein, and Susan Sgorbati.

Integrated yet Independent: Penny Campbell

After their time at Bennington, Penny Campbell and Susan Sgorbati went on to create their own ways of working with dance improvisation greatly influenced by Dunn's and Dixon's ideas. Campbell has collaborated with musician Arthur Brooks, Bill Dixon's musical protégé, since 1983 and currently collaborates and coteaches with composer and multi-instrumentalist Michael Chorney at Middlebury College.

Campbell's Performance Improvisation work has come to include vocal work and text as well as music, especially through the influence of Peter Schmitz, colleague, collaborator, and choreographer-dancer-actor. In these works, sound and movement are integrated while their independence as unique disciplines is respected. "Every action and sound is rooted in the instant of its emergence but, of course, also steeped in the history, experience, training, and personality of each improviser."[4] Through the work, students develop their ability to mix disciplines while recognizing and working within the limits of their individual training.

When they coteach, Chorney and Campbell ask a beginning ensemble of dancers and musicians to improvise together, working independently and simultaneously in the dance space. Chorney will give his musicians a particular

exercise, Campbell another. Sometimes they find a combination of these practices work well in ensemble. At other times, they ask dancers and musicians
to use the same structure, such as "Don't Say No" (dancers and musicians
stick to whatever material comes up initially then allow shifts in the material
to occur as they arise) or "Follow the Leader" (dancers follow musicians or
vice versa). Chorney's musicians, who often have previous improvisation
experience in which they follow fixed chord progressions, are surprised at
first to be given this kind of instruction, but as the group (both musicians and
dancers) learns to negotiate various situations, an ensemble emerges. The
work develops solo and ensemble playing skills.

An Emerging Duet: Susan Sgorbati

Susan Sgorbati returned to Bennington College for a master's degree in
dance and later to teach. As a student she had met Arthur Brooks, who
was part of the Black Music division, and with whom she later collaborated
and cotaught for many years. An improvisational music ensemble remains
an integral part of Sgorbati's dance work, and she continues to coteach an
improvisational composition class, as Dunn did, with a current member
of the music faculty at Bennington. In her recent body of work, Emergent
Improvisation, Sgorbati investigates how forms emerge in improvisation
simultaneously and cocreatively between dancers and musicians and what
kinds of signaling or cuing systems operate between them.[5]

In the Emergent Duet, for example, a dancer and musician improvise a
dance with music (or music with dance!) from the forms that emerge during their play. Framing the duet as between the dancer and musician rather
than, for instance, between two dancers with an accompanying musician,
emphasizes the coequal partnership at work. One partner may begin or enter
and the other may join, or if the two are working simultaneously, one might
become silent or still. Each listens to or watches the other's output and
responds, whether through imitation or contrast, qualitatively or formally,
depending on what he or she picks up on in the other's offering. Ultimately
dancer and musician play off of one another, creating a discourse in the discovery and exploration of the emerging forms.

A Dialogue of Forms: Richard Bull

Richard Bull's dance work was inspired by music, though not in the common
way of making a dance to it. Trained as a jazz pianist, Bull loved the dialogue

of form that happens when jazz musicians play. His interests lay in recreating that dialogue in the discipline of dance. To enable this dialogue, Bull believed a dancer needed an understanding of the underlying "grammar" of movement. He began investigating various possibilities of form in dance and created his Choreographic Improvisation technique to train dancers in this skill.

In Choreographic Improvisation, dancers train to think choreographically while remembering elements of the dance as they build it in real time. Traditional compositional elements such as spatial formations (like diagonals or circles, flocks or mirroring), theme and variation (like repetition or retrogrades, canons or fugues), attention to phrasing and quality of movement, and relationship of movement to music were emphasized to develop dancers' basic choreographic tools.[6] The skills needed to be quickly and fluently accessible to reference and dialogue with the material as it arose during the improvisation. This focus pushed development of the dancers' movement memory skills. Dancers learn to be speedy and precise with vocabulary—inverting, retrograding, and transposing it—creating variations on a moment's notice. Attention to larger choreographic frames of reference (such as movement themes and group spatial composition) made the dialogue of forms possible. To further this compositional dialogue among the dancers and also to let the audience in on it, Bull developed the device of having the dancers give spoken commentary on the shifting elements of the dance as they saw it taking shape. A prototype for this work was called *The Dance that Describes Itself* (1977). Many variations followed (see also chapter 2). Though Bull is known more for his innovation with spoken rather than musical accompaniment, it was his interest in jazz music that launched his dance-making career.

Minimalists: Nancy Topf and Jon Gibson

Jon Gibson is a composer and musician (woodwinds) who took part in the development of the minimalist movement in music while also playing in the works of other minimalist composers, such as LaMonte Young, Steve Reich, Terry Riley, and Philip Glass. Minimalists reduced music to basic elements (harmonic chords or intervals, regular pulses or drones, and figures or motifs) and focused on small differences between them by amplifying them through repetition and juxtaposition, for example. They opted for processing and investigating the basics rather than using existing musical forms.[7] Gibson composed music for many choreographers, including Merce Cunningham and Lucinda Childs. Initially he was quite surprised that Cunningham literally did not want him at rehearsals. Gibson confesses to peeking once or twice at the dancers while he played during performances, to enjoy the synchronicities when they occurred.

Gibson collaborated with, and later married, dance improviser Nancy Topf, who shared a similar minimalist aesthetic. Topf believed that dance at its most basic was an investigation of anatomical form. For her, composing meant finding the form for a dance inferred from movement explorations of anatomy. For instance, in an improvised dance on the theme of "the body is round," she found that the arising dance had a tai chi–like quality, or that a dance based on the exploration of the sacrum had a quality of weightedness and punctuated rhythm. Movement explorations involving the sternum tended to have a lighter, floating quality because of the reach of the arms anchored by the sternum. The form of the dance was based on process and investigation and echoed the qualities of the elements under investigation.

Jon Gibson and Nancy Topf performing at the Cloisters, Fort Tryon Park, New York City, November 1971. Photo © Ben Topf

Topf often used Gibson's music in classes (usually recorded) and for performance (often live). The music Gibson created for Topf, while distinctive, doesn't insist on a particular rhythm or movement quality, allowing dancers' investigation of an anatomical theme to surface.

MAGPIE MUSIC DANCE: KATIE DUCK

Katie Duck studied modern dance at the University of Utah, then joined the Salt Lake City Mime Troupe and toured Europe with them. She became interested in the experimental dance and improvisational music scene there and stayed on, touring and making dances with improvising musicians. The musicians she worked with also used text, so together they developed a hybrid form, incorporating text with music and dance. During her first year in Europe, she met Tristan Honsinger, who plays the cello quite physically, and they became partners and long-term collaborators. Honsinger introduced Duck to music composers who were working improvisationally with ensembles of musicians—some who made scores, like Mischa Mengelberg from Holland, and some who worked freely, like Derek Bailey from England.

Duck notes the influence of Merce Cunningham's and John Cage's work with scores and indeterminacy. In her work with her company GROUPO, which she formed in Italy in the 1980s, she created detailed scores based on what she calls "the aesthetics of chance." She made the pieces to "look" improvised—a casual juxtaposing of a few well-placed simultaneities—but, in fact, they were elaborate set-ups painstakingly created to highlight prefabricated synchronicities between elements in the work.[8] From her work with GROUPO and her experience with ensembles of improvising musicians, she became intrigued to work with an ensemble of purely improvising dancers and musicians, and in 1996 she formed Magpie Music Dance Company, based in Amsterdam.

In a class with Magpie, a dancer is as likely to be critiqued by Mary Oliver, violinist, improvising musician, and artistic director of music, as by Duck, dance improviser and artistic director of dance. Improvising musicians are featured equally with dance as the company name suggests. In a performance duet, for instance, violinist Mary Oliver moves around the space as she plays, incorporating her "musician movements" into Duck's danced image.[9] If an instrument is not mobile (such as a keyboard or laptop), it is included in the "stage-scape." The company dance studios are currently housed in the same building as Kraakgeluiden, a group of improvisational acoustic and electric musicians, which facilitates collaboration.

In Magpie Music Dance's MELT project, the company works and performs with local professionals as part of a residency, leaving behind a model for future interdisciplinary collaboration between local artists. To date, MELT has been held in Spain, New Zealand, South Korea, and the United States. The project also brings artists to Magpie's home base in Amsterdam. Here a Trust Company (Seoul, Korea) dancer performs with Magpie (*from left*: Mary Oliver on violin, Andy Moor from the Ex band on guitar, and Katie Duck) at Bimhuis, Amsterdam, the Netherlands, 2008. Photo © Malgorzata Haduch

Magpie encourages practical dialogue between dancers and musicians—workshops with the company include both dancers and musicians as teachers and students working together, although musicians or dancers might split up by discipline for part of the time. A discussion might start concerning the dancer's "default" relationship with music—the matching of rhythm and/or mood of the music—and go on to suggest and try various alternate possibilities. Inviting both dancers and musicians to voice their interests creates a potentially contentious but dynamic atmosphere for collaboration between the disciplines, the core of Duck's work.[10]

The Music in Movement: Dana Reitz

Most of Dana Reitz's works are performed in silence. She is interested in the musicality built into movement, which she brings out, for example, by improvising with phrasing. Just as a musician listens to the space between the notes, allowing sound to register, Reitz listens to pauses between movements. She finds that listening to her movement as she makes it suggests the amount of time it will need to be registered and be digested by the audience before the next movement is offered.

Reitz advises audiences of the silent nature of her dances. She finds the expectation that music will accompany dance is often so strong that audiences are distracted because they are waiting for the music to come in. Knowing beforehand that there will be no music helps the audience relax and pay attention to the musicality of the movement.

Carrying the Music: Kazuo Ohno

Kazuo Ohno, cofounder of Butoh, likens a dancer's relationship with music to that of a child to his parents. When a child is young, his parents carry him. When the parents become elderly, the child, now an adult, carries them. This image conveys many possible meanings and interpretations, and a dance emerges from its investigation. As a dancer, do I let myself be carried by the music? Or do I anticipate its shifts by changing my dynamics ahead of the music, arriving on top of the music, so to speak? Indeed there might be many different relationships with the music in a given dance.

86 Aspects of Composition: Mike Vargas and Nancy Stark Smith

Mike Vargas, influenced by John Cage among others, treats any sound as fair game when composing music. He plays traditional musical instruments, such as the piano or drums, as well as any object that might make a noise, like a length of plumber's pipe. He sometimes incorporates prerecorded music and sounds in his compositions—from the recognizable and familiar (pop song or dog bark) to the mysterious (Is that noise a stick whipped through the air?).

As a composer, Vargas has developed 86 Aspects of Composition—a spectrum of open-ended and wide-ranging yet practical aspects to consider in the creative process. The list—which starts with "abstraction," "appropriation," and "balance" and finishes with "transition," "variation," and "vibration"—offers one or two elaborating questions for each entry.[11] There are many ways to use the list; it is built to be flexible. In practice it be can applied to music as well as dance or to any creative project, and it can be used before, during, or after the creative process in a variety of ways.

Vargas often teaches with Nancy Stark Smith, dancemaker and developing collaborator of Contact Improvisation. They might use Vargas's 86 Aspects as an interdisciplinary tool to aid Contact Improvisers, who are usually focused on the physical sensations of a Contact duet, in finding other relationships available in the dance space, including awareness of alternative relationships to a soundscape. For example, one or a few Aspects might be chosen as a reference to consider throughout the progression of Stark Smith's Underscore (see chapters 3 and 4) or used during the "harvest" period as a lens to help focus dancers' reflections of the event. For alternatives to the conventional relationship of "simultaneous" and "similar" between music and dance, Vargas suggests these possibilities: "questioning," "challenging," "contrasting," "agreeing," "anticipating," "hesitating," or "resisting."[12]

⤳ FIELD NOTES ⤶

Music motivated me to dance initially; as a child I loved to improvise to the music my parents played, recorded or live—from symphonies to honky-tonk piano, Broadway musicals to opera (and my brother was a country music fan!). Later, I enjoyed coordinating the physical dance skills I had mastered and the choreographies I learned with the rhythms and melodies of music. Once in a company, it was a delight to perform the same dance many times, which allowed investigation into the nuances of a particular piece of music through movement.

In the ballet company, especially among corps members who were dancing synchronously, there were often heated debates about how the placement of a movement fell on the count of the music. We would each have our favorite ways of musically placing phrases and would argue like lawyers for our interpretation to be taken up by the group—citing historical precedent, convenience, common usage, whatever we could come up with to make our case. And taking sides. In one fell swoop, a director or choreographer might change the execution and we would be forced into compliance until the next remembering of the choreography for the next performances or season. Then the debates would begin again, with new coalitions forming.

It was a thrill to come upon Kazuo Ohno's exercise of carrying the music many years later. Looking back at my friends in the ballet company, I saw that we had often stuck to our preferences: one dancer was always "carrying her parents," while I was happy to be carried, and therein lay the tale. Now I learned to challenge myself to be ahead of the music and enjoy the difference.

A large issue for me in my transition from classical to postmodern dance was learning to stop dancing in time to the music, that is to stop imitating the music's rhythms and melodic qualities. I realize now that not dancing to the music is as much a learned skill as dancing to the music. For me, this transition from one aesthetic to the other was greatly eased by the inherent rhythms I found in Topf's anatomical work and also by the artistry of Jon Gibson's music, which we often used for accompaniment. Its openness allowed us dancers to fill in, almost as if we were the visual harmonics to what was laid down musically. It was very satisfying to be offered a new approach to being with music; I hardly felt the loss of the old relationship. I found that "not dancing to the music" didn't mean not listening to it, but rather listening in another way.

After many years of dance study and viewing, this postmodern aesthetic played itself out. I needed to give myself permission to dance to music again, to enjoy that primal urge of rhythmic play and to witness its effect ripple through my body. Integrating the traditional music-dance relation back into my palette felt like a homecoming. My musical relationship now feels respectful—no longer a support but an active partner, offering me a key to access my slipstream of movement.

PRACTICES FOR FURTHER RESEARCH

1. While dancing to music, notice if you tend to lay back behind it or ride on top of it. Stick with one relationship for a while to see if it feels comfortable or not. Also try switching back and forth quickly. Can you tell which relationship you are using? If possible, work with both prerecorded and live improvised music.

2. Do you tend to work rhythmically with music, or catch an atmosphere or mood of the music and translate that into your dancing? Maybe you don't use music at all or use it as a background for movement. Consider your past predispositions for working with music. Experiment with another relationship.

3. Find an improvising musician and work together. Discover the expectations and desires you have for the relationship between music and dance. What relationships do you fall into? Is there a tendency to work with matching qualities and rhythms? Try pushing the envelope you create together. Do any new forms or relationships of working together emerge for you? Consider degrees of contrast and counterpoint, mixing differing amounts of stillness or silence, types of responding—questioning, challenging, agreeing, for starters.

4. In an improvisation, play with the idea of partnerships—with the floor, another person, the space, music.

⤙ INTERLUDE ⤚

Notes to Myself: Listening

Since I know nothing at all, I shall do whatever occurs to me.

—C. G. JUNG, *Memories, Dreams, Reflections*

There seem to be two parts to listening with the body. First, there is listening to the phenomenon, but then there is listening to the body's response to the phenomenon to see what flash I get. I tend to listen and then calculate. But instead I could learn to hear what the first flash is and pay attention to that. For some reason I often put off acting on the first thing I hear, but when I put it off and then do it, it's already old.

In improvisation, I need to practice listening and then listening to what occurs to me. And then I need to just go and not get involved with my judgment or calculation, because I can't be everywhere at once and know what is going to happen and if I wait it isn't fresh news. I have to catch the tail and hang on. The more I learn to trust catching the tail, the easier it is to catch the ride, I imagine.

If I enter knowing what I am going to do (planning) then I miss (shut down to) all the reads and what is actually going on. If the body plans, what does that feel like? It seems like the body can alter its course very quickly because of the reflexive tuning it uses to plan. In the end, there aren't any absolutes. I can just use everything all the time—whatever occurs to me. What else is there?

7

The Eyes

Are your eyes open in such a way that your soul can come and go without hindrance? . . . Pay careful attention to the way you gaze about you, for it's possible to create a dance solely with the eyes. They are a world unto themselves.

—KAZUO OHNO, *Kazuo Ohno's World*

IN SOME DANCE TRADITIONS, especially those of India and Asia, eye movements are choreographed. In contemporary Western concert dance, while the gaze is an acknowledged part of the presentation of a dance, it is often left up to the individual dancer to figure out where he or she will look while dancing. A choreographer or dance teacher might give some cues, like "look out to the back of the theater," as a guideline. This question of how to use the eyes while dancing has led to the creation of specific improvisation practices that consider the eyes' relationship to movement.

THE FIVE EYE PRACTICES: BARBARA DILLEY

Barbara Dilley's interest in the eyes began with a friend's comment about a trend of blank looks and stares on the faces of dancers performing contemporary dance choreography. Dilley found that when dancers improvised there were also difficulties with the usage of the eyes—though in a different way. In improvising movement, she noticed that dancers tended to put so much interior focus on the sensation and creation of movement that they generally worked with their eyes half-open, often looking down at the floor.[1] It was enough to manage the body in space and generate movement; the eyes were left out of the picture.

To bring awareness to the usage of the eyes, Dilley developed the Five Eye Practices to offer dancers options to a habitual interior or a fixed exterior gaze. *Closed eyes*, a way of looking within, also rests and refreshes the eyes. *Peripheral seeing* uses a soft focus to allow seeing out of the corner of the eyes.

Dilley describes the third practice, *infant eyes*, to be the way babies move their eyes around with a freedom of looking without analyzing—"seeing before naming." The fourth practice, *looking between things*, asks improvisers to focus their eyes on the empty space between people and objects in the room. This suggests spaces to move into and becomes quite a kinetic and energizing score for improvisation. The last practice, *direct looking*, is not about looking someone directly in the eyes, says Dilley in an interview for *Contact Quarterly*. Rather, she explains, "I talk about not looking in each other's eyes yet, but you just look at the light on somebody's face, or the creases of their arm, or the way they hold their hand . . . to look from the back of your head rather than to push through the eyeballs. . . . It takes a lot of pressure off of the seeing." The five are practiced individually to give an experience of each, to bring awareness to the individual's particular habit, and as options to the habitual. With familiarity, they become a common reference point for an ensemble, part of the "language for the practice" of improvisation—an articulation of the eyes.[2]

These practices came out of a performance piece, *Naked Face* (1997), which Dilley developed in residency at the Djerassi Foundation with the Mariposa Collective. Dilley marks *Naked Face* as her first work of Dharma Art, a work that created an equal exchange between audience and dancer, without setting up the dancer as special somehow—as the creator or carrier of the art—but that included the audience and invited it to take part in the making and framing of the work as well.[3]

Originally the Five Eye Practices were given to the audience on cards as suggestions for ways to view the piece, while the performers worked with another kind of imaginative visioning process, which Dilley called projection. This looked into the psychological component of seeing—how we often see what we want to see because of our inner desires and conditioning. The dancers worked with three types of projections. First, a dancer could look at another and see someone she knew well, a friend perhaps, or someone she disliked, like the bully down the street from when she was a kid. Second, she might look at someone as if she were a deity of some sort, a person placed on a pedestal. The third option was to look with no projection. What would it be like to discover the naked face? The piece took place in an art museum amid a sculpture installation and was quite still and spacious, with the dancers perhaps sitting, standing, or lying down except when they shifted position. The audience was free to walk among the dancers, choosing the style of viewing with which they wished to experiment, creators of their own visual art.

ENGAGING THE EYES: KATIE DUCK

Katie Duck often starts her workshops by calling attention to the eyes. She asks dancers to use their eyes "to bring the space with them" as they move across the floor—actually to see the space that they are in as they dance.[4] Duck notes that when not dancing we naturally use our eyes in various ranges depending on the task as well as the type and speed of our movements. But oddly, when we dance we don't always shift our gaze in this way. So Duck reverse engineers what she calls a natural gaze in her training for improvisers. Normally she finds a close or short-range gaze to be used for more internal types of movements based on sensation, for example, soft touch between partners. The eyes are focused close in, as if on a hand in front of the face. A second, mid-range gaze (around three feet into space) is used for inter-action with other dancers; this is normally our social mode—most dance movement falls into this category. A longer gaze that takes in the edges of the space—the far walls, the ceiling, and beyond—is a third possibility, used in large movements and broad gestures that reach beyond the dancer's personal space and take in the entire room and what is occurring in it.

Improvisers experiment with each gaze range in turn, noticing what kinds of movement the gaze elicits and vice versa—for example, a long-range gaze invites traveling through the space, and duets often give rise to a mid-range gaze. The ensemble members improvise together, experimenting with all three gazes to notice how individual patterns of eye usage jibe or not with dance movement. It would be an unusual and dramatic choice for a person to get up off the floor while using a long-range gaze, something that might be choreographed but that isn't routine. However, when dancers are impro-vising they tend to revert to their performance habits at first, and rather than using their eyes in a relaxed, everyday manner, they mix gazes and types of movement, creating awkward, stiff coordinations. Duck asks dancers to develop awareness about their eye habits and suggests returning to more nat-ural patterns.

She encourages dancers to use their eyes directly to connect with their partners; she calls this eyeballing. Eyeballing creates an excitement by in-voking "biology," an interpersonal chemistry between the dancers, that pulls the audience in and gets them involved in the exchange empathetically or, she suggests, even hormonally. She also encourages dancers not to be afraid of getting close to the audience or to another dancer to elicit a rush; play with this sense of biology; and create interpersonal interest, empathy, and excitement. Duck doesn't want her audience members to sit back and read a performance solely visually and in an emotionally detached way like they might read the newspaper; she wants them to be involved with the play of the improvisers on a gutsy, hormonal level. The focus of the eyes can be crucial in creating this effect.

THE KINESTHETICS OF SEEING: LISA NELSON

Lisa Nelson grew up dancing and choreographing—as a teen at the Juilliard School in New York and then at Bennington College in Bennington, Vermont. She turned her focus to improvisational dance when she turned nineteen, working with musicians and theater artists and eventually joining Daniel Nagrin's improvisation company, The Workgroup, in New York in 1971. But, a few years later, frustrated with the dance scene and not sure how to get what she was interested in from it, she stopped dancing entirely. Serendipitously, she picked up a video camera when they were first becoming publicly available and began producing community TV and teaching videodance at Bennington College. At that time, she documented much of the local Vermont and downtown New York dance scene, including Steve Paxton's early years of Contact Improvisation and Judith Dunn's Compositional Improvisation ensemble with Bill Dixon at Bennington College. In 1977 she began video documenting the work of Bonnie Bainbridge Cohen, creator of Body-Mind Centering, an approach to experiential anatomy and movement reeducation, as Cohen researched developmental patterns with brain-injured and normally developing infants.

Nelson found that videotaping entailed the process of relearning to see through the camera, an artificial eye that comes between the body and the image, magnifying and distorting the mechanics of seeing. She became fascinated by the experience. Using the video camera pointed out to her how intertwined movement is with the act of seeing, whether it involved getting into a sometimes awkward position and holding still or following a movement in order to get a shot. She noticed how her visual desires reflexively prompted her own movement through space and that often it was a change in the environment that she hadn't been aware of until she watched the playback of the video that had actually prompted her shifts. She realized that seeing was a kinesthetic activity. Eventually, she found her way back into dancing through her interest in deconstructing and reconnecting the act of seeing with the movements her body made to satisfy her eyes.[5]

What exactly is a visual desire? Desires of the other senses seem some-how more easily defined: a taste for sweets, a yen for a massage, a particular piano concerto, or favorite perfume. At first it may seem difficult to identify a simple visual desire. We are always looking; the choice to close tired eyes is one kind of visual desire, if a negative one. But try sitting in a partial-view seat at a dance concert and have your desire to see thwarted, or try staring at someone's ear while they are talking to you; in each case you really notice how desire relates to your vision. Call up one of these experiences (or one like them), and you may find that packaged with the memory is the bodily desire to move—either your eyes or your body—to satisfy your desire to see. Nelson asks students new to her work what they like to look at—it's not surprising that often movement is entwined in their tastes.

Nelson developed Tuning work to explore movement as a response to environmental influences—both the external and the internal (e.g., sensa-tions in the body, memory). Somewhat like a violin string is micro-adjusted to sound a certain pitch, the body tunes its movement to the current condi-tions of the task at hand—for example by adjusting stance and muscle ten-sion in anticipation of taking weight or by tilting the head to turn a good ear toward a speaker. These movements made to organize the body for spe-cific activities often prove difficult to observe in oneself, as they happen just under awareness. This exploration led Nelson to develop performance works such as *Dodo* (1982), *The Part One Hears* (with collaborator Christina Svane, 1984), *An Abondanza in the Air* (with collaborator Cathy Weis, 1990), *Ball Room* (with collaborator Daniel Lepkoff, 1990), and site-specific *Observato-ries* (with Image Lab: Karen Nelson et al., 1990s). These works play with the senses of sight, sound, and touch and with kinesthetics, and they investigate the codependence between the senses and the moving body.

The Tuning Score, developed as an ensemble work in collaboration with Image Lab, offers an opportunity to examine the connections between ob-serving and moving. The participants, "players," are both movers and view-ers, alternately and at the same time. Some of the players create a moving image from various starting points such as the Single Image Score (described in chapter 5) or the Blind Unison Trio (described in chapter 2). Then both viewers and movers are free to use verbal calls, for example, "reverse" or "end," to tune the dancing image to their taste as it unfolds (see chapters 3 and 5 for call descriptions). A player might call "reverse" because he or she didn't want a grouping to split up just yet. Or maybe a viewer likes seeing the dancers think backward on their feet. Sometimes an interesting interaction between dancers can be revisited through the "reverse" call. "End" stops the action and clears the space. "End" is usually a call for which players have already developed a particular taste relating to a sense of composition and duration. A viewer may have a different perspective on the "end" from the dancers in the image space (the preselected area for the dance), all of which is up for investigation in the course of the play.[6]

Based on both choreographic organization and the functions of video shooting, playback, and editing, the calls affect the piece in predictable and unpredictable ways. Because they interrupt and interact with the play of the image, the calls create an opportunity for players to investigate seen or felt desires—what they want from a dance.

Players enter and exit the image space, moving or observing, responding to the calls. It quickly becomes clear that the calls are much more than a tool to test performers' ability to follow directions, as are the calls in a Square Dance. For example, a mover might be motivated to use the call "pause" to get a better feel for where the other dancers are in the space. However, a viewer might call "pause" to satisfy his or her desire to enjoy a moment in the dance that he or she found pleasing visually or to change the rhythm of the dance. The call "repeat" is another way the viewer could ask to enjoy the moment, but with an emphasis on the dynamics of the movement. The calls do not have entirely predictable consequences. For instance, the movers pick their own segments to repeat. What a particular call actually elicits from the dancers may vary as the play evolves; the players may adapt their interests and explorations as they go.

The calls become a device for the players to examine what is satisfying to them about the action—whether it gets fulfilled as anticipated or not. At first, the players use the calls at face value, but after experiencing the consequences of each communication, they soon begin to explore ways to satisfy the layers of desires that arise while watching the dance performance. As in the example above, a viewer might at first use "pause" to enjoy a visually pleasing moment, and in so doing discover that "pause" may also be used to shift the rhythm of the dance. Used deftly, the calls become tools for examining the pleasures of any given moment in the unfolding of the action.

A particularly informative call is "replace," which asks the viewers to replace the activity in the image that is absorbing their attention at the moment the call is made (all the current movers must exit). A viewer now becomes a mover and experiences a shift from visual to kinesthetic perception. Different activities in the image become magnified if they've caught more than one player's attention. An image may have many movers replacing a single figure, and other parts of the image may have vanished completely. The "replace" call informs movers about the importance of their movement in the viewing field. In pointing out the overall interest, "replace" also shifts the playing field. For example, what was interesting as a solo activity may play out completely differently as a choral unison. The various calls become a device to explore not only these compositional desires but also how effective the choices made were in satisfying those desires and whether other players share one's desires for the dance.

In the Tuning Score, choices are mutable; through the calls they can be reworked according to taste, and even be taken back with a "reverse" call. The usual relation of cause and effect are up for negotiation by the group. Choosing becomes playful rather than weighty. This atmosphere allows the players to learn as much from the calls that misfire and the navigation of unexpected results as from calls that satisfy expectations. In the ensuing dialogue set up by the tuning of the image, players define and refine their tastes, and by following the interplay of sensory delights they learn something of the nature of seeing, and seeing dance in particular, in the process.

Brussels group in a Tuning Score Observatory, a proposition by Lisa Nelson, Brussels, Belgium, 2005. Photo © by Raymond Mallentjer

The practice of the Tuning Score is a practice of performance, as the play-ers are also assuming the role of audience. Nelson also welcomes an outside audience to the practice, calling it an Observatory. In witnessing the players edit the action, the audience is let in on the process. Even when the viewers are not actively involved in making calls or movements, they become caught in the growing suspense over how the action will play out. For the audience, there is a feeling of satisfaction when their own desires are fulfilled by one of the player's calls or actions—a recognition of a shared aesthetic. From Nelson's viewpoint, the play educates the audience about their own tastes. She says in the program notes, "The Observatory is an invitation into the nature of your own seeing."[7]

The Eyes as an Image of Depth: Nancy Topf

Nancy Topf was especially interested in the eyes for the image of depth and dimensionality they gave to our bodies. First, she would have dancers look at and feel the shape and depth of the eye socket on a skeleton. Then she would ask them while lying down to imagine their eyes sinking to the very bottom of the sockets, and to feel the eyes as heavy. Topf found that imagery helped people to find sensation in places they weren't used to feeling.[8] Another image Topf used to create a sense of depth in the eyes was that of the optic nerve running from the back of the eye deeply into the brain through to the optic lobe at the back of the cranium. In suggesting these images, she gave students a sense of their eyes as something besides flat screens for vision. She reminded students that the eyes had shape and connection and showed them how to use these new feelings to dive deep beneath the surface to discover a sensation of depth in the body.

This sensation was important to Topf because, as her teacher Barbara Clark pointed out, "the body proportion needs depth."[9] Dancers (and people generally) are aware of their bodies' heights and widths from side to side, but depth is not a dimension in which we get much of a sense of ourselves from daily life. Dancers work in front of mirrors, watch themselves on video, and often think in terms of the proscenium stage, all experiences that tend to flat-ten the image created. Yet the mechanics of moving a two-dimensional object through space are quite different than that of a three-dimensional one. Topf believed that giving dancers a felt sense of depth in their bodies helped them find better mechanics in their moving and dancing. Improvising movement based on images of depth helps to change the image of body by bringing physical sensation into that dimension.

One of the improvisations Topf used to further investigate the eyes and depth of the body involved an image based on the anatomy of the skull. In her anatomy lecture that preceded the improvisation, Topf pointed out the heaviness of the head (around eight pounds).[10] She contrasted the cranial bones, the large bones of the skull that encase the brain, with the "lacy face," referring to the facial bones in front. The facial bones are mostly smaller and more numerous than the cranial. They make up the face, shot through with holes, and house specialized sensory organs. The facial area seems very light in comparison to the cranium. The image of the lacy face reversed the usual pattern of vision-driven (frontally driven) head movement. That the weighty head supports the face creates a sensation of depth and suggests a more centrally supported mechanics for head movement, one that frees the neck. In Topf's work, the eyes were both windows and doorways to the depth of the body.

PLAYING THE FIELD: NINA MARTIN

"Big/Small" is the name that Nina Martin gives to an eye practice that investigates the manipulation of the scale of the dancing image (from the audience's perspective). The dancer needs to be consciously aware of how the size of the image he or she is creating gets shifted through movement, from big (this is up to interpretation—it could mean up close or a full-body view) to small (farther away or partial-body view) and back again. The practice is done in pairs, with an observer and a dancer, who moves to create the shifting image.[11]

A number of strategies may develop to create this shift; clearly moving closer or farther in the observer's field of view is key, but many variations are revealed in the course of the improvisation. For example, the dancer, without moving closer or farther away, might negotiate a switch of the observer's attention from foreground to background. The dancer could be standing in front of and very close to a seated observer, blocking the view of the space with his or her body, filling the foreground. With a simple shift of the hips to the left and a crook of the arm to the right, the dancer creates a window through which the viewer is invited to observe the background. Or the dancer might choose to change the scale of his or her movement to cause the observer to zoom in (a nose scratch) or out (a grand jeté).

While most of Martin's Ensemble Thinking exercises focus on composing physical space around and about the dancers, this exercise from her Articulating the Solo Body work offers its own curious solution to composing the space of the dance from the vantage of the observer's eye.

PERIPHERAL VISION: STEVE PAXTON

While many improvisers have created movement practices based on the activity of the eyes, the practice of Contact Improvisation necessitates a different usage—an emphasis on peripheral vision. Frontally based vision is not very helpful when the body is tipping quickly and unexpectedly, upside down, sideways, and backward through all 360 degrees around its center of gravity. Fortunately, our bodies understand this and instinctively know to look in a different way. Peripheral vision gets developed through the practice and with it a mode of peripheral sensing as well: the back, sides, and underside of any surface of the body become potential transmitters of navigational information. This is a big change from our pedestrian mode of being, where a frontal orientation is most significant, and other sensory information, which, though still there and always available, is in the background of consciousness.

An interesting thing about peripheral vision is that if you focus on the periphery too much, too consciously, you lose it—vision becomes frontal. To keep this switch from happening, a certain amount of relaxation, what feels like an opening or expansion of consciousness, is required. This heightening of peripheral sensation creates a shift of being, and may be one of the reasons for the form's popularity among practitioners. Steve Paxton says, "My training of Contact Improvisation dancers highlights peripheral vision, on the premise that it leads to peripheral mind, which intensifies peripheral sensing."[12]

CLEANING THE WINDOWS OF PERCEPTION:
SUPRAPTO SURYODARMO (PRAPTO)

Prapto asks his students to use their arms to make windows to look through by opening and closing the shoulder, elbow, wrist, and finger joints as they move in space. Later the legs, the back, and the whole body are included in the activity. The windows open and close as the body moves, giving different views.

Prapto believes that we can get stuck in our perception, always looking out, but not registering what we see in ourselves. Changing perspectives brings

circulation to our perceptions and helps us to clear our minds of habitual attitudes and responses.[13]

⇥| FIELD NOTES |⇤

Scene 1: Interterm at Bennington College with Lisa Nelson. We are in the
cavernous Martha Hill Dance Theater, an oversized black box with a gor-
geous rich-brown wooden floor. It's February, it's Vermont: the six or seven
dancers are wearing down jackets or layers of wool. I am totally intrigued by
Nelson's practice. When she describes her research I am on the edge of my
seat; it makes some kind of intuitive sense. But perhaps because I have little
experience with a video camera or because I am less of a visual learner, I find
it difficult to cross-reference the logic of certain statements she makes with
my experience. It's perhaps the most foreign approach of any that I have
come across. I have to put months, even years of dogged investigation into it
to finally have an "aha" moment.

We sit huddled on the floor positioning ourselves strategically in the stage
lights for warmth and talk about what makes us feel "physicalized" while dancing. As a group we discuss rolling on the floor, physical exertion, yoga, muscles versus bones, what it means to be embodied, and whatever else comes
up. Then we take turns making solo improvisations researching the physicalized state. As viewers, we signal when we feel the solo dancer is achieving
physicality in his or her dancing; viewers have differing opinions. After the
practice, in which she also participated by dancing and reporting her viewing,
Nelson says that something about the way she uses her eyes makes her hook
into her physicality while dancing. I have no idea what she could be talking
about! This statement is about as far removed from my experience as I can
imagine. Yet I must have seen something in the watching—I am determined
to figure out what she could mean by it.

Jump cut to scene 2: The Festival of Interactive Physics, Toronto, four
years later. Early spring, the fifteen or so dancers are again clad in wool and
down: the second floor space is bright and airy, but the floor is cold. We are
in the middle of a long weekend workshop with Nina Martin on her group
work Ensemble Thinking. Now she teaches us Big/Small, an exercise that
she says is not part of the Ensemble Thinking toolbox, that is, not about
composing an improvisation with a group, but one that she finds related. I
thoroughly enjoy this exercise, which the group does all at once, in pairs. My

partner, from Ottawa, makes luscious buttery falls to the floor in her dance at unexpected intervals, and I, in my turn, feel completely engaged in directing her focus through my movement choices. Martin's response is surprise. She says, "It's very strange—the space seemed composed, but it shouldn't have!" Because of my Tuning experience with Nelson, it seemed perfectly reasonable that the group appeared composed, though we considered only our partners and no one else in the space. We had been "tuning" in the sense that we had a group focus and were investigating those ultimate composers, the eyes. I had stepped into my own movie-making: my movements, the director; my partner's eyes, the camera. Here I experienced directing from the other side of the lens.

Fade to scene 3: It's August at Earthdance in the wooded hills of Western Massachusetts two years later; Prapto teaches a ten-day workshop called the Prayer of the Butterfly. It is hot and buggy; we work in the forest by a stream, on the lawn, and in the round studio with the windows wide open. We learn a dance in which we use our limbs to create frames to look through, and this action creates a continually shifting perspective. I ask if the dance is done to invoke a shift of perspective, to bring on a quality that I don't have and don't know how to attain but wish to acquire. Prapto smiles. He is onto my desire of explaining process. He accedes that a dance may invoke, but he always leaves a trail of "and also . . . ," leaving space for multiple possibilities. How I would like to expand my perspective! It seems to me that some of these dancemakers have their feet firmly planted in another reality, their movements here a trace of that place. I am hopeful that my perspective will broaden because of the dancing we do in this incredible week with Prapto.

Black out, scene 4: Dusk at our local studio, the Wildlife Sanctuary, in Florence, Massachusetts, nine months later. I am leading a Tuning investigation with my coworker and another friend. We do some simple eye warm-ups, noticing how our eyes track objects in the room. Later in our practice, I suddenly develop the ability to "surf," by which I mean that somehow my eyes are feeding their kinesthetic experience to my body, and it comes out in movement. I feel like I am pulled along by the ride—vision informs movement shifts vision—endless and effortless. And somehow it is a familiar feeling; I have always known how to do it. It feels like it feels when I am carried by the music, but my eyes have triggered the experience. "It's important what we feed our eyes," Nelson says. Aha!

PRACTICES FOR FURTHER RESEARCH

1. Next time you are listening to someone speak, notice how you are paying attention to them with your eyes. Change what you do, and see how long you can maintain the change.

2. Catch yourself in your daily life using close-, medium-, and far-range gazes. Observe yourself in a dance class or while improvising, and see what kind of gaze you tend to use.

3. Create an improvisation from a score for the eyes.

4. While doing your chores, close your eyes but continue doing what you were doing. Do your eyes move to follow your movement in the same way they did when they were open? Go back and forth from eyes open to eyes closed and observe whether and how the eyes move when they are closed. Try this exercise while you are improvising movement as well. Observe the differences about your movement between when your eyes are open and when they're closed.

5. Find any comfortable position in the room you are in. Notice where your eyes fall. Holding your body in the same position, shift your eyes and focus on something specific in the outer range of your field of vision. Hold the new focus. Notice if your physical comfort shifts. Now, holding your eyes steady, shift your body into a new comfortable position. Do several rounds, shifting the eyes then shifting the body. What might make you change levels (sitting to lying down) or travel around the room? Consider the possibility of shifting the depth of field of your focus as well.

⤚{ INTERLUDE }⤙

Notes to Myself on Catching It Out of the Corner of My Eye

I have to catch it out of the corner of my eye because movement patterns happen mostly subconsciously. If I look directly, I am not seeing the subconscious ones, only the conscious ones. I want to see my habit patterns, not my made-for-TV moves.

I remember trying to catch myself out of the corner of my eye in one of Lisa Nelson's Tuning exercises. She asked us whether we thought we used our eyes first to see where we were going when we switched directions. It seemed like you would, sure. So then we tried it, walking around the room, changing directions. Did the eyes move first, or did the body lead? We had to try to catch ourselves in the habit. One thing she suggested was to try doing both and see which felt more familiar. I had to trick myself into not paying attention just enough so I could see what I did habitually. And it had a way of coming back later in the day when I was going about my business— a residual state of hyperawareness. The whole thing was like playing tag with my shadow.

8

Partnering Science

The critical difference [between artist and scientist] is that the artist measures
from his intuition, his feeling. In other words, he uses himself as the measure.
Whereas the scientist measures out of an external logic process and makes his
decision finally on whether it fits that process in terms of various external
abstract measures.

—ROBERT IRWIN, in Lawrence Weschler, *Seeing Is Forgetting the
Name of the Thing One Sees*

I n contemporary culture, science is often used to validate experience, as
in, "It is scientifically proven that . . ." The following dancemakers have
found other ways to relate to science, using it to inform rather than con-
firm. Science instead becomes a partner that suggests new ways of thinking
about, working with, and articulating an avenue of inquiry.

COMPARATIVE ANATOMY OF A MOVING BODY:
JENNIFER MONSON

Jennifer Monson's multiyear BIRD BRAIN project studies navigation and
migration patterns of animals such as birds and whales. She and her dance
improvisers camped out along migration routes and observed the animals
interacting with their particular habitats. Through teaching dance workshops
based on navigation and sensory explorations, performing for the local community, and engaging in conversations with ecologists, park rangers, and hik-
ers, Monson and her group use dance as a vehicle for observing and engaging
in local ecosystems and for uncovering their importance to migrating species.

Monson devises dances based on the strategies of the migrating animals
she follows. She shares some of these dance ideas in her community classes:
basic navigation exercises like finding north, facing toward home, remembering pathways, and flocking practices. She peppers these exercises with

examples of how scientists think birds and other animals are adapted to accomplish these tasks (magnetically sensitive metal deposits in their brains, North Star celestial navigation, polarized light, weather pattern recognition, or low frequency sounds).[1] Perhaps we humans take our navigation skills for granted, have forgotten them through disuse, or think that only other animals have them. Monson challenges us to navigate and become aware of how we do it.

These simple exercises reveal a wealth of research possibilities for anyone interested in movement. For example, how do we refind a location? Visually, or kinetically through muscle memory? How do the senses combine to accomplish the task? What other senses play roles? What does home feel like? How do we know when we've hit our mark? Landmarks reveal themselves as a nexus of sensory information. In the end, no matter how the birds or whales do it, we reflect on our own latent capacities.

Monson points out that the concerns of migrating animals are similar to those of the dancer. Both share the same baseline, movement. For example,

Jennifer Monson's *Flight of Mind* (2005), a component of BIRD BRAIN, her multiyear navigational dance project, East River, Williamsburg, Brooklyn, New York. *From left*: Katy Pyle, Jennifer Monson, and Alex Escalante. Photo © Bob Braines

a dancer's landmarks are created against a backdrop of moving bodies. Dancers may be unaware of how they build and remember these marks. Comparing experiences with another order of intelligence suggests nuances and potentials for skills dancers might never have considered or challenged themselves to develop if left studio-bound.

Questions regarding group dynamics arise: How are transitional states between movement and stillness negotiated in a group? What's the difference between departing from and arriving into stillness and a moving state? How is a moving state established and agreed upon? Switching the discussion from a sedentary to a moving frame of reference opens up a world of comparisons. For workshop participants, empathy arises for animals in a changing environment. For the performing dancer, the investigation of animal navigation offers a comparative study from which to consider and create movement.

In her *Urban Migrations*, a scored improvisation, Monson asks dancers to include everything they find in the environment in the evolving dance, the natural as well as the man made—like migrating birds do when they use an abandoned concrete pier as a landing pad. Dancers likewise create an ecosystem of the available in their dance, considering manmade objects from a perspective of adaptability. That buildings, streets, and lampposts might have functions other than the obvious piques a curiosity and responsibility toward those other functions. Monson's dances help us—dancers and viewers alike—experience the interconnectivity of the natural and the manmade and question the distinction between the two. In doing so, we begin to reconnect and take responsibility for our place in a larger ecosystem.[2]

Embodying Complexity: Susan Sgorbati

As a dance professor at Bennington, a progressive liberal arts college, Susan Sgorbati is in a unique position to create an exchange of ideas with scientists. She was inspired to do so upon hearing about the relatively new scientific paradigm of complexity that has revolutionized areas of evolutionary biology and neuroscience. She recognized that the language of complexity and the ideas around it described what she had observed in dance improvisations over her many years of involvement with the art form. She teamed up with colleague Bruce Weber, an evolutionary biologist, and began developing work to explore complexity theory and how it informs the practice of dance improvisation. She has also been inspired by and consulted Nobel Prize–winning neuroscientist Gerald Edelman and evolutionary biologist Stuart Kaufmann. The result is a body of work—training, practice, performance—Sgorbati calls Emergent Improvisation.

Three key components of complexity theory inform Emergent Improvisation: self-organization, ordering or structuring that comes from within a given system; emergence, "an outcome or property of self-organization, the process by which some new form, some new ordering, some new pattern, or some new ability arises to move something toward the creation of another idea, opening up or exposing the potential for something new"; and complexity, "a structuring at the edge of chaos, where there is enough order to recognize a pattern yet enough openness to be adaptable to new information leading to the creation of a new property or outcome."[3] In her work with Emergent Improvisation, Sgorbati looks for certain initial conditions—improvisational structures—that will lead to this state of complex self-organization where there is enough going on to feed the dance and to keep it reinventing itself. One prerequisite she finds is that the dancers must be aware and adaptable enough to sustain a self-inventing movement vocabulary while retaining enough awareness of their surroundings to respond to conditions as they develop. A certain level of improvisational dance ability is necessary to create and maintain this self-organizing yet complex state. Her dance training addresses methods for building these skills. (See chapters 1 and 2.)

One such structure, which Sgorbati calls "the Memory Form," is based on Edelman's concept of a "remembered present." Edelman and his coauthor, Giulio Tononi, explain: "The ability of an animal to connect events and signals in the world, whether they are causally related or merely contemporaneous, and, then, through reentry with its value-category memory system, to construct a scene that is related to its own learned history is the basis for the emergence of primary consciousness. . . . The ability to construct a conscious scene is the ability to construct, within fractions of seconds, a remembered present."[4]

In the Memory Form, dancers create a short improvised sequence and then repeat it over and over. This is not so easy to accomplish with a group! To re-create the interactions that occurred in the sequence, dancers need to remember their own movements as well as their timing in relation to others. The audience members watch the dancers' re-creation of the sequence and test their own memory, delighting when a memorable action from the original sequence (like a collision) is duplicated, or when it is not, and another solution, slightly off the original, presents itself.[5] For example, originally person A tips over, raising his leg, while person B ducks under it. But the next time, B is late. A's leg is already coming down. B catches A's leg and still accomplishes the maneuver—a variation of necessity arises in the moment.

While remembering the dance, the dancers are also researching—learning more about the original movement elements in the dance through repetition and variation. At another level of complexity, after several repetitions of the sequence, each dancer takes on the role of another dancer and repeats the sequence from this new perspective. More than one dancer can take on a particular role. Skills of remembering movement, timing, spatial awareness, and shifting perspectives are challenged and developed, as is a sense of when to let go of the memory of the initial sequence and adapt to present circumstances, incorporating past experience into current activity and creating new material. In the final section, the dancers are free to enter and exit the memory and to draw on any element of the event, the memory of the event, or the subtext that they thought was buried in the origin of the event or its consequences.

The Memory Form, currently one of four distinct forms of Susan Sgorbati's Emergent Improvisation project, performed at Bennington College, 2006. Carson Efird lifts Keith Thompson while Zornitsa Stoyanova looks on. *Floor, from left*: Jaamil Olawale Kosoko, Katie Martin, and Nicole Pope Daunic. Photo © Paul Kyle

Complexity theory gives Sgorbati a comparative language to help her investigate what makes an improvisation develop and what elements go into making a "successful" improvisation. She is interested in the dialogue with the scientists: Could the scientists experience and witness the complex systems that she sees in improvisation? Could a dance in a studio shed light on scientific investigation? In 2006 the Neurosciences Institute in La Jolla, California, directed by Edelman, brought the Emergent Improvisation Project to the West Coast for performances. According to Sgorbati, many scientists have been thrilled to see the principles of complexity at work on the stage.

Physics for the Body: Steve Paxton

Before Contact Improvisation became the socio-cultural dance phenomenon that it is today, it was initially a question of physics. Or a question of redefining physics. Newton articulated the force of gravity as a mathematical concept: $G=(gMM_2)/r^2$ where g equals gravitational constant and r equals the distance between the two bodies in question. In Contact Improvisation, Steve Paxton suggested a dance form that articulated the force of gravity through kinesthetic sensations, the feelings of the body in falling, momentum, and centripetal force. How could two bodies negotiate the sharing and bearing of weight around a physical point of contact? In the soundtrack for the video *Fall after Newton* (1987), Paxton says, "Being essentially objective, Newton ignored what it felt like to be the apple."[6] Now the skills of Contact (surfing, flying, and spinning spiral shoulder lifts), the community created around the "jam" (the open space forming and reforming duet practice of Contact Improvisation), and the thirty-five-plus years of history of the form have obscured the initial inquiry to a degree, although it is still there to be found in any moment—a fall, a spin, a surprise change of direction.

Contact Improvisation heightens a dancer's dialogue with gravity by placing the body in a situation that challenges certain reflex responses. The body is pushed to the edge of its ability to respond to weight and speed by asking it to handle slightly more than it is used to handling, and to do so unexpectedly. All this happens simply by virtue of following the point of contact with another moving body. Contact's dialogue with gravity is not so much about defying or controlling it (as do dance forms that develop balances, leaps, or rhythms) as it is about following gravity—in the taking of weight, rolling, and falling in connection with another body—to chart what ends up being a not so predictable path. Contact improvisers become gravity experts within their particular field of inquiry—touch and kinesthetic sensation, the language of the body.

A Research Proposal: Simone Forti

"It seems to me that when the polar bear swings his head, he is in a dance state. He is in a state of establishing measure, and of communion with the forces of which he is a part."[7] In an early phase of her long career investigating movement and making dances, Forti studied the various gaits of zoo animals as they paced in their pens or cages and made dances from them, capturing something of the essence of each animal in its dance. She has studied crawling and made dances of the way we humans bank when we run in a circle or figure eight. There's a way our physical bodies measure out the world for us as we move about, especially noticeable in cyclical movements like gaits, which set up rhythms that act like a clock or metronome. Our bodies, engaged in movement, speak to us of the laws of physics, whether we know them intellectually or not, through direct experience.

It is this "being in the knowing" of forces through the body that Forti attributes to her "dance state":

> There's something I experience that I call the dance state. It is a state of enchantment. As in chant. Or the French *chanter*, to sing. A kind of being besonged. I have experienced it as a state of heightened awareness where one possibility after another presents itself like an unfolding path. As I rise, sink, and turn, my eye catches the shadow play of leaves on the far wall, suggesting the next move. I think it's a state of being. Like sleeping, figuring out, or panicking are states of being. The dance state can occur in performance of choreographed work. Improvisation depends on it. When it is flowing very strongly, it is as if an angel were dropping the improvisation into your lap. When it's not, you have to bring your skills into play in a more methodical way. It still works. But part of becoming an improviser is getting to know what material is currently inspiring you to the point that it can induce this state.[8]

Forti takes to task a prevailing attitude that improvisational dance comes out of nowhere and is made up on the spot, instantaneously. For her, a structure for an improvisation develops out of some personal interest or study and has a depth of experience behind it. Preparation—research and rehearsal—

is part of improvised performance, "a wave which will crest into the lap of the audience."[9] This physical preparation sets up the context for "the communion of forces" to occur; the practice, she says, is to get the research to move, to enter the dance state through it and because of it.

Research for her group dances in the past has included watching the sunrise over Manhattan, a Circle Line boat tour, a geology lecture, and a day at the botanical gardens, with plenty of physical interaction along the way.[10] The research process often includes writing about the experiences, for example, in timed free-writes.[11] This research creates a pool of common experience, a focus of shared imagery, memory, and physical experience, a base from which the group moves—and speaks, in the case of Logomotion, her latest body of work. Forti sees an improvised dance not in isolation but as part of a series of improvisations that inform, refine, question, regroup, and direct the next dance, and so on—a series of references, a context, a body of research. The research then moves and responds—a growing body of knowledge, written in movement.

⨭ FIELD NOTES ⨮

Science as we know it today is based on objective, "third-person" accounting of phenomenon, relying on repeatable, corroborative data collected visually or sometimes aurally. As understanding shifted in twentieth-century science, the ability to be objective was called into question; the Heisenberg uncertainty principle describes the inherent limits of measuring with photons.

Other possible models for research practice have emerged, especially from the human sciences. One model is "first-person" science, suggested by Eugene Gendlin, which allows first-person accountings of experience as data in research. This possibility posits new scientific language based on process rather than standard measurement.[12] First-person science opens the way for sciences to be based on the other senses, such as the kinesthetic. Already technology is driving such growth; data can potentially be delivered faster than we can take it in solely visually through the current computer monitor interface.[13] Kinesthetic sensory specialists—dancers and others—may find themselves atop the scientific wave of the future. The research is already being done.

Contact Improvisation's presentation of the traditional laws of mechanics is immediate and intimate. There is no being "outside" these laws in CI; the dancer experiences them firsthand, with no interpreter. Like Alice in

Wonderland down the rabbit hole, here there is no introduction; the dancer finds him- or herself right inside the centrifuge of the ongoing experiment.

In Sgorbati's work, there is a sense of separate disciplines dialoguing and informing, observing and gleaning. The findings of one field inform the discourse of another and suggest further avenues of investigation, mutually supportive, hand in hand.

Monson's work combines elements of these two approaches. She places the human being in the natural world—while pointing out that "human" is also of the natural world. The dancer observes and studies the plants, birds, whales, and insects navigating their worlds and, in so doing, finds his or her own unique abilities and coping strategies. There is both immersion and translation at work in Monson's renegotiation of the boundaries between the human and natural worlds.

Forti's approach is pure research—an investigation of what it means to research in a particular medium. Her work doesn't have to do with science in and of itself but speaks to science in that she points so clearly to the phenomenon of research and humanity's predilection to quest for knowledge through experience. The translation of research into a culturally unusual medium such as dance informs through example.

Forti seems to take remarkable advantage of the "law," if you will, of synchronicity in her improvising. In performance, she seemed able to count on it, and it came through for her. Though she is unassuming, her mastery and easy confidence were awe-inspiring. I wrote in my journal during her Logomotion workshop: "There seems to be something I am understanding around the nature of chance—that chance isn't random but something to be tapped into." After the workshop, I revealed my big discovery to Forti: "Chance isn't random! It seems to be some kind of information or to have some order to it." "Well," she replied, "it's bigger." The true researcher—not speculating, just telling it like she finds it!

PRACTICES FOR FURTHER RESEARCH

1. "Starting by defining a point of origin and a destination point, traverse an open space in a straight line. At each destination, choose another point and continue traversing the space several times. After you have moved through six to eight points come to a stop, close your eyes and remember in your mind's eye your journey. Once you have a clear memory of it, retrace your steps back to your point of origin. If you are working with other people, it is useful here to discuss what was

difficult about the task. How did the experience of memory change your perception of the points you chose? Was it easy or difficult to remember? Do you remember more by the points or the passage of the journey? Next, try the same thing, but this time make curved pathways through the space. Again after six to eight points, stop, close your eyes retrace your journey in your mind's eye and then physically. How was this experience different from the one with straight lines? Again, discuss this with your comrades. You can also experiment with changing speed. If you are running, is it easier to remember? In the arcs, do you remember the pathway more than the point? What is your relationship to the other bodies moving? (This exercise could be done indoors, but it's especially nice done outside.)"—Jennifer Monson, a Navigation Score

2. Take a "blind walk" (close your eyes) with a group of people—down a corridor, across a field in the rain, pick your spot—and then do a ten-minute free-write focused on the experience. Share your writings with each other. How do experiences overlap and how do they differ? Pick a contrasting environment and repeat.

3. Moving with a group of people (this is especially fun with a large group), maintain equal distance from your adjacent partners at all times. Try this with chemists! Ask them how it simulates molecular behavior. (Nancy Topf referred to this as the "Equidistant Score.")

4. Start standing back to back with a partner, mutually sharing your weight through a point of contact. Now cross the space together, allowing the point of contact to roll between you. Check in with your partner afterward, each of you describing where your attention was drawn or something that you noticed. Next time, close your eyes. Check in again. Did your experience and attention shift? If so how?

⤐ INTERLUDE ⤖

Notes to Myself on Not Knowing

As an improviser, I'm building something, but I don't know exactly what. I'm only knowing it as I build it. There is a phase of not knowing, and that can feel extremely disconcerting because generally in our lives we know what we're about or at least have plans. We may be fooling ourselves, but we operate as if we do know what we're doing. So in improvisation, when I throw myself into a possibility of being somewhere and not knowing what I am doing there, I can feel very lost. Developing a tolerance for being lost, or, another way to say it, a tolerance for ambiguity, is a useful skill in improvisation.

Then, the recognition phase can be very exciting: "My God, I had no idea where I was, and look where I am!" Suddenly it happens that I recognize where I am because I have been lost long enough to make some sense of my surroundings. My surroundings give me information about where I am, and either I recognize it because it is familiar, or I just recognize that I AM somewhere, even if I haven't been there before. And that is exciting.

Then I arrive somewhere, and it can be, "Oh no, not here again!" But that is more about snapping to a judgment about a place—anticipating it without entering into it and living in it. What does it have to tell me today? With some improvising skill I can sometimes negotiate and shift my destination within an ensemble. "Not that diagonal again!" There's a recognition and then a response to realize it or divert.

There is also this thing that can happen where I am improvising and I am lost, that is, not knowing where I am at or what I am doing. But again, suddenly I find that I have been lost long enough that I can dance that "lostness." My lostness brings me into a dance state in the Simone Forti sense, which, after all, is what we were looking for to begin with. Found.

9

The Magical Object

My experience of working with objects with the senses brings me more to the preverbal state of children. It is a magical state because it precedes naming.

—LISA NELSON, in Jeroen Peeters, "Dialogue with Lisa Nelson on Communication with Objects"

WE TAKE OBJECTS FOR GRANTED—a banana is a banana and a shoe, a shoe. But is that all there is to it? Molly Shanahan, a Chicago-based dancemaker, writes: "I think about how objects appear in my life and in my home and how they transform over time: that rock from the 2002 trip to Lake Huron, which I remember less in accuracy and more in the sense of how my body feels/felt in the instance of noticing . . . the footfall . . . the bending to gather . . . the decision to gather some objects and not others . . . the sense of not needing. That for me is documentation. The object is an arrow that points to past and memory."[1] At the same time, this history of interaction informs, colors, and instructs our future interactions with the object and things like it, till those actions are mostly habitual—accompanying sensations mere corroborators rather than collaborating investigators.

How do we unlock that archive of primary sensation held in the objects that we hold or touch, that our eyes fall on and spill over? How do we unlock these sensations—and with them the movement implied in the initial discovery of each object? For objects are vast libraries of movement memories—objects are directors, choreographers! The following improvisers make dances in interaction with objects, touching on an object's intimate connections with sensation, movement, language, and memory. There is more to an object than meets the eye. . . .

TAKING INSTRUCTION FROM OBJECTS: LISA NELSON

An object—take a banana. This is not just a detail in the field of vision but a rollercoaster of information to take in through the eyes. A quick slide down the peel, pause for a quirky detail, a change in light attracts attention with a hop. The eyes are on the move; even when they are still they shimmy back and forth. According to some neuroscientists, biologists, psychologists, and philosophers who study consciousness, our seamless field of vision—which appears to be like a movie on a screen that we can zoom into for detail—is an illusion constructed by the brain in coordination with the eyes.

Lisa Nelson had stopped dancing and had taken up videography when she began reading psychologist J. J. Gibson's groundbreaking *The Senses Considered as Perceptual Systems* (1966). Gibson, a psychologist interested in perception, proposed that the senses worked together in interwoven ecologies rather than as à la carte individuals used on an as-needed basis—which was the prevailing view. For Gibson, movement and the senses are intertwined and to study them separately was to misunderstand the very nature of perception. Vision, for example, is not a series of static snapshots developed on the retina and processed by the brain but a stream or array of visual information gathered through movement in response to feedback from all the senses. Nelson found Gibson's views on perception to be similar to her own thinking and experience from her work in movement and video.

Gibson classifies a detached object as having a closed surface, distinguished by the way its edges occlude what lies behind it when the observing eye, head, or body moves. This information communicates the shape of the object, and indeed its objectness to the viewer. The other senses work simultaneously—collecting streams of information through movement over time while they feed back information in response to prompts from the object itself for further sensory investigation.[2] Memory comes into play; present and past associations may stimulate further investigation and confirmation. Or not. We might dismiss the object as "banana" and move on. But just beneath the surface of that label, whether Chiquita or Dole, lie seas of sensation, waiting for their depths to be plumbed.

Nelson foregrounds this underlying dialogue of the senses in her performance works in which objects are featured, such as *Ball Room* (a physio-ball), *An Abondanza in the Air* (TV-sized video monitors), and *GO* (a table, chairs, and other objects big and small such as a bowl or stick, chosen before each performance). *GO*, developed in collaboration with Scott Smith in 2002, starts with a "conversation" through the movement of situating and resituating objects on a table using the Tuning Score verbal calls to tweak the play. The table appears to be a miniature stage or a poker table. A player might be attracted to use an object as a tool in an ordinary way, but, more likely, the shape, feel, look, or sound of the object is the motivator for action. Whatever aspect of the object the player tunes into is offered as a communication to the other through a discrete movement interaction with the object in the space. The partner doesn't necessarily read the action as intended but responds as the situation appears to him or her and makes tuning calls to affect the movement of the player or the object, the sound, or the visual image.[3]

The circumstances create a context for the play, and the play builds. The scope of action may shift as the table and the movement of the players become objects in the play. In an interview by Jeroen Peeters, Nelson says, "Taking instructions from the objects and listening to them is really what I've been busy with, which includes the objects of the space—the architecture. In a way, I don't think I improvise, I follow the instructions of the space. There are no such things as impulses. There are reactions, but no impulses that just come out of nowhere: what we think of as impulses often concerns reaction to the local environment, to the signals that exist but that we're not so attentive to, although they are very powerfully moving us."[4]

In a performance at the Flynn Theater in Burlington, Vermont, in 2007, the audience's first glimpse of GO is dramatic—just a table and two pairs of hands are lit and appear to float in the blackness of the theater space. A hand places an object, an odd-shaped stick, on the table. The owners of the hands utter one-word comments—"end," "pause," "reverse"—and the stick responds. A nose or a cheek slips into the light, revealing something of one of the people behind the hands. What is going on? Some kind of barter? Attention is high as we search for clues about this exchange. As the play continues, other objects are introduced, more of the bodies of the players are revealed, more light is added, and our floating table lands firmly in the stage space. But only briefly, for the table soon becomes fair game in the conversation, scraped back and forth across the floor, lifted, or tilted, affected by the whimsy of the short directives delivered by the players.

These calls seem related to the actions—exactly how, we ponder. How the players' actions inform us about the calls becomes our Rosetta Stone. The correspondences are unpredictable; they shift and build off of one another. The personality of each player is revealed through his or her responses—one player examines the sound of the scraping table, the other plays with the perspective of the stage space. As we come to know their tastes through their actions, characters develop and a drama unfolds: there is humor, there is tenderness. At one point, after following the logic of the calls, the players find themselves in an embrace, which seems romantic at first but lasts a bit too long, becoming comic, then poignant, as it evolves into a clutzy waltz, conjuring a variety of relationship metaphors. Have we just seen a play? Or was it our imagination that filled in the cracks of random coincidences? We continue to ponder.

RE-REIFY: MARY OVERLIE

When Mary Overlie teaches, she jumps from theory to a performed demonstration of a principle back to theory so fast it may even make a dancer dizzy, but then, shifting viewpoints is her game. She uses her Six Viewpoints as tools to deconstruct and reframe the theatrical experience for the audience. On her website Overlie says, "Applying the concepts of 'reification,' 'redefining meaning', and 'making language' automatically brings the presence of the audience into focus. . . . This conceptual frame is a meditation on how art works and depends on the degree to which an audience can follow—reify, un-reify and re-reify."[5]

That's the theory; here is her quick demonstration of it: in her Invisible Dances workshop, Overlie holds out her arm and says, "Watch, how long does it take to become art?" She's borrowed this example from John Cage, one of her influences. Overlie has a practice with objects that works on the reify, un-reify, and re-reify principle (and that catches some of her quixotic personality). She places two objects on the table, then turns away to give them time to "talk" or "arc." When she turns back, she arranges the objects according to this dialogue, whether imagined, projected, or real.

The play with objects accesses the intuition perhaps, bringing out relationships we weren't aware of initially. Just as her arm turned to sculpture before our eyes in the demonstration, now cup and camera—random objects on a table—become camera on top of cup, no longer quite the same objects, no longer random. There is new information about cup and camera to be read from this arrangement, not simply a spatial rearrangement, but also one suggesting a narrative or movement (Did someone take a self-timed picture?) or an unusual shape (rectangle on cone) or intimating a sequence of events (Where is the photographer now?), colored by personality or emotion (the Styrofoam cup strains under the weight of the bulky old 35mm camera). Here are the Six Viewpoints at play in their many combinations and permutations, informing the sculpture. Watch as Overlie turns this play with objects into an interactive philosophy lecture on the nature of things.

ANIMATE DANCING: SIMONE FORTI

Early in her life, Simone Forti had been interested in painting. Married to visual artist Robert Morris in her twenties, she experimented a bit with abstract expressionism. But her focus shifted to movement and dance when she discovered Anna Halprin, who was just beginning to explore the teaching of dance improvisation in San Francisco in the late 1950s. Forti became a student of Halprin's during these early investigations, studying with her for four years.

Later in a development of Logomotion she called "animate dancing," Forti found a way to connect her visual interests and movement practice through the physicality of drawing. An object is "known" in a kinesthetic way when it is transferred from eye to hand through pencil to paper. There is a physicality in the rhythm of the lines drawn, for example, whether long lines or short squiggles, and a correlation to the object drawn. Forti makes quick sketches of an object to create a link between what is seen and a felt experience of

Simone Forti in *Animation* at A Cappella Motion workshop in Northampton, Massachusetts, 1995. Photo © Bill Arnold

the object. This experience of drawing opens up other physical memories of interaction with the object as well—picking it up, using or handling it—and even associations that might come through language. She then uses this physical research to embody the object in question through movement. Forti explains, "For us, the drawing of the objects was a bridge, and as we came to be intimate with the drawing, it worked as an analogy. If we could draw what we saw, we could 'body move' what we saw, with all the kinetic stimulation that can come from the developing page now coming from our movement in itself and in its relationship to its source: a torn box, a balcony of repeating arches, a corner where steam pipes disappear into the wall."[6]

In her solo improvisations, she often works with what she calls an arbitrary object, something she finds on the day of the performance—a washtub, a gong stand, a full ten-gallon Arrowhead water bottle. This practice came out of a cycle of improvised dances called *News Animations* (see chapter 1), where the newspapers become world maps, shelters, a forest floor, or heaps of trash—temporary sculptural objects referencing their written content.

Drawing Dances: Dana Reitz

Dana Reitz often draws the dance she is in the process of choreographing. Influenced by the study of calligraphy, she has developed a process of catching the character and nuance of a dance or dance phrase with charcoal or ink on paper. She finds that drawing a dance reveals hidden potentials of its movements and brings them to life; a drawing might suggest options for what is needed next in a dance's development—options that weren't otherwise apparent.

Reitz also uses the method with her students to teach observational skills as well as to develop their dances. Students make drawings of their own dances (just after they run them) and one another's dances (while watching them). In "Drawings and Dances" for *Contact Quarterly*, Reitz says, "The collection of drawings from a class clearly indicates the various perspectives and attentions of those watching. Both performers and viewers begin to notice potential for emphasizing, shading, or fine-tuning, and, consequently, the enormous range of possibilities that includes boldness and subtlety, clarity and finesse."[7] Translating an event that takes place over time (the dance) into a two-dimensional object (the drawing) creates a new point for comparison and discussion.

WIGGLE ROOM: WILLIAM FORSYTHE

Traditional ballet has a set vocabulary. Glissades are glissades and arabesques, arabesques. From Russian to French, they may vary slightly stylistically but are still recognizable across styles—like an apple is an apple whether it is a Red Delicious or Granny Smith. Ballet vocabulary is made up of clearly defined individual movement components. They have a solidity, like objects; they don't change. The steps of ballet arranged in sequences and permutations speak by telling stories or through abstractions. These atoms of ballet delight us, and at the same time they give us our bearings, making a dance recognizable as ballet.

William Forsythe plays with the idea of the solidity of ballet vocabulary. He thinks of movements as prescriptions or algorithms. What was a "solid object"—a glissade—to him is a formula to be tweaked, a little bit—or a little more. A glissade or arabesque warped, perhaps beyond recognition. When does it stop being ballet? Opinions may vary! Some see the play on words, the old steps in the new, or the reference to an older grammar; some see the new dance. Others miss the days when a rose was a rose was a rose.

Regarding a fluidity of the steps and positions of ballet, Forsythe says:

People think of prescriptions as a sort of linguistic form that has no space in it. A bit like a pen: I can't do anything with this pen on the table here—it is solid and it is fixed. But it's language, a linguistic prescription. Language is malleable and suggests change already. Because I like to think algorithmically, I like to think of these prescriptions as little language machines that produce these things called arabesques and tendus and pirouettes. . . . Why not look at it as a research project and ask, "What happens if the prescription is altered by one word, two words, and we replace this with that, what emerges?" Basically, it is curiosity.[8]

BYTES: POOH KAYE

Pooh Kaye is a choreographer trained as a visual artist who makes live stop-animation dance films as well as dances. In some cases, when making a dance Kaye will choreograph small fragments that have a singular quality of movement, like a sudden poke of an arm, a pop off the ground, a twist, or an arch backward. Then in performance, she improvises with these choreographed bytes of movement, assembling and reassembling them in different combinations, changing facings and timings, too. The affect is like holding a gemstone up to the light and studying its facets to understand its composition, strengths, and flaws. The surprise of a movement may not show up until—click—just the right combination of bytes fall into place and one of them pops out like a jack-in-the-box.

Kaye also makes dances with objects in interactive installations for the stage, for example, bricks in *Home Life of a Wild Girl* (1979), sticks in *The River Sticks* (1983), and trashcans in *Swept Up* (1985). In her animated films, objects come to life in jerky movements of their own alongside live stop-animated human dance partners. Fancy a dance with your mattress upon waking (*Wake Up Call*, 1987–89)? A ride down a city street on a wooden beam (*Sticks on the Move*, 1983)? Tumbleweed dancers blow through a warehouse, attracting junk like magnets (*Inside the House of Floating Papers*, 1984). Bodies become objects, and objects come to life in the magical mix.

OBJECTS IN SPACE: NANCY TOPF

Nancy Topf suggested that students treat their bodies like toys when working with the images she offered them in her Anatomical Release Technique classes. The body and its mechanics are puzzles with their own logic and particular solutions like a Rubik's Cube. To grasp the mechanics of a particular area, dancers studied its structure both visually and tactilely through anatomical images and investigated it through sensation produced in movement. This "body toy" comes with built-in instructions in the form of sensory feedback. Play in the form of movement improvisation is important in discovering how to read those instructions.

In a structure Topf called Space Walk usually performed outside, dancers place their bodies as "objects in space" along a predetermined path. The directions for the Space Walk: "See the space. Imagine yourself in it. Go there directly. Be present. Watch and wait. Follow the next persistent impulse. Progress along the path from point A to point B."[9] Dancers might respond to the environment and the bodies in it from a design perspective, either spatially or sculpturally—a body shape between two rocks. Or they might respond from a more emotional perspective, either narratively or relationally—joining a lone figure in a meadow. With some grounding in Topf's anatomical release work, choices mirrored anatomical images—"that split in the tree trunk reminds me of the feeling of opening my chest and sternum."

Pooh Kaye in her dance *Unexplainable Efforts*, performed in the historic Federal Treasury Building, New York City, 1982. Photo © Lona Foote

The image in nature would suggest a movement in the body that had a simi-lar feeling sense. Through comparison, echo, and metaphor, Space Walk created a bridge between the felt interior world of anatomical forms and the exterior world of shapes. Topf, in suggesting this unique correlation of inner and outer, engaged the composing mind.

Not Only for Yourself: Min Tanaka

As an improviser, always dancing from your own concerns can be limiting; always presenting "yourself" in a performance situation narrows your options. Being somebody or something else, a character, lets you explore movement outside of your own movement. Min Tanaka suggests that dancers "bring a prepared body" for performance. In an interview with Petra Vermeersch, Tanaka says, "At least once a dancer should try to put his body there as an object, not only for himself."[10]

Following is an early practice exploring the body as an object as Tanaka describes in the newsletter regarding his Body Weather training, called "end-less paper Drive On":

Last year I danced in water streams three times in Sapporo, Toyama, and Matsumoto, and I tentatively call it "stream dance." It is very interesting as well as difficult: it is better if the stream is running fast. You lie down in a shallow part of the river and just wait for the body to start flowing like an object. Try to see what is around you with your eyes open. You hear the sounds from within water and sounds above ground at the same time. Various hydraulic patterns are formed around the body. As you gradually abandon conscious control of the body, you will begin to feel no resistance to the stream in the wrists, elbows, ankles, knees and other parts of the body. It is most difficult to be free of resist-ance in the head part, but if you try for a long time, even that is possible. It does not work if you get totally immersed in it and get desperate, but if you can look at your body and your surroundings and grasp their real feelings, your body will start flowing. That is, make your body alert to things around you, rather than concentrating on your ego. You might feel frustration between the feeling of the water and that of the body. Suppose you get stuck by a rock, and not being able to do anything, you just wait and see. The body will turn around the rock and start flowing again like water.[11]

⊰ FIELD NOTES ⊱

The Space Walk (or its indoor cousin, Objects in Space): I think it was everyone's favorite structure of Nancy Topf. We did it every year at our weeklong retreat at Windhover in Rockport, Massachusetts. Directed toward the surrounding environment, it was a respite from the deep, internally directed work of Topf's approach. But more than teaching us about composition in the space around us, Space Walk opened us to an experience of permeability with Nature, a "we are one" state—lying on a rock for twenty minutes, feeling the light and surf shift around the body, then moving to another vantage point, again, again. Simple, magical, profound. My body is an object among objects; indeed it is made up of the objects of its anatomy, which I can feel. The Space Walk became a Buddhist treatise on detachment.

Never having studied with Tanaka himself, I am nonetheless thrilled when I read his exercises and comments on movement. He is from such a vastly different culture than I, yet his words remind me of something I have experienced in watching certain ballet dancers, Ulanova or Fonteyn, for instance. That transcultural synergy feels like a truth to me. Tanaka says, "Let your body be there as an object not only for yourself"—there was a way that a good dramatic ballerina could remove her personality from her execution of the role and allow the vocabulary to speak on its own through her body, through those particular steps. Forsythe speaks of ballet as a syntax: "The most important thing is how you speak with the language, not what you say."[12]

That objects might be communicating with us and that we could enter that world and receive information from them through drawing and dancing was the portal to an artistic world I longed to climb through. Spending time with Mary Overlie—disappearing on the subway platform with her or "waiting for something to happen" in a café with her—and observing the imaginative ways she shifted and expanded her proscenium to include all of what went on around her was an instructive delight. Her occasional tip-offs as to how she was viewing the scene were helpful, if not necessary, for me to catch that ride.

PRACTICES FOR FURTHER RESEARCH

1. Next time you are at a party with a friend, each of you choose an object that might get picked up and moved around and about. Place them in conspicuous spots, but don't tell anyone else what you are up to. See whose object travels the farthest by an appointed time.

2. Try this exercise from Susan Rethorst, based on a game she learned from Simone Forti (to be published in *A Choreographic Mind* by Susan Rethorst):

The Game consists of moving five objects between two people one at a time by turns. The playing space is defined by the space between the two persons sitting on the studio floor, and should remain more or less constant. The objects are ordinary things that might be found in a handbag or student's backpack, none much larger than a watch or pair of scissors, but different as to shape, color, texture and function. The first step is to gather more objects than are needed into a pile from which each couple chooses five to take to a playing spot. The game has no goal or ending, only the ongoing placing and replacing of these objects one by one in relation to one another. Attempts to make it something other than this are beside the point. I sometimes say, "If it bores you, be bored."

3. Select two objects. Make an arrangement with them for each of Mary Overlie's Six Viewpoints: space, shape, time, story, emotion, and movement.

4. Pick an object and research it for a half hour. Research could include moving with it, finding out how it moves or might be moved, and also what stories or memories it evokes for you. Then, based on your research, improvise a three- to five-minute duet for you and your object. If you do this with a group, perform your duets for each other. This exercise is from Keith Hennessy, Performing Improvisation/ Improvising Performance workshop (Earthdance, Plainfield, Massachusetts; Fall 2006).

⊁ INTERLUDE ⊰

The Objects Begin to Speak

Walking along the road with my dog, Nellie, I asked myself about objects— I wanted to teach myself about them. Lisa Nelson says that objects communicate to us, we take instruction from them. I understand that in a sense, but I don't feel it yet. What can I learn about objects right here, right now? I am on the road, and I follow the path. The path defines where I walk—the path instructs me where to walk. I got that much!

I look at things on the path to work with. A thorny bramble. No, too prickly. A log, what would I do with it? It has a crack with dirt in it. I could touch it, but I don't feel like bending over to pick it up. Then Nellie is panting and I want her to drink from the stream ahead. We go down the bank, but it is too shallow right there. I see a deeper pool clogged with branches. I call to her and start clearing the area, throwing the branches onto the bank. I catch myself reaching for another branch—OH! Aha. I had just rejected similar interactions with a bramble and logs. But now. . . . I wanted something. I needed to clear the pool. I picked up the branches and threw them.

Objects are talking to us all the time, telling us how to use them. Sit like this on me; pick me up with two hands; don't touch me, or I'll stick you. It is so automatic that we forget that they are speaking to us with their shapes. We read them, their shapes and their uses, infer what an interaction will be like, then try it out and adjust accordingly.

It was this weird moment—mid-reach, when I caught myself engaged in activity with a branch—that it became clear to me. Things in my environment were calling. I kept missing them when I tried to arbitrarily create an interaction. I had to catch myself midstream, out of the corner of my eye.

Epilogue

Developing Your Practice

But isn't it the height of self-contradiction to give exact steps for how not to follow instructions? Indeed. One often needs several attitudes at once.

—EUGENE GENDLIN, *Focusing*

T HIS IS A BOOK OF ARTISTS' PRACTICES—to be more precise, a snapshot in time of any given artist's development of his or her work.[1] These practices didn't spring out of the blue—the work that went into informing them, sometimes years of it, remains unspoken of here except for a few biographical details and some context. While these methods, structures, and scores imply a certain permanence on the page, their practice requires living breathing bodies to inhabit them, and thus adaptation, refinement of ideas, growth, and change.

How do you develop your own practice? An obvious thing to do: Make time in your schedule to work in the studio. Studying with artists who have developed practices can be inspiring and informative, but in the end, it comes down to asking questions from your own particular vantage point, living with them and in them physically, learning how you question and answer through the body. Find a space and the time to work, and obtain anything else that might facilitate your research: music, dancers, a studio notebook, and any other peripherals that might be useful to you.

The amount of time you need in the studio will be an individual decision, of course, and vary upon circumstance. One way to discover your own predilection for working is to try out what has worked for others. If something doesn't work for you, use it to point you in a direction that might. Deborah Hay advises "practicing performance" daily for an hour. (See "Performance Practices: Deborah Hay" in chapter 2.) If you are involved in regular study—with an artist of special interest to you, in a program at an institute or conservatory, or a dance major at a university—Nancy Topf suggests spending a few hours alone in the studio each week to integrate and digest the material.

There is room for variations on the theme. Some artists love spending long hours alone in the studio. Others find working by themselves to be excruciating and need to have people around—whether to work with them or simply be together simultaneously in the space while working.

Susan Sgorbati offers a solo practice schedule that I find helpful as a starting place: fifteen minutes to prepare the space (arrive, set up, sweep); fifteen minutes to warm up, attending to your body; fifteen minutes to focus on work, which could include developing your personal vocabulary and giving attention to the material of the day; fifteen minutes to write. Keeping ambitions low—for example, aim to find just a few moments from the practice that interest you—helps maintain a nonjudgmental attitude toward practicing, if that's an issue.

Eventually you may begin to get a sense of your work cycle—how long it takes you to process ideas physically and produce work.[2] A work cycle could be an arc of weeks, a few months, or several years. And, of course, there are arcs within arcs—an overarching idea is worked out, returns, and reinvents itself over many work cycles. An arc could be months, years, a lifetime, or even lifetimes, if you are working within the lineage of a dance form. In the current culture, the work cycle may be driven by the college semester or the producer's schedule; being aware of the nature of your work cycle may prove helpful in navigating imposed deadlines.

The Architects—an improvisational dance group made up of Katherine Ferrier, Lisa Gonzales, Jennifer Kayle, and Pamela Vail—are graduates of Middlebury College who studied Performance Improvisation with Penny Campbell. They have developed their own way of making improvised dance for performance based on their studies, which they offer in a workshop: Movement Intensive in Compositional Improvisation (MICI). Musician Michael Chorney joins them as a fifth Architect.

The group suggests four rules for dance improvisation, which they discovered in a book by anthropologist Angeles Arrien in which she describes four principles arising from shamanic cultures:

1. Show up.
2. Pay attention.
3. Tell the truth.
4. Don't get attached to the results.[3]

Though otherwise unconnected to Arrien's work, the Architects have adapted these rules for use in dance improvisation. They inform their students that the rules aren't simply "general procedures" to be used in order for any given session, but are nonlinear—to be applied at any moment while improvising. As such, they support the multilevel awareness necessary for negotiating dance improvisation. In developing your own practice, consider how these four rules might support you.

The Architects in *YOU-ARE-IN-MY-EYES* at Movement Intensive in Compositional Improvisation (MICI) at Franklin & Marshall College, Lancaster, Pennsylvania, 2007. In this piece they explored a compositional form they called a "charge," in which some aspect of the material (movement and text) gained momentum, range, or volume in space and/or time. *From left*: Pamela Vail, Katherine Ferrier, Lisa Gonzales, Jennifer Kayle. Photo © Stephen Aubuchon

⤜ A FINAL FIELD NOTE ⤛

My ballet teacher Peter Saul was fond of saying that ballet training was in its essence about learning to stand up—both literally and figuratively. I believe improvisational dance study is in its essence about learning to be. Barbara Dilley modeled this clearly for me one spring in a Fearless Dancing workshop she led at the Shambhala Center in New York City. I found Dilley down-to-earth—no superstar airs. Fearless?

Some of the students in the workshop were meditators and valued silence during our improvisations. A few of the students were dancer improvisers who worked with a sounding and movement practice. Uh oh. The situation came to a head after a few days of working together on Dilley's scores. There was a heated discussion, and everyone put in their two cents; if there wasn't a clear preference for silence or the need to sound, we offered solutions that had worked in the past to handle similar situations.

Dilley listened to both sides—and didn't decide anything! She suggested that we were all adults, and shall we continue? That was what the practice was for: the dynamics of the group to work themselves out. All our desires and needs, our aesthetics and methodologies rubbing up against one another—all our differences—became so poignantly apparent in the improvisation through our reacting to one another, in proving ourselves. That the dynamics of the group would "work themselves out" meant literally that: "come to the surface" not "be solved." In clarifying the elements of the group, the improvisation created its alchemy. Reoriented then, assuming some fearlessness—but maybe not always comfortable—we danced toward being.

A FINAL PRACTICE FOR FURTHER RESEARCH

You have come to the end of the book. Flip through its pages, find a practice that interests you, GO . . . and keep going!

Meet the Artists

Dancemakers' Biographies

Twenty-six dancemakers and their approaches to making work are covered in this book. This section gives some background information on each, including the context in which I encountered their work. Unless stated otherwise, the artists have reviewed my writing on their artistic process for this book. In some cases, with permission, I have reprinted portions from their biographies used for press releases and from program notes, to catch the precise wordings of their approaches. This material will appear in quotation marks, without endnotes. Bold names and terms have entries in this section or in the glossary.

You might use this section either to familiarize yourself with each artist before venturing into the main text of the book or as a home base for a more detailed investigation of a particular artist. Below each artist's name you will find the chapter and page references for the artist's work.

RICHARD BULL (1931–98)

chapter 1, page 22; chapter 2, page 43; chapter 4, page 76; chapter 6, page 109

In his **Choreographic Improvisation technique**, performers improvise with choreography-based compositional principles to create a dance in real time. Bull was known to borrow compositional devices from other disciplines as well, especially literature. Trained as a jazz musician, he was interested in the dialogue of form that arises through improvisation. He began making work in New York City contemporaneously with but independently of the **Judson** choreographers and later collaborated extensively with his wife, Cynthia Novack, dancer, anthropologist, and author of *Sharing the*

Dance: Contact Improvisation and American Culture, and Peentz Dubble, now a certified Iyengar yoga teacher and teacher trainer.

Their company, formed in 1978 and directed by Bull, was called the Improvisational Dance Ensemble, later renamed the Richard Bull Dance Theater. While teaching at New York University in the 1960s, Bull made dance works for his New York Chamber Group in New York City. He later chaired the dance department at SUNY Brockport and headed the graduate studies program in movement at Wesleyan University, in Middletown, Connecticut. He created the Warren Street Performance Loft in New York City, which served as a venue for improvised dance, theater, and music performances from 1978 through 1998. Bull died in 1998, a few years after Novack did, each of cancer. De Facto Dance (New York City), founded by Kelly Donovan, Meg Fry, and Aggie Postman, continues the work.

I first happened upon Bull's work in a rehearsal. The choreographer, Pedro Alejandro, introduced some of Bull's improvisation methods while he was developing material for the piece. The work was exacting; I had never thought so hard or fast on my feet in an improvisation before. In 2002, while attending a performance of a friend's work at a benefit for Improvised and Otherwise in Brooklyn, I saw De Facto Dance perform their new work *Beginnings*, inspired by Bull's *Making and Doing* (1970). Then, serendipitously, a former Richard Bull Dance Theater company member, George Russell, was assigned to be my teacher-training mentor at massage school. He invited me to join a summer course on Bull's methodology, which included archival video research from the dance collection of Wesleyan University, where Bull had taught. I never met Bull or Novack, but spoke with Peentz Dubble in preparation for this book.

Penny Campbell (1948–)

chapter 1, page 16; chapter 2, page 49; chapter 6, page 108

Campbell's **Performance Improvisation** is a practicum in improvisational dance for both dancers and musicians with the goal of performance. The direction of study arises from the interests of the group and includes tried-and-true practices Campbell has developed. Inspired by her study of **Compositional Improvisation** with **Judith Dunn** and Bill Dixon (musician) at Bennington College, in Bennington, Vermont, Campbell works closely with musicians, and includes the spoken word as well. Campbell's collaborators have included Peter Schmitz (as 2 P's in a Pod); and Schmitz plus **Susan Sgorbati**, Terry Creach, and visual artist Sue Rees (as the Giants of Sciants) with musicians Arthur Brooks and his ensemble of improvising musicians, and multi-instrumentalist Michael Chorney.

Campbell has been a member of the dance faculty at Middlebury College, Middlebury, Vermont, since 1985. In 1996, with other members of the Giants of Sciants, she cofounded Work in the Performance of Improvisation (WIPI), which continued for ten years at Bennington College. WIPI has since transformed into MICI (Movement Intensive in Compositional Improvisation), led by former students, the Architects (Katherine Ferrier, Lisa Gonzales, Jennifer Kayle, and Pamela Vail) with musician Michael Chorney, who also make improvised performance works. Campbell's current interests include Afro-Caribbean dance and Dominican Carnival traditions, contemporary Cuban art dance, and cultural studies through movement.

>∤ ∤∢

My first encounter with Campbell was at a symposium on science and art collaboration at Bennington College, where I was a graduate student. Campbell spoke eloquently about the practice of adopting metaphors from science as artistic research tools. After graduating, I participated in a summer session of WIPI, and in 2005 I saw a performance Campbell gave at the Western Massachusetts Moving Arts Festival at Earthdance, in Plainfield, Massachusetts, where I attended a workshop with her a year later. More recently, Campbell articulated the benefits of improvisational dance practice on a panel, "Dance in the University Setting," at Bennington College's Seventy-fifth Reunion.

Barbara Dilley (1938–)

chapter 1, page 14; chapter 2, page 55; chapter 3, page 69; chapter 4, page 77; chapter 5, page 92; chapter 7, page 118

Dilley's work in improvisational dance is imbued with her practice of **Shambhala Buddhism** and contemplative arts training. She developed **Contemplative Dance Practice**, a score that explores **open space improvisation**— an invitation for spontaneous dancing. She also developed a collection of improvisational dance structures, which serve the dual purpose of mindfulness or awareness practices and tools for improvised dance training.

Once a dancer with the **Merce Cunningham** Company (1963–68), Dilley was influenced by **Judson** choreographer Yvonne Rainer, whose piece *Continuous Project Altered Daily* (1970) transformed into a well-known dance theater improvisation collective, the **Grand Union** (1970–76), of which Dilley was a member. She directed the Natural History of the American Dancer: Lesser Known Species (1971–74), in which she developed scores for performance, such as the grid. She cofounded the downtown dance presenter DanceSpace at St. Mark's Church in New York City in 1974. She designed the Dance/Movement Studies Program at Naropa University in Boulder, Colorado, at its beginning in 1974, at **Chögyam Trungpa Rinpoche**'s invitation, and served as the university's president (1985–93). She cofounded the performance group the Mariposa Collective (1994–99) with Diane Butler, Carol McDowell, and Polly Motley. She continues to teach improvisation and meditation at Naropa University, where she directs the dance.art.lab in the summers.

My first contact with Dilley was through the mail: a compelling packet of reading materials including a biographical newspaper article and her booklet on Contemplative Dance, sent in response to my query in 2003, when I was commissioned to write this book. A year later, I set out to study with Dilley and collaborator Steve Clorfeine when she came east to teach a workshop at Sky Lake Lodge, a Shambhala Buddhist retreat center in Rosendale, New York. Later that year I took a trip to Boulder to interview her and watch videos of her early works, such as *Sets* (1975), performed at DanceSpace.

My first editorial project at *Contact Quarterly*, the dance and improvisation journal, was transcribing and editing an interview by Nancy Stark Smith with Dilley on her improvisation structures. In 2005 I attended a workshop with Dilley at the Shambhala Center in New York City, and two years later, traveled to Boulder to discuss this book and watched her in rehearsal with MFAs in Naropa University's Contemporary Performance Program. I've also seen videos of some of Dilley's performances with the Grand Union.

Katie Duck (1951–)

chapter 1, page 18; chapter 3, page 60; chapter 4, page 87; chapter 6, page 112; chapter 7, page 120

Influenced by the **Cage-Cunningham** aesthetic, Duck is interested in what she refers to as the "aesthetics of chance." Her current company, **Magpie**

Music Dance, a collaborative of dancers and musicians, is the working model of and research base for her improvisational dance principles. The company performs improvised dance, often with live improvised music, and sometimes incorporates text.

Duck, originally from Oxnard, California, studied modern dance at the University of Utah and toured with the Salt Lake Mime Troupe, leaving the United States in 1976 to live and dance in Europe. Deeply affected by the experimental music scene there, in 1979 she formed the dance company GROUPO in Italy, for which she made choreographed dances. In 1995 she founded Magpie Music Dance in Amsterdam to address her interest in purely improvised dancing. Since 2006 Magpie has expanded from a dance company into an umbrella organization that supports improvised experimental dance and music projects. She taught at and headed the choreography program of Dartington College of the Arts in the United Kingdom and currently teaches in Amsterdam at the School for New Dance Development and for the Magpie Umbrella Program, comprising summer workshops and an apprentice program. Besides participating as a performer and composer touring and collaborating internationally, she has initiated numerous dance and music improvisation projects in her three bases: Holland, Italy, and England. Websites: katieduck.com and magpiemusicdance.com.

→¦ ¦←

Initially I ran across two online interviews with Duck, one conducted by Tangente, a dance producer in Montreal, and the other in *Proximity*, an Australian dance magazine. I became fascinated with the prospect of decoding Duck's writings on improvisational dance. She had developed a terminology emphasizing such concepts as On, "exit and dance," Biology, and the aesthetics of chance. My curiosity grew when I overheard some attendees of her workshop at the Improvisation Festival in New York City heatedly discussing her performative approach to improvisation and her provocative teaching style. It wasn't until December 2004 that I finally experienced the action behind the language; I attended a workshop she gave at the University of California, San Diego, and her performance at Sushi downtown later that evening.

Judith Dunn (1933–83)

chapter 6, page 107

Dunn called her work **Compositional Improvisation** and sometimes improvisation/composition. She believed improvising was composing and performing simultaneously while taking into consideration structure, order, space, time, materials, and tone. Dunn danced in **Merce Cunningham**'s company from 1958 through 1963. She assisted **Robert Ellis Dunn** (her husband at the time) and influenced the composition classes he presented at the Cunningham Studio from 1960 through 1962. She was a participant in the **Judson Dance Theater** as well. In 1965 Dunn met Bill Dixon, an African American musician (trumpet, piano) and composer influential in the experimental music scene, and they began to collaborate on performance works as well as coteaching composition and improvisation to musicians and dancers at Bennington College, Bennington, Vermont. Later Dunn combined Compositional Improvisation with improvised text in collaboration with her second husband, linguist-activist Peter Lackowski, in work with The Dance Company (**Penny Campbell**, Barbara Ensley, Cheryl Lilienstein, Erika Bro, and Robert Kovich). Sadly, she died at fifty of brain cancer.

I never met Dunn, but as a graduate student in dance at Bennington College I learned of her through her legacy (and Dixon's) there—stories told by my teachers who studied and danced with her and continue her work and the thriving collaborations between experimental musicians and dancers that are core to the Bennington dance experience. Penny Campbell, **Susan Sgorbati**, and **Lisa Nelson** shared their memories of Dunn's work with me.

Eiko (1952–) and Koma (1948–)

chapter 2, page 39

An important aspect of Eiko and Koma's **Delicious Movement** approach to improvising movement is that it be enjoyable, delicious, to the individual mover. They use imagery and layers of imagery as sources for generating their movement, generally characterized by a slow, mesmerizing quality. While they improvise movement in performance, Eiko and Koma work with set narrative structures.

They met in 1971 in Tokyo in Tatsumi Hijikata's company but soon developed an exclusive partnership. They also studied with **Butoh** cofounder **Kazuo Ohno**. However, they never studied traditional Japanese dance or theater forms. Their interest in Neue Tanz, the German modern dance movement, and their desire to explore nonverbal theater took them in 1972 to Hanover, Germany, where they studied with Manja Chmiel, a disciple of Mary Wigman, the noted pioneer of expressionism in dance. They came to the United States in 1976 at the suggestion of Lucas Hoving of the José Limón Dance Company and gave their first performance, sponsored by the Japan Society, in New York City. They have since become permanent U.S. residents.

They have presented their works at theaters, universities, museums, galleries, and festivals across North America, Europe, and Japan. They also work in dance video and have presented their work on the television series *Alive from Off Center* (1989) and at the Dance on Camera Festival at Lincoln Center (2001). Recently Eiko and Koma have worked with students and graduates of the Reyum Art School in Phnom Penh, Cambodia, and continue the collaboration. Website: www.eikoandkoma.org.

I first saw Eiko and Koma perform at Cornell University when I was an undergraduate studying physics. I had never seen or *felt* anything quite like their dance before. It's hard to explain: Like driving around a bend in the road, it was as if they could open up a new vista through a simple action, invoking a physical sensation of revelation. I was surprised that dance theater could have such effect on me in the audience, and I resolved to uncover this invisible action-at-a-distance. I have attended several of their performances since: *Grain* (1983), *Night Tide* (1984), *Rust* (1989), *Snow* (1999), *The Caravan Project* (1999), and *Be With* (2001) with **Anna Halprin**. I took a Delicious Movement workshop at Earthdance, in Plainfield, Massachusetts, and attended talks Eiko gave at Wesleyan University, in Middletown, Connecticut, where she was a Center for Creative Research artist-in-residence.

WILLIAM FORSYTHE (1959–)

chapter 1, page 28; chapter 3, page 68; chapter 4, page 86; chapter 9, page 149

William Forsythe is a ballet choreographer who creates his unique vocabulary partly through improvisational means and sometimes uses improvised movement in his ballets (for example, *Limb's Theorem*, 1990; *Eidos:Telos*, 1995). He calls this approach **Improvisation Technologies**, as described on his CD-ROM *Improvisation Technologies: A Tool for the Analytical Dance Eye*, which is used as a training tool to familiarize dancers new to his work. An American working overseas, especially in Germany, Forsythe is known for "reorienting the practice of ballet from its identification with classical repertoire into a dynamic twenty-first-century art form." He was the director of the Frankfurt Ballet for twenty years and now directs an independent ensemble, the Forsythe Company, also based in Germany. His works are featured in the repertory of major ballet companies throughout the world—the Kirov, the Royal Ballet Covent Garden, the Paris Opera Ballet, and the New York City Ballet. Website: www.theforsythecompany.de.

⁂

As a ballet dancer with New York Theater Ballet, New York City, I wasn't exposed to improvisation as a formal training. I was quite curious to find out how a ballet choreographer might approach the topic. Besides viewing an interview of Forsythe with Celia Ipiotis from the television series *Eye on Dance*, I watched several of his ballets, including *Eidos:Telos*, one of his many works that include improvised material, and early video footage of some of his Improvisation Technologies at the New York Public Library for the Performing Arts, Lincoln Center, New York City. I also viewed his CD-ROM *Improvisation Technologies: A Tool for the Analytical Dance Eye*. In April 2005 I attended former Ballet Frankfurt principal Helen Pickett's Forsythe Improvisation Technologies workshop at the Boston Cyberarts Festival: Ideas in Motion—Innovations in Dance, Movement and Technology. I interviewed Pickett about her experience working with Forsythe, from her early career with the San Francisco Ballet Company to her time at Ballet Frankfurt.

SIMONE FORTI (1935–)

chapter 1, page 13; chapter 8, page 138; chapter 9, page 147

Forti's **Logomotion** explores the ties between movement and language. Forti studied with **Anna Halprin** in the late 1950s and in the early 1960s attended **Robert Ellis Dunn**'s composition classes and was part of the **Judson Dance Theater**, becoming known for her minimalist dance constructions. Her later works included an in-depth series of animal movement studies, news animations, and "animate dancing," which led to the development of Logomotion.

Based in Los Angeles, California, Forti performs and teaches worldwide, often at the University of California, Los Angeles. Her published books include *Handbook in Motion* (1974), "an ongoing personal discourse and its manifestation in dance"; *Oh Tongue*, a collection of experimental writings (2003); and *Unbuttoned Sleeves* (2006), writings by Forti, Terrence Luke Johnson, Sarah Swenson, and Douglas Wadle, generated from work on two performance projects.

⇥ ⇤

I studied Forti's work in dance history and composition; I read her *Handbook in Motion* and her many articles; and I saw video clips of her works, for instance, her *News Animations* as part of an *Eye on Dance* interview with Celia Ipiotis. In summer 2004 I met her at her home in Vermont, improvising with her and others while a film crew shot a documentary on Canadian composer-violinist Malcolm Goldstein, a collaborator of Forti's. I took a Logomotion workshop with Forti at Earthdance, in Plainfield, Massachusetts, and she treated us to a retrospective video screening of her *News Animations* as well as performed with us in an evening concert.

ANNA HALPRIN (1920–)

chapter 2, page 35

Halprin, currently dancing, teaching, and creating at ninety, is a venerable elder of contemporary Western improvisational dance. After college, Halprin danced professionally for a few years in New York City, before moving to San Francisco to raise a family. She continued to teach dance there, including children's classes. In the mid-1950s she stopped teaching stylized dance technique altogether and began to explore the teaching and performing of dance improvisation in both urban and natural settings. She was an early proponent of improvisation as performance in contemporary Western theatrical dance. Task and the researching of the kinesthetics of movement were among her early favorite exploratory themes.

Another common thread throughout her work has been using dance and theater as a means for bringing disparate elements of a community together. Besides her own innovative work in the field for over fifty years, she has informed the working processes of many other improvisers and dancemakers of note (for example, **Simone Forti**, Yvonne Rainer, and **Nancy Topf**) who have studied with her in the San Francisco Dancers Workshop, or on her dance deck or in her studio at the Tamalpa Institute in Marin County, California. Through her struggles with recurring cancer in the 1970s, she turned her attention to the healing aspects of dance and has created personal, community, and global rituals to that purpose based on her **Five Stages of Healing** process.

Halprin is the author of *Movement Ritual, Moving toward Life: Five Decades of Transformational Dance,* and *Dance as a Healing Art/Returning to Health* and has numerous dance works documented on film. Her husband, Lawrence Halprin (1916–2009), an architect, was a long-term collaborator and supporter. She cofounded the Tamalpa Institute in 1978 with her daughter Daria Halprin-Khalighi. The institute offers training programs developed around Halprin's work. Longer retreats on the Halprin work are held at Sea Ranch (Sonoma County) on the Northern California coast during the summers. Websites: www.annahalprin.org and www.tamalpa.org.

I saw the legendary Anna Halprin perform at the Joyce Theater in an eightieth birthday celebration concert, which included her solo dancing in *Memories from My Closet* and a trio created with **Eiko and Koma**, *Be With* (2001). I've seen archival footage of her early works and the video documentary *Returning Home* by Andy Abrahams Wilson, of Halprin's work in natural settings in collaboration with visual artist Eeo Stubblefield.

Deborah Hay (1941–)

chapter 2, page 38

Hay's long and experimental dance career has culminated in a set of **performance practices** that engage the performer on several levels of consciousness at once. Currently she works in collaboration with highly trained dancers, passing on her nuanced solo works by means of detailed choreographic scores, including these practices, to create both solo and group works. Hay danced briefly with the **Merce Cunningham** Company (1964) and was a member of the **Judson Dance Theater**, going on to create an extensive body of choreographic work that runs the gamut from dances for the untrained (*Circle Dances,* 1970s) to experimental tour de forces for dancers such as Mikhail Baryshnikov (*Single Duet,* 2000). She has authored three books about her work: *Moving through the Universe in Bare Feet* (1975), *Lamb at the Altar: The Story of a Dance* (1994), and *My Body, the Buddhist* (2000).

Hay, who is influenced by Ram Dass, the cross-cultural spiritual teacher and author of *Be Here Now*, is based in Austin, Texas. Website: www.deborah hay.com.

I have been delightfully disoriented and repositioned by Hay's writings in her many books and articles on her dance works and artistic process. I have seen her work on video, including a solo she performed at Wesleyan University after the publication of her book *My Body, the Buddhist*. I coedited an article by Hana van der Kolk for *Contact Quarterly* regarding a performance cycle of Hay's solo commissioning project, *The Ridge*. Subsequently, I saw *The Ridge* and *The News*, another solo commissioning project, in performance by van der Kolk and Layard Thompson in Plainfield and Northampton, Massachusetts, in 2007.

KEITH HENNESSY (1959–)

chapter 2, page 45

Hennessy's interdisciplinary performative research "engages improvisation, spectacle, ritual, and public action as tools for investigating political realities." The Canadian-born, San Francisco-based Hennessy directs the contemporary circus CIRCO ZERO "in intimate spectacles for stage and street." Previously he has performed in collaborative companies: Contraband (1985–94), CORE (1995–98), and Cahin-caha, cirque bâtard (1998–2002) based in France. Hennessy cofounded 848 Community Space/CounterPULSE, a performance space in San Francisco. Hennessy has taught at improvisation festivals in Budapest, Seattle, Stolzenhagen (Germany), Moab (Utah), Vienna, Boulder (Colorado), and at the University of California, Davis, and the University of San Francisco. Website: www.circozero.org.

I first encountered Hennessy's dance-circus-theater in an improvised solo performance he gave at Earthdance, in Plainfield, Massachusetts, in 2005. To make a point about live performance, he collected his snot into a gooey mass and later exited the performance space out of a transom window. I courageously took his workshop the next year and have since seen him perform at CI36, **Contact Improvisation**'s thirty-sixth birthday celebration festival, in *Laugh Scream* at Juniata College in Huntingdon, Pennsylvania, in June 2008.

In February 2009 I saw Hennessy perform in an improvised duet with Ishmael Houston-Jones at Earthdance.

Pooh Kaye (1951–)

chapter 9, page 149

Kaye's dances, influenced by her work in animation, often include small bytes of choreographed movement, whose sequencing is then improvised in performance. For her company Eccentric Motions (1980s), Kaye created installation environments in which the dancers interact. Kaye, dance improviser and choreographer, an animator and filmmaker, also makes special-effect films that use a variety of animation techniques in conjunction with pixilated human movement. The films explore the interaction of the human body with the extraordinary environments only possible with the camera. Her films have been seen on PBS, HBO, and Showtime. Kaye, a visual artist by training, studied and danced with **Simone Forti** and created a documentary film, titled *Four Women in a Tree*, on the mentor-protégé relationship in dance, including Forti as well as **Anna Halprin** (Forti's mentor), and **Jennifer Monson** (who was in Kaye's company.)

→| |←

While still a ballet dancer, I unsuccessfully auditioned for Kaye's company Eccentric Motions in the late 1980s. She gave me some honest feedback—she was looking for more natural movement. It was the first prick in my awareness that there was another realm of movement study available. Later, I was lucky to attend graduate school at Bennington College, in Bennington, Vermont, while Kaye was a research fellow there. She showed her animated films and her documentary, *Four Women in a Tree*, and shared her dancing as part of class assignments and her articulate view on others' dance projects, including mine. Later we developed an improvised duet, which we performed in Woodstock, New York, and at Bennington College.

Daniel Lepkoff (1950–)

introduction, page 5; chapter 4's interlude, page 89

Lepkoff considers "all of our movement as a finely tuned physical dialogue with our environment and explores the form and composition of this interaction." He sees physical improvisation as "a way of composing dance works, a performance practice, and a body of research and knowledge about how to move and live in the world." He played an instrumental role in the development of **release technique** with Mary Fulkerson and **Contact Improvisation** with **Steve Paxton**. Through his travels teaching and performing in the 1970s and 1980s, he helped spread the work worldwide. A cofounder of Movement Research in New York City, Lepkoff has taught and performed his work at dance centers, studios, and schools around the world. His collaborators include Paul Langland, **Lisa Nelson**, Steve Paxton, Oleg Soulimenko, Attila Dora, and Sakura Shimada. He has published articles on his work in dance publications such as *Contact Quarterly*, Movement Research's *Performance Journal*, and with Contredanse (Brussels). Website: www.daniellepkoff.com.

⇥‹ ›⇤

Familiar with Lepkoff's dancing through early videos of Contact Improvisation, Channel Z, and his work with Lisa Nelson, I first saw him perform live at IDEA in Northampton, Massachusetts, in his work ~~PERMANENT RESIDENT STATUS~~ (2006). Subsequently, I studied with him at Earthdance, saw him perform *Land Mass* at the SEEDS Festival, in summer 2008, and the next winter *Divided By Zero* in collaboration with Sakura Shimada, at the Blue Guitar Gallery in Easthampton, Massachusetts. As an editor, I have worked on various writing projects of Lepkoff's for *Contact Quarterly*, always marveling and learning immensely from his exacting articulation of movement ideas.

NINA MARTIN (1953–)

chapter 1, page 20; chapter 2, page 48; chapter 3, page 62; chapter 4, page 82; chapter 5, page 95; chapter 7, page 126

Nina Martin has created a unique group of training practices she calls **Articulating the Solo Body** and **Ensemble Thinking**, which are intended to equip the improvising dancer with the tools of the trade. Articulating the Solo Body concentrates on individual movement choice, and Ensemble Thinking concerns composing with a group of improvisers. Articulating the Solo Body features a somatic approach for repatterning movement that Martin calls ReWire/Dancing States.

Martin developed her training structures out of the improvisation classes she taught at New York University's Experimental Theater Wing, among other places; through her work with Channel Z, 1982–90, a performance improvisation ensemble that used **Contact Improvisation** as a common movement vocabulary (with collaborators **Daniel Lepkoff**, Dianne Madden, Steve Petronio, Randy Warshaw, Robin Feld, and Paul Langland); with Locktime Performance, 1992 (Jennifer Keller, Johanna Meyer, and Alexandra Hartmann); and her work as a founding member of Lower Left, 1995 (with Jane Blount, Karen Schaffman, and Mary Reich, and including Margaret Paek, Andrew Wass, and Kelly Dalrymple), a performance collective originally based in San Diego, California. She continues as part of the collective, which has been instrumental in the development of Ensemble Thinking, from her home base in Marfa, Texas. Also a performer and choreographer, Martin danced, for example, with David Gordon's Pick Up Company and in Martha Clarke's Miracolo D'More, and directed her company Nina Martin/Performance from 1979 to 1994. Her work has been produced internationally. Website: www.lowerleft.org.

I first saw Martin perform with David Gordon's Pick Up Company at Cornell University in the early 1980s. At the post-performance discussion, I naively asked Gordon, a **Judson Dance Theater** choreographer and member of the **Grand Union**, if he thought it important that art have meaning. Gordon, a paragon of postmodernism, passionately pointed out that meaning-making is the audience's responsibility, not the artists'. (I also remember him implying that I was a ninny for suggesting otherwise. Martin and her company-mates kindly consoled me after my first brush with true artistic temperament.)

I saw Martin's work with Channel Z and her own company in video clips, as well as an interview she did with **Simone Forti** and Sally Silvers on improvisation for Celia Ipiotis's *Eye on Dance* television series. I took an Ensemble Thinking workshop with Martin at the Festival of Interactive Physics in Toronto, Canada, in May 2006, when, with **Nancy Stark Smith**, I interviewed her for an article for *Contact Quarterly*. I studied Ensemble Thinking with Martin's Lower Left collaborators at the Trisha Brown Studios in New York City, and again with Martin in a workshop at Earthdance, where she also performed. I saw her perform again with the Lower Left at CI36, Contact Improvisation's thirty-sixth birthday celebration, at Juniata College in Huntingdon, Pennsylvania, in June 2008.

Jennifer Monson (1961–)

chapter 8, page 132

"Monson has created an original approach in experimental dance that combines elements of environmental studies, fieldwork, and improvised dance research and performance." This approach is exemplified in her project BIRD BRAIN (2000–2006), in which Monson and her dancers gave more than thirty free performances following four migratory routes: Gray Whales (Spring 2001) from Mexico to Canada, Ospreys (Fall 2002) from Maine through Cuba to Venezuela, Ducks and Geese (Spring 2004) from the Gulf of Mexico to Canada, and Northern Wheatears (Fall 2007) from the Arctic through Europe to West Africa. The theater piece component of the project, *Flight of Mind* (2005) was performed across the United States.

A graduate of Sarah Lawrence College, Monson has collaborated with musicians and dancers such as composer Zeena Parkins, and dancemakers DD Dorvillier, Yvonne Meier, and David Zambrano. Currently, Monson is a professor of dance at the University of Illinois, Urbana-Champaign, "where she continues her collaborations in environmental studies and encouragement of social discourse on environmental issues." The interdisciplinary Laboratory for Art, Nature, and Dance (iLAND), another brain child of Monson's, "is committed to fostering and supporting creative interactions between movement artists, scientists, and environmentalists as a means of engaging the public's imagination in a kinetic understanding of the urban environment" through residency programs and performance projects. Websites: www.birdbraindance.org and www.ilandart.org.

⋊ ⋉

I studied with Monson and saw her perform at Earthdance's Western Massachusetts Moving Arts Festival in 2006 and SEEDS Festival in 2008 and 2009. I also coedited an interview with Monson by Margit Galanter for publication in *Contact Quarterly*. Besides being committed to pushing the edge of the art form as an artist-educator, Monson is a thrilling performer, able to invoke a sense of the wild even in the artificial confines of theater space.

LISA NELSON (1949–)

chapter 2, page 52; chapter 3, page 70; chapter 5, page 94; chapter 7, page 121; chapter 9, page 143

From her work with video and dance, Nelson has developed an approach to spontaneous composition and performance she calls **Tuning Scores**, which employs calls made by viewing and moving participants based on both choreographic organization and the functions of video shooting, playback, and editing.

Nelson studied dance and composition both at The Juilliard School in New York City as a teen and while attending Bennington College, in Bennington, Vermont. She became a videographer, teaching videodance at Bennington in the 1970s, when the field was just developing. Her long-term collaborators include **Steve Paxton**, **Daniel Lepkoff**, video-artist Cathy Weis, Scott Smith, and Image Lab (K.J. Holmes, Karen Nelson, Ray Chung, Scott Smith, and others). For thirty years, she coedited (with **Nancy Stark Smith**) *Contact Quarterly*, the dance and improvisation journal. She continues to codirect *Contact Quarterly* and Contact Editions, a producer and distributor of nonperiodical new dance literature. Nelson directs Videoda, which produces, archives, and distributes videotapes of improvisational dance. Currently, she travels the world teaching and performing, mainly in Europe.

For graduate work, aiming to make dances based on my experiential anatomy studies, I chose Bennington College. I was quite surprised when the faculty admitted they didn't find much merit in sensation-based work for performance—because of its inner-directedness. Nelson arrived to teach for a month in spring 2001. Her unique emphasis on the action of sensing, the sensual aspect of sensory experience, redirected my inward focus and happily proposed a solution to my dance-making conundrum. That summer I saw Nelson perform her solo *Memo to Dodo* at the International Festival of Arts and Ideas in New Haven, Connecticut. To continue study, I organized a workshop with her at Bennington for winter 2002 interterm.

In subsequent years, I participated in a Tuning workgroup in Seattle and in a laboratory, The Sense of Perception, with Nelson and Bonnie Bainbridge Cohen at Earthdance, Plainfield, Massachusetts; saw her performance of *GO*, in collaboration with Scott Smith at the Flynn Center in Burlington, Vermont; and watched several videos of her works: from her personal collection;

from the New York Public Library for the Performing Arts, Lincoln Center collection; and from the Wesleyan University Library dance collection. In 2005 I coedited my first issue of *Contact Quarterly* with her.

KAZUO OHNO (1906–2010)

chapter 5, page 100; chapter 6, page 114

Ohno, with Tatsumi Hijikata, cofounded **Butoh**, an avant-garde dance form of Japan. Ohno collaborated with Hijikata from 1959 through the mid-1960s in performances that would come to be known as Ankoku Butoh (dance of utter darkness). After a ten-year hiatus from performing, he returned to the stage at the age of seventy-one in his seminal solo work *Admiring La Argentina* (1977), which eventually brought him international acclaim. He was also known for his workshops composed mainly of improvised movement, which he offered from the 1960s until a few years before the end of his life in 2010. Ohno, based in Yokohama, Japan, cowrote a book (now available in English), *Kazuo Ohno's World*, with his son, Yoshito Ohno, also a prominent figure in Butoh. Website: www.kazuoohnodancestudio.com.

⁂

I saw Kazuo and Yoshito Ohno perform *The Dead Sea* (1985) at the Joyce Theater in New York City. I've also seen Kazuo Ohno's work on video, including Michael Blackwood's *Butoh: Body on the Edge of Crisis*, and I have heard accounts about his workshops from fellow dancers who have attended them: Melinda Ring (in Los Angeles) and Hiroko Ishimura (in Japan). The "Workshop Words" section in *Kazuo Ohno's World* gives a fabulous taste of the artist's teachings. John Solt, scholar of Japanese avant-garde culture, reviewed my writing on Ohno for this book.

MARY OVERLIE (1946–)

chapter 1, page 25; chapter 2, page 51; chapter 3, page 62; chapter 4, page 85; chapter 5, page 102; chapter 5's interlude, page 105; chapter 9, page 146

Mary Overlie's **Six Viewpoints** (space, time, shape, emotion, movement, and story) are compositional lenses through which to consider dance or theater. Rather than defining them for students from the perspective of the prevailing aesthetic, Overlie lets the Viewpoints define themselves through specific practices she has developed that give experiential knowledge of each.

The Viewpoints form the base of her method, which has influenced American theater, for instance, through the works of directors Anne Bogart (SITI Company) and Joanne Akalitis.

Originally a dancer and dancemaker, Overlie was a founding member of the Experimental Theater Wing at New York University, as well as of Movement Research (New York City) and St. Mark's Church (a dance presenter and theater showing experimental work). She performs, choreographs, teaches, collaborates in theater, writes, and is a theorist. Her company (1976–80) included Paul Langland, **Nina Martin**, and Wendell Beavers, with whom she continues to collaborate. Website: www.sixviewpoints.com.

⇥ ⇤

I saw Overlie perform an open improvisation at the Shady Corners American Maverick Performing Arts Festival, Milford, New York, in 2005, where she also gave a post-performance question-and-answer session. Later, I attended her Invisible Dances workshop at Movement Research's Open Source Festival. I viewed videos of her early works at the New York Public Library for the Performing Arts, Lincoln Center, and interviewed her in Brooklyn. From my time spent with Overlie, I get the sense that she is always considering the performance angle in any given situation, even, for example, while hopping on the subway.

STEVE PAXTON (1939–)

chapter 2, page 41; chapter 3, page 66; chapter 4, page 79; chapter 7, page 127; chapter 8, page 137

In 1972, during a residency with the **Grand Union** at Oberlin College, Steve Paxton began developing what would become **Contact Improvisation**, now a dance form practiced around the world. The investigation at its root: two bodies sharing weight through a moving point of physical contact. Paxton's most recent body of work, developed over more than twenty years, is Material for the Spine, a training that explores in detail how the body organizes itself for movement around the spine.

A gymnast and dancer from Arizona, Paxton danced for the **Merce Cunningham** Company from 1961 until 1964. He was a member of the **Judson Dance Theater** from 1962 to 1964 and of the Grand Union, a dance theater improvisation collective, from 1970 to 1976. As a choreographer, he weaves back and forth across the lines between dance, performance art, and theater with, for instance, a series of inflatable sculptures incorporating movement, lecture demonstrations, and site-specific works as well as dances made for the concert stage. A few of his works include *Afternoon* (1964), *Physical Things* (1966), *Satisfyin' Lover* (1967), *Magnesium* (1972), *PA RT* (with **Lisa Nelson**, 1979), *Goldberg Variations* (1986), and *Night Stand* (with Lisa Nelson, 2002). Paxton teaches and performs worldwide, annually attending the Breitenbush Contact Jam in Oregon.

⋈

I was introduced to Paxton's and other Judson choreographers' reframing of dance in my undergraduate composition course at Cornell, taught by Peter Saul, who danced in Yvonne Rainer's seminal *Trio A* and had seen many Judson performances firsthand. I particularly remember viewing Paxton's *Intravenous Lecture* (1970) and being simultaneously repelled and intrigued. I have seen Paxton's work on video in early performances of Contact Improvisation, in dances made for the stage such as *PA RT*, *Goldberg Variations*, and *Night Stand*, and his DVD *Steve Paxton: Material for the Spine*, a movement study. I attended a two-week course on Material for the Spine at Earthdance in March 2010.

DANA REITZ (1948–)

chapter 1, page 23; chapter 3, page 65; chapter 4, page 83; chapter 6, page 114; chapter 9, page 148

Reitz refers to her work as the "radical middle," as it falls somewhere in between the worlds of choreography and improvisation. In her dance career, she also found herself between the established and classically inclined "uptown" and experimental "downtown" New York City dance scenes, for example, as a member of Twyla Tharp's company (1970–71)—postmodern choreography with popular appeal, in Robert Wilson's avant-garde opera *Einstein on the Beach* (1976), and later touring her distinctive solo works with Mikhail Baryshnikov (1996).

Her works are mostly performed in silence, revealing the movement's musicality. A visual artist as well, Reitz draws her dances in the process of creating them. Since 1973 Reitz has been making her own work—scores that weave together movement and light. She often creates her own lighting design and has collaborated with lighting artists Beverly Emmons, James Turrell, David Finn, Richard Martin, and, extensively, Jennifer Tipton. Her projects include *Necessary Weather*, a collaborative work with Tipton and dancer Sara Rudner; *Unspoken Territory*, a solo she created for Baryshnikov; and many others. Reitz's works have been commissioned and produced internationally and she tours extensively as a teacher and performer. Reitz has taught at Bennington College, Bennington, Vermont, since 1994.

>¦ ¦<

I studied with Reitz at Bennington College in graduate seminars and in her class Finding Form. Besides seeing some of her work on video, I attended Reitz's showing of a collaborative work-in-progress with Jennifer Tipton and sculptor Michael Singer at Bennington College and have been bewitched by her solo improvisations based on gesture. I coedited an article about her use of drawing in her dance-making process for *Contact Quarterly*.

SUSAN SGORBATI (1949–)

chapter 1, page 17; chapter 2, page 50; chapter 6, page 109; chapter 8, page 134

Inspired by the scientific theory of complex systems that studies emergent phenomenon, Sgorbati calls her training and performance work with an ensemble of dancers and musicians **Emergent Improvisation**. A member of the Dance Faculty at Bennington College, in Bennington, Vermont, since 1983, she collaborates with evolutionary biologist Bruce Weber, a fellow faculty member, as well as others from the scientific community, notably neuroscientist and Nobel laureate Gerald Edelman. She is also a professional mediator for the Vermont Attorney General's Office and the Vermont Human Rights Commission. In 1999 she created Quantum Leap, a program that reconnects at-risk youth to their education.

As an undergraduate at Bennington College, Sgorbati studied with **Judith Dunn**, and later returned for graduate study before joining the faculty. She has had a long-term collaboration (late 1980s–2001) with **Penny Campbell**, Peter Schmitz, and Terry Creach (dance); Arthur Brooks and Michael Chorney (music); and Sue Rees (visual artist), as the Giants of Sciants. In 1995 she cofounded Work in the Performance of Improvisation (WIPI) with the Giants of Sciants, which continued for ten years at Bennington College. Website: emergentimprovisation.org.

>¦ ¦<

Susan Sgorbati was my graduate advisor at Bennington College. I studied and performed with her Improvisation Ensemble for Dancers and Musicians and attended graduate seminars that she led and lectures with scientists that she sponsored. I coedited an article on her Emergent Improvisation Project for *Contact Quarterly* and have seen her solo improvisation and group work in performance. Sgorbati's advice to me has always been practical—and compassionate. When the going gets tough, she enthusiastically points out any progress, no matter how small the scale.

NANCY STARK SMITH (1953–)

chapter 3, page 67; chapter 4, page 80; chapter 6, page 114

Stark Smith, developing collaborator of **Contact Improvisation**, found as a teacher of Contact Improvisation that particular warm-up exercises and movement activities were helpful in bringing dancers to a state of body and mind preparedness for engaging in a Contact duet. Stark Smith's **Underscore** is a scored collection of those exercises and activities, complete with pictographs that represent each phase and subphase in its progression. The Underscore culminates in an open-score phase, which includes improvised dancing and Contact Improvisation. Stark Smith first trained as an athlete and a gymnast, leading her to study and perform modern and postmodern dance in the early 1970s. She was greatly influenced by **Grand Union** and **Judson Dance Theater** performances and graduated from Oberlin College with a degree in dance and writing.

In 1972 she danced in the first performances of Contact Improvisation in New York City and, as a dancer, teacher, performer, organizer, and writer-publisher, has since been central to its development, working extensively with **Steve Paxton** and others. In 1975 she cofounded *Contact Quarterly*, an international dance and improvisation journal, which she continues to coedit and produce, as well as codirecting with **Lisa Nelson** Contact Editions, which produces and distributes nonperiodical new dance literature. Her own writing appears in the books *Taken by Surprise: A Dance Improvisation Reader* (2003) and *Caught Falling: The Confluence of Contact Improvisation, Nancy Stark Smith, and other Moving Ideas* (2008) with David Koteen. Her dancing is featured in the DVD *Fall after Newton* (1987). Stark Smith teaches and performs around the world, often collaborating with composer and musician Mike Vargas. Website: www.nancystarksmith.com.

My first contact with Nancy Stark Smith was through a portion of writing I had contributed to *Contact Quarterly*. She asked me a couple of questions in an e-mail, and before I knew it my piece had been seamlessly edited. Little did I imagine that some years later I would be spending hundreds of hours learning that magic from her first-hand.

I began my study of Contact Improvisation out of desperation. After leaving New York City for the suburbs in 1995, I found there were scant dance opportunities for adults, until I bumped into the proverbial local Contacter—the one who teaches everyone she meets how to do it so that she will have partners to dance with. (In my case, her name was Leslie Cohen-Rubury.) Familiar with Stark Smith through her early Contact dances on video, I became curious about her Underscore and took a workshop with her at Movement Research in New York City in 2002. Later, I attended her intensive three-week January workshop on Contact Improvisation at Earthdance in Plainfield, Massachusetts. Since then, I have attended a few Global Underscores and have seen scores for performance Stark Smith created for her students. I started working as an editor for *Contact Quarterly* in 2005.

Suprapto Suryodarmo (Prapto) (1945–)

chapter 2, page 53; chapter 7, page 127

Prapto, from Java, Indonesia, calls his improvisational movement practice **Joged Amerta**, which stems from his study of free movement, Vipassana and Javanese Sumarah meditation. Prapto sees this approach as more than an improvisation technique, rather as cultivating an attitude toward life. In 1986 he created his own school, Padepokan Lemah Putih, in his uniquely land-scaped garden in Mojosongo, just north of Solo, Central Java. He offers a series of month-long workshops that also include practice in historical and cultural areas of Central, West, and East Java; West Sumatra; Samuan Tiga-Bedulu, South Bali; Tejakula, North Bali; and Sulawesi.

Prapto began performing in the mid-1970s and has taught and performed internationally, creating intercultural art events in Europe, the United Kingdom, Australia, the United States, Mexico, Japan, India, and the Philippines. He initially brought his work to Europe in 1982, establishing many ongoing movement events there. For example, Sharing Time, first held in Köln, Germany, in 1993, takes place every other year in different places throughout the world. Each locale creates its own theme and approach for sharing art and the cultural environment. The event Sharing Movement (1997) arose so mature practitioners could share their development of Joged Amerta within the many different areas of their professional inquiry (e.g., therapeutics, performance, spirituality, psychology). Prapto performed in the United States for the first time at Jacob's Pillow in Becket, Massachusetts, in 1993 and has returned since, for instance, sharing his work at the Naropa University in Boulder, Colorado; the Commonweal Center in Bolinas, California; and Earthdance in Plainfield, Massachusetts. Website: www.lemaputih.com.

> ⃰| |⃰<

Intrigued by an article I read about Prapto by Andrea Morein in *Contact Quarterly*, I sought out one of his students, Margit Galanter, and interviewed her to learn more about him. I watched a video of Prapto teaching at Bennington College, in Bennington, Vermont, as part of the Jacob's Pillow International Improvisation Workshop, and a DVD by Ana Godinho de Matos of Prapto teaching and performing in London in 2006. Also, I read an informative personal account of study with Prapto at his school in Indonesia by Susan Bauer, later published as an excerpt in *A Moving Journal*. In 2008 I attended the SEEDS Festival at Earthdance, cocurated by Galanter, at which Prapto performed, spoke on a panel, and taught a workshop. He gave his all to each interaction—including dancing with each workshop participant daily as well as chanting and playing music for our practices.

Min Tanaka (1945–)
chapter 3, page 63; chapter 5, page 101; chapter 9, page 152

Tanaka founded the **Body Weather** Laboratory in 1978, connecting the idea of the body with the weather and its ever-changing relationships. Tanaka says, "A dancer indeed embodies the 'body weather.' An ideal state of a dancer is that his/her center is blurred and that his/her self is outside of the body." Tanaka has held Body Weather workshops internationally and at Body Weather Farm, on an exquisitely beautiful, remote landscape in Hakushu, Japan, where participants come to work on the farm, live close to the land, and study dance with Tanaka. His trainings combine complex imagery, subtle as well as physically demanding exercises, and farm labor, giving students the opportunity to know the body's limits and spectrum of ability, as well as to develop a flexible attitude toward training and what it might encompass.

A trained dancer and athlete, Tanaka saw Tatsumi Hijikata, cofounder of **Butoh**, perform *Revolt of the Flesh* (1968) and was greatly impressed. (Tanaka later worked with him, from 1982 to 1986.) But instead of imitating him, Tanaka says in an interview in *Theme Magazine,* "Does a true master teach his disciple how to dance like himself? I wanted to learn from Hijikata how I could be as marvelous a being as him in dancing" (2006). Tanaka's interest is in distilling the essence of dance. In the *Theme* magazine interview he asks, "What is the unique element of dance? What distinguishes dance as dance, aside from physical movement and gestures? It is invisible. Dance consists of things invisible as well as visible." He has an extensive career as a solo dance improviser and he has created group works for his companies Maijuku and Tokason. Tanaka tours internationally and currently is involved in a solo improvisation project, *Locus Focus,* performed in the United States at P.S. 1 Contemporary Arts Center in Long Island City, New York, with which he has a longstanding performance association. Website: www.min-tanaka.com.

Because of my interest in **Eiko and Koma**, I became curious about Tanaka. I had seen some of his early work on video and read about it in reviews. Fortunately, one of my fellow graduate students at Bennington College, Melinda Ring, had studied with Tanaka at his Body Weather Farm in Japan. Ring, a choreographer, was actively engaged in investigating what she received through her studies with Tanaka. We practiced some exercises that she had learned at the farm, and she shared something of the sensibility with which Tanaka's work is imbued.

I saw Tanaka's company perform *Los Caprichos* at Bennington College, in Bennington, Vermont, and later saw him perform his solo *Locus Focus* at P.S. 1 in Long Island City, New York. Afterward, there was a post-performance lecture in a gallery with a retrospective photo exhibit by Masato Okada of Tanaka's works. The choreographers in the audience questioned Tanaka about the specifics of his dance-making process through his interpreter-producer Kazue Kobata. The enigmatic Tanaka skirted them deftly. However, a museum security guard who was privy to the entire series of site-specific performances throughout the museum was luckier. Asking several basic and pointed questions, the guard soon had Tanaka talking about aspects of spirituality in his dancing. I also spoke with former Tanaka company members Roxanne Steinberg and Dana Iova-Koga regarding my writings on Tanaka, and I interviewed Kobata.

NANCY TOPF (1942–98)

chapter 1, page 24; chapter 3, page 66; chapter 5, page 97; chapter 6, page 110; chapter 7, page 125; chapter 9, page 150

Topf pioneered **Anatomical Release Technique**, a **movement education** and repatterning work, with collaborators Marsha Paludan, John Rolland, and Mary Fulkerson. The four met in 1968 at the University of Illinois, Urbana-Champaign, as teachers or students of dance and subsequently studied independently with Barbara Clark (1889–1982), their major influence, who in turn had studied with Mabel Todd (1880–1956), movement educator and author of *The Thinking Body*. Topf, Rolland, and Paludan created the Vermont Movement Workshop (circa 1972–85), which became a teaching laboratory for their ideas. Over a period of thirty years, Topf developed her own approach to Anatomical Release Technique, which she called **Topf Technique** and **Dynamic Anatomy**. These approaches could be experienced in a private hands-on bodywork session or a movement class that incorporates the hands-on work. These programs are certified by ISMETA (International Somatics and Movement Education Therapy Association).

Topf studied Dalcroze Eurythmics as a child, at the Martha Graham School as a teen, and with Margaret H'Doubler in the dance program at the University of Wisconsin. Upon graduating she moved to New York City and trained with José Limón and at the **Merce Cunningham** School and danced professionally with Viola Farber and Katherine Litz. Topf was drawn to the technical aspects of dance training and was teaching Cunningham technique at the University of Illinois, where she met her collaborators in Anatomical Release Technique. Besides teaching her own work in the United States at such schools as the Laban-Bartenieff Institute of Movement Studies and Movement Research in New York City, she taught at Dartington College of the Arts in the United Kingdom, the School for New Dance Development in Amsterdam, Instituto Nacional de Bellas Artes in Mexico, and at dance studios in Geneva and in Stockholm. She also choreographed and performed, sometimes with her husband, Jon Gibson, a composer and multi-instrumentalist. At the time of her death in 1998, in a Swiss Air airliner crash, Topf had just completed the first draft of an introduction to Topf Technique called "The Anatomy of Center," as yet to be published. Website: www.dynamicanatomy.org

⋊⃰ ⃰⋉

Last on this list but first in my heart is Nancy Topf, who introduced me to the rigors of formal improvisational dance training: when I left the ballet company, I wandered from modern dance studio to modern dance studio looking for the home that I had felt in my body studying ballet. After two years, I was at a loss and developing a persecution complex at the hands of modern dancers who smelled my ballet training from a hundred yards away. Then, in 1991, one of my college dance buddies invited me to come with him to a new class he liked. The first session showed me such a new way of working; I remember telling him, "Either she's completely crazy or she really knows her stuff."

Thus began a two-year period of intensive training with Topf: weekly classes, monthly intensives, private bodywork sessions, a summer workshop, and performances. The classes were rigorous; there was technique—something to dig into, a way to measure yourself and learn. When I moved from New York City, I stayed in touch with Topf as she developed her training certificate program in Topf Technique and began writing her book. Sadly, she died before her time, in a plane crash, leaving her students to carry forward the work she had given us. Since then, I have found that there are many people working in a larger field of dance improvisation. Topf was part of a movement, a time, a way of working with the body that is perhaps always a possibility.

Glossary of People
and Terms

NOTE: Bold names and terms have entries in this glossary or in the Meet the Artists section.

Additional contributors in the improvisation dance-making field. The twenty-six dancemakers included in this book are not an exhaustive list of those working in the field of dance improvisation, though many are major players in and have helped define it. Here is a further (nonexhaustive) list of improvisational dancemakers and performers who have made important contributions to the field by expanding its scope and/or through their definitive performance qualities. Their names are set in small caps.

From the early generation of dancemakers: YVONNE RAINER, also well-known for her experimental filmmaking, is a **Judson** choreographer whose piece *Continuous Project Altered Daily* (1970) transformed into **Grand Union** (1970–76), the well-known improvisational dance theater collaborative. DANIEL NAGRIN's (1917–2008) collaborative Workgroup (1970s) explored emotional and psychological motivation for movement to create social and political commentary. DIANNE MCINTYRE founded the troupe Sounds in Motion (1970s and 1980s), which pushed the limits of improvised dance vocabulary to encompass the rhythms of free jazz through study of existing African American dance forms. PAULINE DE GROOT in Amsterdam established the new methods of experimental choreography and performance improvisation that she had been exposed to in New York City in the 1960s and carried them on, developing the basis for the **New Dance** scene that has since flourished there. JULYEN HAMILTON, now based in Spain, trained in London during the radical experimentation of the 1970s and has been a proponent of performance improvisation since then, working with improvised text, light, and dance.

An independent artist since 1970, SARA SHELTON MANN danced with the **Contact Improvisation**–based Mangrove in San Francisco and started her own company, Contraband, for which she continues to create works often influenced by studies of **Body-Mind Centering**. Since the mid-1970s ANDREW DE L. HARWOOD (Montreal) has been involved in improvisational dance performance, first cofounding the dance troupe Fulcrum, a Contact Improvisation–based performance group, with Peter Bingham (Vancouver, British Columbia) and Helen Clarke (now in Lapin, New South Wales, Australia), and currently his own company AH HA Productions, in his home base of Montreal. PETER BINGHAM cofounded EDAM (Experimental Dance and Music) in Vancouver in 1982, including both choreographed and improvised work. Since the late 1970s EVA KARCZAG has been a dancemaker, dancer, dance improviser, and educator based in Europe and influenced by studies in tai chi, Alexander Technique, and Ideokinesis who danced with Richard Alston (United Kingdom) and Trisha Brown (United States).

ALESSANDRO CERTINI and CHARLOTTE ZERBEY and Company Blu, based in Tuscany, Italy, have been creating, presenting, and experimenting with improvised performance since 1979. YVONNE MEIER, originally from Switzerland and now based in New York City, has been making improvised works since 1979 and has developed a Score Technique inspired from her work in **Authentic Movement** and **Skinner Releasing**. In the early 1980s AL WUNDER started the Theatre of the Ordinary in Melbourne, Australia, which investigates open improvisation—combining movement, words, sounds, and music—and invites the participation of people of all levels of performance experience. KIRSTIE SIMSON, who trained at the Laban Center in London and danced with experimental British choreographer Rosemary Butcher, is a Contact Improviser and performance improviser who, since the 1980s, has had an extensive performing and teaching career throughout Europe and the United States.

K.J. HOLMES, a dancemaker, improviser, singer, and poet based in New York City, has been weaving interdisciplinary collaborative works influenced by studies in Body-Mind Centering and Contact Improvisation since 1981. YOSHIKO CHUMA, experimentalist and choreographer from Japan now based in New York City, is an interdisciplinary master collaborator through her company the School of Hard Knocks, founded in 1984. Since the mid-1980s KAREN NELSON, based in Washington State, has combined dance improvisation, performance, and meditation in work that includes persons of diverse ages and abilities; in 1987 Nelson and cofounder ALITO ALESSI created DanceAbility, a dance company and training that uses dance improvisation to explore and promote artistic expression and relationships between people with and without disability. ISHMAEL HOUSTON-JONES, choreographer, writer, dance performer, and improviser based in New York City, is known for his performance physicality and presence as well as his works that, since the 1980s, have expanded the field's territory, tackling gender, race, and other social and political issues.

STEPHANIE SKURA, now based in Auburn, Washington, and influenced by **Skinner Releasing**, is a choreographer who, beginning in the mid-1980s, has worked with imagery, text, poetry, and improvised movement. MEG STUART, director-choreographer of the Brussels-based dance company Damaged Goods, has developed improvisation projects such as *Crash Landing* (1996) and *Auf Den Tisch!* (2005). SCOTT SMITH is a United Kingdom–based music- and dancemaker who works with mixed ability groups and collaborates with other artists, including **Steve Paxton**, **Lisa Nelson**, and Charlie Morrissey. CHRIS AIKEN, assistant professor of dance at Ursinus College in Collegeville, Pennsylvania, has taught and performed improvisation, Contact Improvisation, and composition studies since the mid-1980s, currently collaborating with artistic and life partner ANGIE HAUSER, a member of Bebe Miller Company.

DAVID ZAMBRANO, from Venezuela and based currently in Amsterdam, since the late 1980s has been a performance improviser, choreographer, dancer, and teacher known for his Flying Low technique. Also in the late 1980s, Middlebury College graduates KATHERINE FERRIER, LISA GONZALES, JENNIFER KAYLE, and PAMELA VAIL formed The Architects, a **Performance Improvisation** group including musician Michael Chorney. CYRUS KHAMBATTA has been performing Contact-inspired choreographed works and improvisation internationally since the 1990s with his company Phffft! Dance Theatre, now Khambatta Dance Company, based in Seattle, Washington. And De Facto Dance—based in New York City and formed in 2000 by KELLY DONOVAN, MEG FRY, AGGIE POSTMAN (members of the **Richard Bull** Dance Theatre), and LEE SHAPLEY—works with Bull's **Choreographic Improvisation technique** in the creation of their works.

Anatomical Release Technique works with images based on human anatomy—particularly the shapes of the bones and the mechanics of their articulations and weight bearing. Some deep support muscles, such as the psoas,
are considered as well. The **movement education** technique developed by
Mary O'Donnell Fulkerson, Marsha Paludan, John Rolland, and **Nancy
Topf** in the late 1960s was greatly influenced by their studies with Barbara
Clark (1889–1982), who worked in the tradition of Mabel Elsworth Todd
(1880–1956). Inspired by their work with Clark, the Anatomical Release
Technique pioneers introduced movement investigation, often based on the
developmental path (the stages through which the baby learns to locomote,
including rolling, creeping, crawling, sitting, standing, and walking) and
incorporated dance improvisation into the **movement repatterning** process. Each of the four colleagues went on to refine individual articulations of
the work, teaching in the United States and abroad. John Rolland (1950–93)
published *Inside Motion: An Ideokinetic Basis for Movement Education* (1984).
Writings by Mary O'Donnell Fulkerson may be found at releasedance.com.

Articulating the Solo Body is one of **Nina Martin**'s training practices (the
other is **Ensemble Thinking**). It concentrates on individual movement
choice and features a somatic approach for **movement repatterning** that
Martin calls ReWire/Dancing States.

Authentic Movement is a therapeutic improvised movement discipline
developed by Mary Starks Whitehouse and further developed and named
by Janet Adler (1970s). The practice includes solo improvised movement
following impulses arising from within, usually with eyes closed and a witnessing partner. People may practice in groups with multiple movers and
witnesses working simultaneously. Authentic Movement is practiced for a
variety of purposes: personal growth, creative process, psychotherapy, or as
a community ritual. (See Mary Ramsay, guest ed., Authentic Movement issue
of *Contact Quarterly*.)

Body-Mind Centering, created by Bonnie Bainbridge Cohen, is an approach
to movement analysis and reeducation that works with touch, movement, and
the body-mind relationship. The study includes "cognitive and experiential
learning of the body systems—skeleton, ligaments, muscles, fascia, fat, skin
organs, endocrine glands, nerves, fluids; breathing and vocalization; the
senses and dynamics of perception; **developmental movement**; and the art

of touch and re-patterning," says Bonnie Bainbridge Cohen in *Sensing, Feeling, and Action: The Experiential Anatomy of Body-Mind Centering.*

Body Weather is the name of **Min Tanaka**'s training, which combines complex imagery, subtle as well as physically demanding exercises, and farm labor, giving students the opportunity to know the body's limits and spectrum of ability, as well as to develop a flexible attitude toward training and what it might encompass. Tanaka has held Body Weather workshops internationally and at Body Weather Farm, an exquisitely beautiful, remote landscape in Hakushu, Japan, where participants come to work on the farm, live close to the land, and study dance with him.

Butoh, a dance form cofounded by Tatsumi Hijikata (1928–86) and collaborator **Kazuo Ohno** (1906–2010), arose in Japan during the period of economic and cultural turmoil after World War II. The first Butoh piece, Hijikata's *Kinjiki* (Forbidden Colors), which was inspired by the book of the same name by Yukio Mishima, premiered in 1959 and dealt with social taboos of homosexuality. Hijikata considered Butoh a new kind of activity, something that was different from dance as it had been previously understood, especially different from the Western dance that had been recently introduced to Japan. "He would find the essence of butoh even in nonhuman creatures including plants," according to **Min Tanaka** (in an interview with Jiae Kim, "Min Tanaka's Butoh").

There are a lot of misconceptions around what Butoh is, what it might look like, and whether particular artists consider themselves Butoh. Butoh is often identified with slow movement, white body paint, and grotesque and distorted imagery, but it needn't be any of these. It has been perhaps most aptly described as "the body on the edge of crisis" (e.g., *Butoh: Body on the Edge of Crisis*, directed by Michael Blackwood). It is up to the individual artists to find their relationships to the form, and to reconsider it with each new expression in performance.

John Cage (1912–92) was an influential U.S. composer and experimental musician of the twentieth century, whose effect was felt in the field of dance as well as through his long-term collaboration with **Merce Cunningham**, the modern dance choreographer. Cage did not care for improvisation as a compositional tool; he found it mostly led to repetition of the familiar. He was interested in indeterminacy, in making something he had never experienced before. He explored this through the disciplined use of chance operations, creating scored events that give players particular degrees of freedom so that he could not foresee the specificities or the relationships that would arise in a composition. He says, "What I would like to find is an improvisation that is not descriptive of the performer, but is descriptive of what happens, and which is characterized by an absence of intention" (*Conversing with Cage*, 222). Though Cage did not recommend improvisation as a compositional method, his methods created a climate of experimentation among dancemakers applying his methods to movement (especially the **Judson Dance Theater** choreographers), some of whom began to work with improvisation.

Choreographic Improvisation is **Richard Bull**'s training technique in which performers improvise with choreography-based compositional principles to create a dance in real time. Traditional compositional elements such as spatial formations (like diagonals or circles, flocks or mirroring), theme and variation (like repetition or retrogrades, canons or fugues), attention to phrasing and quality of movement, and relationship of movement to music are emphasized to develop dancers' basic choreographic tools. Dancers also develop a keen movement memory through the work in order to be able to reference and dialogue with the material as it arises during the improvisation.

Compositional Improvisation, also known as improvisation/composition, is the name **Judith Dunn** gave to her work. Dunn believed improvising was composing and performing simultaneously while taking into consideration structure, order, space, time, materials, and tone.

Contact Improvisation (also known as CI or Contact) is a movement investigation initially developed by **Steve Paxton** and further developed, refined, and expanded upon in collaboration with many dancers over the years, notably **Nancy Stark Smith**, **Daniel Lepkoff**, and Nita Little. The first Contact performances were held at the John Weber Gallery in New York City in 1972. In Contact Improvisation, two moving bodies follow the point of contact between them, creating an improvised dance of weight sharing and bearing. The basic form is a duet, but Contact is adaptable to accommodate larger numbers. The Contact jam is a group of Contact dancers who come together to practice as musicians might. Jams may last a few hours or stretch over a week or two, that is, as a retreat jam like the Breitenbush Jam, held at the Breitenbush Hot Springs in Oregon.

Contemplative Dance Practice (CDP), developed by **Barbara Dilley**, is a score for the exploration of **open space improvisation** that employs the tools of meditation and body-mind awareness practices. Composed of three sections, CDP starts with sitting meditation, moves into a personal warm-up phase, and then allows time for open space improvisation—an invitation for spontaneous dancing. Participants sit around the edge of the space with a meditative attention when they aren't working in it. A short final sitting meditation and time for group discussion end the practice, which is designed to take about three hours but may vary in length.

Merce Cunningham (1919–2009), the iconoclast modern dance choreographer, was a lead male dancer for the Martha Graham Company. He began the Merce Cunningham Dance Company based in New York City in 1953. His collaboration with **John Cage** led to experimentation with unusual compositional methods incorporating chance operations using choreographed material. Championing Cage's methods, Cunningham created a new dance aesthetic, which, for example, considered music and movement unrelated, independent events and was marked by an equally weighted, unbiased use of the stage space as well as lack of conventional dramatic effect, that is, narrative and climax or anti-climax. **Robert Ellis Dunn**'s famous composition class that led to the forming of the **Judson Dance Theater** was held at Cunningham's studio.

Delicious Movement, Eiko and Koma's approach to improvisational movement, encourages the individual to find movement that is enjoyable, "delicious." Eiko and Koma use imagery and layers of imagery as sources for generating movement.

Developmental movement or the **developmental path** are the stages through which a baby passes in learning to locomote including rolling (turning over), creeping, crawling, sitting, standing, and walking.

Robert Ellis Dunn (1928–96), musician and protégé of **John Cage**, taught composition classes to dancemakers at the Cunningham studio in the early 1960s. Dunn's class introduced them to Cage's methods of structuring music through their relevancy to movement. With these students, he formed the **Judson Dance Theater**. In 1972, at the Dance Notation Bureau in New York City, Dunn completed his Laban training, which informed his subsequent teaching of movement observation, choreography, composition, and improvisation to several generations of dancers, dancemakers, and teachers.

Emergent Improvisation is **Susan Sgorbati**'s training and performance work inspired by the scientific theory of complex systems that studies emergent phenomenon. Sgorbati works with an ensemble of dancers and musicians investigating forms that emerge in improvisation and their self-organizing properties. Currently she cites four distinct emergent forms in her practice: the Emergent Solo, the Emergent Duet, Complex Unison, and the Memory Form.

Ensemble Thinking is a collection of training structures designed by **Nina Martin** to help improvisers read what is going on in the dance space during a group improvisation and to make choices based on that reading. The training structures focus dancers' attention on various aspects of form as it relates to the ensemble: spatial arrangement, functional groupings (e.g., solo, duet, trio), the place in the space where the viewers' attention is being drawn at any given moment, and the shifting dynamics of the developing dance. Martin's complementary training for developing a dancer's personal vocabulary is called **Articulating the Solo Body**.

Five Stages of Healing (Identification, Confrontation, Release, Change, and Assimilation) is a process designed by **Anna Halprin** that deals creatively with a variety of difficulties and contemporary issues, including individual health and personal growth, family, community, and the environment. Developed through Halprin's own experience of recovery from recurring cancer, it includes individual expression, community ritual, movement, and other expressive arts.

Free improvisation. See **open improvisation**.

Free Writing is a writing practice sometimes used in conjunction with movement improvisation practices as a support to the creative process. Natalie Goldberg in her book *Writing Down the Bones* (1986) suggests: "1) Pick an amount of time, ten, twenty minutes to an hour, 2) Keep your hand moving, 3) Don't worry about spelling, punctuation, or grammar, 4) Lose control, 5) Don't think, don't get logical, 6) Go for the jugular (Dive into whatever is naked or scary)."

Grand Union (1970–76), an improvisational dance theater collective, formed out of *Continuous Project—Altered Daily* (1970), a piece by Yvonne Rainier, a **Judson Dance Theater** choreographer. In the later years of the Grand Union there was no preplanned material for performance, though ideas might be recycled from one performance to the next. Material was taken from whatever was available—sets, props, costumes, and music were improvised, as well as movement and text. Regular Grand Union members included Becky Arnold, Trisha Brown, **Barbara Dilley**, Dong (Lincoln Scott), Douglas Dunn, David Gordon, Nancy Lewis, Yvonne Rainer, and **Steve Paxton**.

Improvisation Technologies are ballet choreographer **William Forsythe**'s techniques for developing his unique vocabulary through improvisational methods. He sometimes uses improvised movement in his ballets (for example, *Limb's Theorem*, 1990; *Eidos:Telos*, 1995). His CD-ROM *Improvisation Technologies: A Tool for the Analytical Dance Eye*, available to the public, is used as a training tool to familiarize dancers new to his work.

Joged Amerta movement is the name of Indonesian dancer **Prapto**'s (Suprapto Suryodarmo) improvisational dance practice. *Joged* is a quality of spontaneous, childlike play and also refers to this quality in an artist who possesses technical mastery. *Amerta* means "nectar of life." Joged Amerta stems from his study of free movement, Vipassana and Javanese Sumarah meditation, and placing of these practices in the nature, temple, and human field. He sees this approach as more than an improvisation technique, rather as cultivating an attitude toward life.

Judson Dance Theater (1962–68): **John Cage**'s student and protégé **Robert Ellis Dunn** offered composition classes to dancemakers at the **Merce Cunningham** studios in New York City in the early 1960s. Dunn's class introduced them to Cage's methods of structuring music through their relevancy to movement. The students needed a venue to show their new works and with Dunn formed the Judson Dance Theater, named for the church that housed it. This particular period of experimental dance-making and many of the choreographers involved in it—such as Yvonne Rainer, Trisha Brown, David Gordon, **Deborah Hay**, and **Steve Paxton**—have become synonymous with the rise of the **postmodern dance** movement in the United States.

Klein Technique is a **movement education** technique developed by Susan Klein and collaborator Barbara Mahler. The work incorporates anatomical study with experiential movement exercises, which emphasize the sacrum, coccyx, and pelvic floor, whose proper mechanics, once grasped, lead to healthy sequencing of movement and ease of support. Klein technique, or loosely related variations thereof, is often offered as a warm-up in **release technique** classes. Despite its popularity in that venue, Klein does not consider this "release technique." Klein finds her work is applicable to any style of dance—ballet, modern, or **postmodern**, for example—or to athletics and movement studies generally.

Laban Movement Analysis (LMA) comprises the theoretical foundation of Rudolph Laban's (1879–1958) notation system, Labanotation, as well as a collection of movement retraining exercises, Bartenieff Fundamentals, developed by Laban's disciple Imgard Bartenieff. In the early twentieth century, Laban, a Hungarian-born choreographer and movement theorist, developed Labanotation, an abstract symbol system, to notate all types of movement, originally as a means of preservation and documentation of dances. LMA has a myriad of applications: **movement education** for children, evaluation for effective placement of factory workers, helping corporate workers understand the decision-making process, a psychotherapy tool, physical rehabilitation, and dance-making, to name a few. (For further information, see Groff, "Laban Movement Analysis.")

Logomotion, **Simone Forti**'s work, explores the deep ties between movement and language—the kinesthetic imagery we often use in storytelling and its accompanying body language. In Forti's work, this body language is not a grace note added to a story as it is told, rather a preverbal embodiment that helps invoke language.

Magpie Music Dance is **Katie Duck**'s collaborative company of dancers and musicians, a working model of and research base for her improvisational dance principles influenced by the **Cage-Cunningham** aesthetic. The company performs improvised dance, often with live improvised music, and sometimes incorporates spoken word or text.

Movement repatterning or **movement education**: underlying all movements are basic habituated patterns of movement not directly under conscious control. To effect a change in a given movement (for purposes including improved performance, increased efficiency, recovery from injury, aesthetics, as well as enjoyment and well-being), these underlying movements may be repatterned through a variety of approaches. The ones that include movement repatterning are often referred to as "movement education" or sometimes "movement therapies," for example, Alexander Technique, **Anatomical Release Technique**, Bartenieff Fundamentals, **Body-Mind Centering**, Feldenkrais, **Klein Technique**, and **Laban Movement Analysis**.

New Dance is a confusing term with similar issues as "modern dance"; it has come to represent an interest in the experience of the body over aesthetics and stylized dance techniques. Arising in England and on the European continent in the 1970s, New Dance is roughly contemporaneous to and shares influences with **postmodern dance** in the United States. As a method of training, New Dance is eclectic, including experiential, hands-on work and **movement education** such as **Body-Mind Centering** and **release technique**, as well as improvisation. (For more information, see Clarke and Karczag, "What We Use in Our Training and Why"; Bales and Nettl-Fiol, *The Body Eclectic: Evolving Practices in Dance Training*.)

Open improvisation, also **open space improvisation** (**Barbara Dilley**) or free improvisation (**Prapto**), is an improvisation with no predetermined structure, rules, or limitations.

Pedestrian movement refers to everyday movements, such as walking, sitting, standing, or lying down and moving in and out of them and simple movements involved in daily tasks—pushing, pulling, reaching, or picking something up, as opposed to stylized movements of more formal dance techniques.

Performance Improvisation, Penny Campbell's work, is a practicum in improvisational dance for both dancers and musicians, with the goal of performance. The direction of study arises from the interests of the group and includes tried-and-true practices Campbell has developed. Inspired by her study of **Compositional Improvisation** with **Judith Dunn** and Bill Dixon (musician) at Bennington College, in Bennington, Vermont, Campbell works closely with musicians and includes the spoken word as well.

Performance practices are an integral part of **Deborah Hay**'s current choreographed work, which focuses a performer's attention on presence. Examples of performance practices include "What if where I am is what I need?" (1995–96) or "I imagine every cell in my body invites being seen perceiving no movement wrong, out of place, or out of character" (1985). (See Hay, *My Body, the Buddhist.*) Hay's dancers engage in a performance practice to navigate them through a given dance. The meditations are practiced simultaneously with the dancing of the score and affect the dancers' action and commitment to the movement.

Postmodern dance is connected with the rise of the **Judson Dance Theater** in the United States and its associated choreographers (Trisha Brown, Lucinda Childs, **Simone Forti**, **Deborah Hay**, **Steve Paxton**, Yvonne Rainer, and others) and subsequent generations of similar-minded choreographers. Postmodern dancemakers share interests in experimentalism and a questioning of form and convention and are generally concerned with process, structure, meta-narrative, and how meaning versus content, narrative, or message is communicated. The postmodern dancemaker may employ improvisation as a vehicle for questioning the dancer's and viewer's relation to structure. **Release technique** is often used as training tool in postmodern dance classes.

Release technique is an umbrella term for an approach to teaching dance and movement, used most often, but not exclusively, in **postmodern dance** classes. The approach culls from a variety of **movement education** approaches to suggest alternate and more functional pathways of movement in order to release excess effort. A release technique class might start by focusing on particular principles from **Body-Mind Centering**, **Anatomical Release Technique**, **Skinner Releasing**, **Klein Technique**, yoga, or a tai chi lesson as a warm-up. Improvisation and/or learning movement sequences influenced by the warm-up might follow. Note that these movement education techniques are particular and specific techniques in and of themselves—they are not "release techniques" necessarily—even though the word "release" may appear in their title.

Further complicating the terminology, there is a style of dancing referred to as "release," characterized especially by a few particular qualities of movement: sequential movement through the joints (as opposed to simultaneous initiation) and a preference for flowing, less effortful movement. Although the various movement education techniques used in release technique classes may address the execution of this type of movement as well, their scope of practice isn't limited to any particular way of moving. (See Clarke and Karczag, "What We Use in Our Training and Why"; Bales and Nettl-Fiol, *The Body Eclectic*.)

Score and structure refer to the rules or instructions decided on before an improvisation that delimit its movement content and govern its progress.

Shambhala Buddhism is a lineage of Tibetan Buddhism that also follows teachings and practices of **Chögyam Trungpa Rinpoche** (1939–87), focusing on mindfulness and awareness meditation. Trungpa Rinpoche's embodiment of "crazy wisdom" was embraced by hippy culture and many artists and intellectuals of the era, including Beat poet Allen Ginsberg.

The Six Viewpoints (space, time, shape, emotion, movement, and story), compositional lenses through which to consider dance or theater, form the basis of **Mary Overlie**'s method. Rather than defining them for students from the perspective of the prevailing aesthetic, Overlie lets the Viewpoints define themselves through specific practices she has developed that give experiential knowledge of each.

The **Skinner Releasing Technique** was created by Joan Skinner, a dancer in the Martha Graham and **Merce Cunningham** companies in the 1940s and 1950s. In the 1960s she developed the Skinner Releasing Technique, an approach to dance and movement training that uses poetic imagery to affect **movement repatterning**. Skinner's school is based in Seattle, Washington. Her work has influenced many contemporary choreographers, such as Stephanie Skura, **Jennifer Monson**, and Yvonne Meier.

A **structural improvisation** follows a predetermined **score**.

Topf Technique and **Dynamic Anatomy** are **Nancy Topf**'s developments of **Anatomical Release Technique**, in which dancers study a specific image of a particular anatomical structure, both visually and through sensation, and then research these images through movement. In exploring an image physically, the dancer follows sensation, investigating through movement and the kinesthetic sense what he or she had experienced through sight and touch. Topf's work could be experienced as a private, hands-on bodywork session or as a movement class that incorporates the hands-on work. They are International Somatics and Movement Education Therapy Association (ISMETA) certified programs.

Chögyam Trungpa Rinpoche (1939–87) was a teacher in the Kagyu lineage of Tibetan Buddhism. He came to the United States in 1970, and founded Naropa University in Boulder, Colorado, in 1974. Naropa is famous for its Jack Kerouac School of Disembodied Poets, where among other notables Beat poet Allen Ginsberg served on the core faculty. **Barbara Dilley** studied with Trungpa Rinpoche, taught at Naropa beginning in 1974, and became president of Naropa University from 1985 to 1993 at his behest. **Shambhala Buddhism** follows Trungpa Rinpoche's teaching and practices.

Tuning Scores, **Lisa Nelson**'s approach to spontaneous composition and performance, evolved from her work with video and dance. They employ calls made by viewing and moving participants based on both choreographic organization and on video shooting, playback, and editing.

The **Underscore** is **Nancy Stark Smith**'s scored collection of particular warm-up exercises and movement activities that are helpful in bringing dancers to a state of body-mind preparedness for engaging in a **Contact** duet. The Underscore culminates in an open score phase that includes improvised dancing and Contact Improvisation. Stark Smith has created a visual score for the Underscore, pictographs that represent each phase and subphase in its progression.

Notes

INTRODUCTION

1. The e-mail exchange resulted from an evening of dance (Movement Research at Judson Church, 2003) at which John Japserse and Juliette Mapp collaborated to create an improvised duet. Daniel Lepkoff and Steve Paxton, "Between the Lines: Re: Presenting Improvisation. An email volley between Daniel Lepkoff and Steve Paxton," *Contact Quarterly* 29, no. 1 (Winter/Spring 2004): 47.

2. Daniel Lepkoff, e-mail to author, September 2007.

3. Lepkoff, e-mail to author, September 2007.

4. See Susan Leigh Foster, *Dances That Describe Themselves: The Improvised Choreography of Richard Bull* (Middletown, CT: Wesleyan University Press, 2002), 73–84, 85–93, 99–106.

5. "Judith Dunn and the Endless Quest," *Dance Magazine* 41 (November 1967): 51.

6. Sally Banes, *Terpsichore in Sneakers: Post-Modern Dance* (Boston: Houghton Mifflin, 1980), 203–7.

7. For example, see Constance Valis Hill et al., "Expanding the Canon," in *Taken by Surprise: A Dance Improvisation Reader*, edited by Ann Cooper Albright and David Gere (Middletown, CT: Wesleyan University Press, 2003).

8. For an in-depth look at the cultural influences behind Western improvisational dance see the chapter "Genealogies of Improvisation" in Foster, *Dances That Describe Themselves*, 19–68.

CHAPTER 1. MATERIA PRIMA

1. For more on the various ways that dancemakers create meaning through movement, see Susan Leigh Foster, *Reading Dancing: Bodies and Subjects in Contemporary American Dance* (Berkeley: University of California Press, 1986), chaps. 2 and 3.

2. For an account of Forti's early dance exploits, epiphanies, and explorations, see Simone Forti, *Handbook in Motion* (Halifax: Press of the Nova Scotia College of Art and Design; New York: New York University Press, 1974).

3. Simone Forti, "Animate Dancing: A Practice in Dance Improvisation," *Contact Quarterly* 26, no. 2 (Summer/Fall 2001): 36.

4. For an engaging account of learning Logomotion, see Carmela Hermann, "Hearing/Miraculously/Structure: An Apprenticeship with Simone Forti in Logomotion," *Contact Quarterly* 26, no. 1 (Winter/Spring 2001): 15–25.

5. John Cage and Christian Wolff, liner notes for *John Cage/Christian Wolff* on the track "Cartridge Music" (New York City: Time Records, 1962), as cited in Richard Kostelanetz, *Conversing with Cage* (New York: Routledge, 2002).

6. Barbara Dilley, "Creative Process and Meditation: Two Streams," *Contact Quarterly* 15, no. 3 (Fall 1990): 40–41.

7. Ibid., 41.

8. Chögyam Trungpa, "Dharma Art Letter," in *Visual Dharma Sourcebook I* (1974), reprinted in Dilley, "Creative Process and Meditation," 43.

9. Barbara Dilley, "Two Streams: Many Ways," *Contact Quarterly* 29, no. 2 (Summer/Fall 2005): 37.

10. Ibid., 36.

11. Penny Campbell, "Riding the Wild Ephemerid: Glimpses into a Preparation for Dance Performance Improvisation" (master's thesis, Wesleyan University, 2000), 4.

12. Susan Sgorbati, Improvisation Ensemble for Dancers and Musicians, Bennington College course, 2000–2001, 2001–2.

13. Katie Duck, workshop at the University of California, San Diego, December 2004.

14. Bonnie Eldred, report from Katie Duck, workshop, "Text/Dance/Music, Choice = Chance = Collaboration," Magpie Music Dance, Amsterdam, The Netherlands, August 2004.

15. David Corbet, "Katie Duck: An Interview," *Proximity* 2, no. 4 (1999): http://proximity.slightly.net/v_two/ve4a2.htm.

16. Nina Martin, Ensemble Thinking workshop, Festival of Interactive Physics, Toronto, ON, May 2006.

17. Nina Martin, e-mail to the author, August 2007.

18. George Russell, Choreographic Improvisation technique course, Graduate Liberal Studies Program, Wesleyan University, Middletown, CT, summer 2002.

19. Peentz Dubble, phone conversation with the author, June 2007.

20. Dana Reitz, Phrasing course at Bennington College, Bennington, VT, spring 2002.

21. Nancy Topf, Topf Technique and Dynamic Anatomy classes in New York City and Windhover, MA, 1991–93.

22. Mary Overlie, Invisible Dances workshop, Open Source Festival, Movement Research, New York City, December 2005.

23. Mary Overlie, "The Six Viewpoints," in *The Training of the American Actor*, ed. Arthur Bartow (New York: Theatre Communications Group, 2006), 199.

24. Ibid., 202.

25. Ibid., 206, 208.

26. John Tusa, "Interview: William Forsythe, Director, Ballet Frankfurt," BBC Radio 3, February 2, 2003, transcript at http://www.ballet.co.uk/magazines.

27. Helen Pickett, Forsythe Improvisation Technologies workshop, "Ideas in Motion: Innovations in Dance, Movement & Technology," part of the 2005 Boston Cyberarts Festival, Boston, MA, April 2005.

28. William Forsythe et al., *Improvisation Technologies: A Tool for the Analytical Dance Eye*, CD-ROM, ZKM Karlsruhe, 1999; Pickett, Forsythe Improvisation Technologies workshop.

CHAPTER 2. DANCING TAKES SHAPE

1. Anna Halprin, phone conversation with the author, August 2007.

2. Anna Halprin, "My Experience of Cancer," *Contact Quarterly* 26, no. 1 (Winter/Spring 2001): 50–53; Anna Halprin, *Moving toward Life: Five Decades of Transformational Dance* (Hanover, NH: Wesleyan University Press, 1995), 65–69.

3. Halprin, *Moving toward Life*, 66, 67.

4. Ibid., 52.

5. Halprin, *Moving toward Life*, 226–36.

6. The *Earth Run* score is described in Halprin, *Moving toward Life*, 237–39.

7. Richard Schechner, "Anna Halprin: A Life in Ritual," interview, in Halprin, *Moving toward Life*, 253.

8. Deborah Hay, *My Body, the Buddhist* (Hanover, NH: Wesleyan University Press, 2000), 103–4.

9. Deborah Hay, e-mail to the author, July 2007.

10. Hana van der Kolk, "All at Once: Dancing the Ridge in New York City Parks," *Contact Quarterly* 32, no. 1 (Winter/Spring 2007): 19–25.

11. Eiko Otake, quoted in Joyce Morgenroth, *Speaking of Dance: Twelve Choreographers on Their Craft* (New York: Routledge, 2004), 125.

12. Jennifer Dunning, "It's a Cave? A Temple? It's a Mystery," *New York Times*, November 29, 2000.

13. Eiko and Koma, "FAQ," http://eikoandkoma.org/index.php?p=ek&id=1777.

14. Eiko and Koma, Delicious Movement workshop, Earthdance, Plainfield, MA, summer 2002.

15. Eiko, e-mail to the author, August 2007. See also Paula Josa-Jones, "Delicious Moving," *Contact Quarterly* 11, no. 1 (Winter 1986): 10–15.

16. Steve Paxton, e-mail to the author, July 2008.

17. In fact, Paxton has evolved a training system, Material for the Spine, out of his work with Contact Improvisation. In a course description for a workshop at Earthdance, Plainfield, MA, he says: "Begun in 1986, Material for the Spine is a simple dancing system based in sensation and evolved self-imagery for the skeletal elements of head, spine and pelvis. In other words, an exploration of the center of the body. The Material is abstracted from Contact Improvisation, but Material is more technical and meditative, with emphasis on breathing and precise exercises done solo. Connections may be noticed to extant dance techniques, and their mostly unstated use of the pelvis. Material for the Spine cannot avoid the rest of the body: so far it has extended to the hip sockets and thighs, the shoulder blades and arms." See http://www.earthdance.net/programs/paxton10.htm.

18. Richard Bull, "The Joyce of Choreography," *New Observations* 38 (1986), repr. in *Contact Quarterly* 24, no. 1 (Winter/Spring 1999): 35.

19. See Susan Leigh Foster, *Dances that Describe Themselves: The Improvised Choreography of Richard Bull* (Middletown, CT: Wesleyan University Press, 2002), esp. 3–17.

20. Ibid., 209, 211–12.

21. Keith Hennessy, Performing Improvisation/Improvising Performance workshop, Earthdance, Plainfield, MA, September 2006.

22. Keith Hennessy, e-mail to the author, June 2008.

23. Nina Martin, Ensemble Thinking workshop, Festival of Interactive Physics, Toronto, ON, May 2006.

24. See also Nina Martin, "Ensemble Thinking: Compositional Strategies for Group Improvisation," *Contact Quarterly* 32, no. 2 (Summer/Fall 2007): 13–14.

25. Penny Campbell, "Riding the Wild Ephemerid: Glimpses into a Preparation for Dance Performance Improvisation," *Contact Quarterly* 29, no. 1 (Winter/Spring 2004): 35.

26. Ibid., 35–36.

27. Ibid., 36.

28. Susan Sgorbati, Intermediate and Advanced Improvisation Ensemble for Dancers and Musicians, Bennington College course, 2000–2001, 2001–2.

29. Susan Sgorbati, "The Emergent Improvisation Project: Embodying Complexity," *Contact Quarterly* 32, no. 1 (Winter/Spring 2007): 40–46.

30. Mary Overlie, Invisible Dances workshop, Open Source Festival, Movement Research, New York City, December 2005.

31. Mary Overlie, Open Improvisation with actor Rich Brown, First Annual Shady Corners American Maverick Performing Arts Festival, Milford, NY, September 25, 2005.

32. Lisa Nelson, Tuning work, Improvisation Ensemble for Dancers and Musicians, Bennington College course, April–May 2001.

33. Christina Stelzer and José Mulder van de Graf, "Talking about Walking," an interview with Suprapto Suryodarmo at Aryatara Buddhist Institute in Munich, Germany, 1985. Published by *Kemongo*, Solo, Java (1987) and reprinted in part in Andrea Morein, "A Practice called 'Road': 'Movement in Meditation' with Suprapto Suryodarmo in Central Java, Indonesia," *Contact Quarterly* 19, no. 1 (Winter/Spring 1994): 29–31.

34. Suprapto Suryodarmo, e-mail to the author, September 2007.

35. Suprapto Suryodarmo, e-mail to the author, May 2008.

36. Margit Galanter, conversation with the author, fall 2004; video of Suprapto Suryodarmo teaching and improvising at the Jacob's Pillow International Improvisation Workshop, video by Lisa Nelson, Bennington College, Bennington, VT, 1993, private collection; Susan Bauer, "Finding the Bone in the Wind: A Journey with Suprapto Suryodarmo in Bali, Indonesia," unpublished manuscript, 2005, private collection.

37. Susan Bauer, "Excerpt from 'Finding the Bone in the Wind': A Journey with Suprapto Suryodarmo in Bali, Indonesia," *Moving Journal* 12, no. 3 (Fall/Winter 2005): 18; Bauer, "Finding the Bone in the Wind."

38. Galanter, conversation with the author; Bauer, "Finding the Bone in the Wind."

39. Suprapto Suryodarmo, in a panel discussion with Anna Halprin and Simone Forti, moderated by Barbara Dilley, quoted in Diane Butler, Evangel King, and Kristine

Maltrud, "Art Human Nature: An International Gathering of Movement Artists," *Contact Quarterly* 28, no. 2 (Summer/Fall 2003): 50.

40. Suprapto Suryodarmo, e-mail to the author, September 2007.

41. Suprapto Suryodarmo, "Web Art Garden—An Idea," *ACE: Art Culture Environment*, 1999, project description for newsletter, private collection.

42. See Barbara Dilley, "Creative Process and Meditation: Two Streams," *Contact Quarterly* 15, no. 3 (Fall 1990): 41.

43. Lisa Kraus, "At Naropa, 3 Generations: Interviews with Barbara Dilley, Irini Nadel Rockwell, and Lisa Kraus," *Contact Quarterly* 15, no. 3 (Fall 1990): 45; Dilley, conversation with the author, April 2007.

44. Nancy Stark Smith, "Barbara Dilley Talks about the Contemplative Dance Intensive," *Contact Quarterly* 6, no. 1 (Fall 1980): 19.

45. Barbara Dilley, Fearless Dancing Project workshop, Sky Lake Lodge, Rosendale, NY, summer 2004, and Shambhala Meditation Center of New York, New York City, 2005; see also Barbara Dilley, "Contemplative Dance Practice," unpublished manuscript developed at Naropa University, 1997 (repr., 2000), private collection.

46. Kraus, "At Naropa, 3 Generations," 46.

CHAPTER 3. TIME MACHINES

1. David Corbet, "Katie Duck: An Interview," *Proximity* 2, no. 4 (1999): http://proximity.slightly.net/v_two/ve4a2.htm.

2. Katie Duck, interview by *Tangent* magazine, Montreal, Canada, probably 2002, http://katieduck.com/Katie%20Ducks%20writing/tangent%20magazin%20montreal.html.

3. Nina Martin, Ensemble Thinking workshop, Toronto, ON, May 2006.

4. Mary Overlie, Invisible Dances workshop, Open Source Festival, Movement Research, New York City, December 2005.

5. Yoshi Oida and Lorna Marshall, *The Invisible Actor* (New York: Routledge, 1997), 39–42.

6. Petra Vermeersch, "AboutButoh: In Research for Its Origin and Actual Meaning, an Interview with Min Tanaka," *Contact Quarterly* 27, no. 1 (Winter/Spring 2002): 24.

7. Min Tanaka, "Quotations: Min Tanaka," trans. Kazue Kobata, Min Tanaka Official Web Site, http://www.min-tanaka.com/wp/?page_id=45.

8. Kristin Kantner, "Min Tanaka at Bennington College," *Contact Quarterly* 19, no. 2 (Summer/Fall 1994): 36.

9. Dana Reitz, Phrasing course at Bennington College, Bennington, VT, spring 2002.

10. Nancy Stark Smith, "January Workshop," Earthdance, Plainfield, MA, January 2005.

11. Ibid.

12. Forsythe et al., *Improvisation Technologies*.

13. Lisa Nelson, Tuning work, interterm workshop, Bennington College, February 2002.

14. T. H. White, *The Once and Future King* (New York: G. P. Putnam's Sons, 1965).

15. Yoshi Oida and Lorna Marshall, *The Invisible Actor* (New York: Routledge, 1997), 33.

16. See also Irmis B. Popoff's *The Enneagrama and the Man of Unity* (New York: Samuel Weiser, 1978).

CHAPTER 4. SPATIAL RELATIONS

1. George Russell, Choreographic Improvisation course, Graduate Liberal Studies Program, Wesleyan University, summer term, 2002.

2. Barbara Dilley, conversation with the author, December 2004.

3. Steve Paxton, "Chute Transcript," *Contact Quarterly* 7, no. 3/4 (Spring/Summer 1982): 16–17.

4. See Keith Johnstone, *Impro: Improvisation and the Theatre* (New York: Theatre Arts Books, 1979).

5. For more on Nina Martin's status work, see Nina Martin, "Ensemble Thinking: Compositional Strategies for Group Improvisation," *Contact Quarterly* 32, no. 2 (Summer/Fall 2007): 15.

6. Nina Martin, e-mail to the author, August 2007.

7. Dana Reitz, Phrasing course at Bennington College, Bennington, VT, spring 2002.

8. Dana Reitz, e-mail to the author, May 2007.

9. Mary Overlie, "Doing the Unnecessary," *Six Viewpoints: A Deconstructive Approach to Theater*, http://www.sixviewpoints.com/Bridge.html.

10. Mary Overlie, Invisible Dances workshop, December 2005.

11. Forsythe et al., *Improvisation Technologies*.

12. David Corbet, "Katie Duck: An Interview," *Proximity* 2, no. 4 (1999): http://proximity.slightly.net/v_two/ve4a2.htm; Duck, interview by *Tangent* magazine.

13. Simone Forti, "The Movement of Attention: An Interview with Daniel Lepkoff," *Movement Research Performance Journal*, no. 29 (Spring 2005): 8–9.

14. Ibid., 9.

CHAPTER 5. THE DANCING IMAGE

1. Trungpa, "Dharma Art Letter," 43.

2. Barbara Dilley, "Two Streams: Many Ways," 42–44; Barbara Dilley, Fearless Dancing Project workshop, Shambhala Meditation Center of New York, New York City, 2005.

3. Lisa Nelson, Tuning work, Bennington College, April–May 2001.

4. Nina Martin, Ensemble Thinking workshop, Festival of Interactive Physics, Toronto, ON, Canada, May 2006.

5. Joan Skinner, "Letters: Releasing Roots," *Contact Quarterly* 16, no. 3 (Fall 1991): 8.

6. Stephanie Skura, e-mail to the author, July 2007.

7. Pamela Matt, e-mail to the author, June 2007.

8. Nancy Topf, Topf Technique and Dynamic Anatomy classes and workshops, New York, 1991–93.

9. Melinda Ring, conversation with the author, December 2005.

10. Kazue Kobata, conversation with the author, New York, fall 2004.

11. Melinda Ring, conversation with the author, December 2005; see also Alissa Cardone, "Killing the Body-Ego: Dance Research with Min Tanaka at Body Weather Farm, Japan," *Contact Quarterly* 27, no. 1 (Winter/Spring 2002): 15–22.

12. Kristin Kantner, "Min Tanaka at Bennington College," *Contact Quarterly* 19, no. 2 (Summer/Fall 1994): 36.

13. Roxanne Steinberg, conversation with the author, April 2008.

14. Dana Iova-Koga, conversation with the author, July 2008.

15. Ibid.

16. Kazue Kobata, conversation with the author, New York, fall 2004.

17. Martha Graham, *Blood Memory: An Autobiography* (New York: Simon & Schuster, 1991), 122.

18. Nelson, Bennington College course, April–May 2001.

19. Yoshi Oida and Lorna Marshall, *The Invisible Actor* (New York: Routledge, 1997), vii–viii.

20. Mary Overlie, Invisible Dances workshop, Open Source Festival, Movement Research, New York, December 2005.

21. Later I found out that Mary Overlie had made a piece where the performers waited on stage for something to happen. Nina Martin mentions it in "Interviews with Nina Martin," *Contact Quarterly* 32, no. 2 (Summer/Fall 2007): 16–17.

CHAPTER 6. THE POSSIBILITIES OF MUSIC

1. Jack Anderson, "Judith Dunn and the Endless Quest," *Dance Magazine* 41 (November 1967): 51.

2. Bill Dixon, "Collaboration, 1965–1972: Judith Dunn, Dancer/Choreographer; Bill Dixon, Musician-Composer," *Contact Quarterly* 10, no. 2 (Spring/Summer 1985): 12.

3. Judith Dunn, "We Don't Talk about It, We Engage in It," *Eddy*, no. 2 (1974): 13.

4. Penny Campbell, quoted in a Middlebury College press release, "Two P's in a Pod Rides Again! This Time: To the Opera," http://community.middlebury.edu/~campbell/2Ps_press.html, November 1, 1996.

5. Susan Sgorbati, "The Emergent Improvisation Project: Embodying Complexity," *Contact Quarterly* 32, no. 1 (Winter/Spring 2007): 45–46.

6. George Russell, Choreographic Improvisation Technique course, Graduate Liberal Studies Program, Wesleyan University, Middletown, CT, summer 2002.

7. Dean Suzuki, liner notes for *Jon Gibson: In Good Company*, compact disc, Point Music, 434 873–2, 1992.

8. Katie Duck, interview by *Tangent* magazine.

9. "Blink," dance by Katie Duck, music by Mary Oliver, Sushi Performance and Visual Art, San Diego, CA, December 2004.

10. See also Jaqueline Oskamp, "Different Codes Seminar," *Contact Quarterly* 31, no. 1 (Winter/Spring 2006): 38–42.

11. Mike Vargas, "Looking at Composition Is Like Painting the Golden Gate Bridge: 86 Aspects of Composition," *Contact Quarterly* 28, no. 2 (Summer/Fall 2003): 28–34.

12. Mike Vargas, conversation with the author, September 2007.

CHAPTER 7. THE EYES

1. Barbara Dilley, "Two Streams: Many Ways," *Contact Quarterly* 29, no. 2 (Summer/Fall 2005): 39–40.

2. Ibid., 40, 41.

3. Barbara Dilley, conversation with the author, December 2004.

4. Katie Duck, workshop at the University of California, San Diego, December 2004; Bonnie Eldred, report from Katie Duck, workshop, "Text/Dance/Music, Choice = Chance = Collaboration," Magpie Music Dance, Amsterdam, The Netherlands, August 2004.

5. Lisa Nelson, "Before Your Eyes: Seeds of a Dance Practice," *Contact Quarterly* 29, no. 1 (Winter/Spring 2004): 20–26; Lisa Nelson, conversations with the author, June 2005.

6. Lisa Nelson, Tuning work, Bennington College, April–May 2001 and February 2002.

7. Movement Research Improvisation Festival program note, 1995; see also Lisa Nelson, "The Sensation Is the Image," *Writings on Dance*, no. 14 (Summer 1995/96): 4–16.

8. Nancy Topf, "The Anatomy of Center" (unpublished manuscript, 1997), 1–2.

9. See for example, Pamela Matt, *A Kinesthetic Legacy: The Life and Works of Barbara Clark* (Tempe, AZ: CMT Press, 1993), 225–61.

10. This figure varies from source to source. See Wyn Kapit and Lawrence M. Elson, *The Anatomy Coloring Book*, 3rd ed. (San Francisco: Benjamin Cummings, 2002), 27.

11. Nina Martin, Ensemble Thinking workshop, Festival of Interactive Physics, Toronto, ON, May 2006.

12. Steve Paxton, conversation with the author, June 2007.

13. Suprapto Suryodarmo, Prayer of the Butterfly workshop, Earthdance, July 2008.

CHAPTER 8. PARTNERING SCIENCE

1. Jennifer Monson, workshop at Western Mass. Moving Arts Festival, Earthdance, August 2006.

2. See also Ishmael Houston-Jones et al., "Cover Artist: Jennifer Monson," *Movement Research Performance Journal*, no. 30 (2006): 15–20.

3. Susan Sgorbati, "The Emergent Improvisation Project: Embodying Complexity," *Contact Quarterly* 32, no. 1 (Winter/Spring 2007): 41.

4. Gerald M. Edelman and Giulio Tononi, *A Universe of Consciousness: How Matter Becomes Imagination* (New York City: Basic, 2000), 109.

5. *The Reconstructed Memory Form*, directed by Susan Sgorbati, Bennington College, March 2006 and October 2007.

6. Steve Paxton, "Fall after Newton Transcript," *Contact Quarterly* 13, no. 3 (Fall 1988): 38–39.

7. Simone Forti, *Handbook in Motion* (Halifax, NS: Press of the Nova Scotia College of Art and Design; New York: New York University Press, 1974), 119.

8. Simone Forti, "Animate Dancing: A Practice in Dance Improvisation," *Contact Quarterly* 26, no. 2 (Summer/Fall 2001): 33.

9. Simone Forti, "Animate Dancing: A Practice in Dance Improvisation," in *Taken by Surprise: A Dance Improvisation Reader*, ed. Ann Cooper Albright and David Gere (Middletown, CT: Wesleyan University Press, 2003), 56.

10. See Carmela Hermann, "Hearing/Miraculously/Structure: An Apprenticeship with Simone Forti in Logomotion," *Contact Quarterly* 26, no. 1 (Winter/Spring 2001): 15–25.

11. See Simone Forti et al., *Unbuttoned Sleeves* (Venice, CA: Beyond Baroque, 2006) for collected writings from the performance process.

12. Eugene T. Gendlin, "Proposal for an International Group for a First Person Science," *The Focusing Institute*, http://www.focusing.org/gendlin_johnson_iscience.html.

13. See Maaike Bleeker and Rob Van Kranenburg, "Corporal Literacy," *Contact Quarterly* 31, no. 1 (Winter/Spring 2006): 49.

CHAPTER 9. THE MAGICAL OBJECT

1. Molly Shanahan, *Glance: Molly Shanahan's Eye Cycle* (Chicago: Links Hall, 2005), 7.

2. James J. Gibson, *The Ecological Approach to Visual Perception* (Hillsdale, NJ: Lawrence Erlbaum Associates, 1986).

3. Lisa Nelson, conversation with the author, February 2007.

4. Jeroen Peeters, "Dialogue with Lisa Nelson on Communication with Objects," in *Materials, Dialogues and Observations on Proximity, Walking about Connexive #1: Vera Mantero*, SARMA, http://www.sarma.be/text.asp?id=977.

5. Mary Overlie, "The Six Viewpoints: A Deconstructive Approach to Theater," "Change of View: The Viewpoints Bridge," "The Piano," http://www.sixviewpoints.com/Bridge.html#.

6. Simone Forti, "Thoughts on *To Be Continued*: A Sketch of a Dance/Narrative Process," *Contact Quarterly* 19, no. 1 (Winter/Spring 1994): 16.

7. Dana Reitz, "Drawings and Dances," *Contact Quarterly* 33, no. 1 (Winter/Spring 2008): 87.

8. John Tusa, "Interview: William Forsythe, Director, Ballet Frankfurt," BBC Radio 3, February 2, 2003, transcript at http://www.ballet.co.uk/magazines.

9. Jon Gibson et al., "Space Walk: Reflections on Nancy Topf's Spacewalk Improvisation," *Contact Quarterly* 25, no. 2 (Summer/Fall 2000): 45; for more description of the practice, see the entire article, 42–47.

10. Vermeersch, "AboutButoh," 25.

11. Reprinted with a collection of articles as Min Tanaka, "Tanaka and the Body Weather Laboratory," *Contact Quarterly* 6, nos. 3 & 4 (Spring/Summer 1981): 6–7.

12. William Forsythe, quoted in Birgit Kirchner, "Good Theatre of a Different Kind," *Ballett International* 7, no. 8 (August 1984): 6.

EPILOGUE

1. The epigraph is a suggestion in experiential psychologist Eugene Gendlin's instructions for Focusing, a "felt sense" form of psychoanalysis he developed at the University of Chicago in the 1960s and 1970s. See Eugene Gendlin, "Instructions for Not

Following Instructions," in *An Introduction to Focusing: Six Steps,* http://www.focus
ing.org/gendlin/docs/gol_2234.html.

 2. Conversation with Terry Creach, Bennington College graduate dance seminar,
spring 2002.

 3. Angeles Arrien, *The Four-Fold Way: Walking the Paths of the Warrior, Teacher,
Healer, and Visionary* (New York: HarperCollins, 1993).

Bibliography

Albright, Ann Cooper, and David Gere, eds. *Taken by Surprise: A Dance Improvisation Reader*. Middletown, CT: Wesleyan University Press, 2003.

Allison, Nancy, ed. *Encyclopedia of Body-Mind Disciplines*. New York: Rosen, 1999.

Anderson, Jack. "Judith Dunn and the Endless Quest." *Dance Magazine* 41 (November 1967): 48–67.

Arrien, Angeles. *The Four-Fold Way: Walking the Paths of the Warrior, Teacher, Healer, and Visionary*. New York: HarperCollins, 1993.

Bales, Melanie, and Rebecca Nettl-Fiol, eds. *The Body Eclectic: Evolving Practices in Dance Training*. Champaign: University of Illinois Press, 2008.

Banes, Sally. *Terpsichore in Sneakers: Post-Modern Dance*. Boston: Houghton Mifflin, 1980.

Bauer, Susan. "Excerpt from 'Finding the Bone in the Wind': A Journey with Suprapto Suryodarmo in Bali, Indonesia." *Moving Journal* 12, no. 3 (Fall/Winter 2005): 14–20.

———. "Finding the Bone in the Wind: A Journey with Suprapto Suryodarmo in Bali, Indonesia." Unpublished manuscript, 2005, private collection.

Benoit, Agnes. *Nouvelles de Danse 32–33: On the Edge—Createurs de l'Imprevu*. Brussels: Contredanse, 1998.

Blackwood, Michael, dir. *Butoh: Body on the Edge of Crisis*. VHS. New York: Michael Blackwood Productions, 1990.

Bleeker, Maaike, and Rob Van Kranenburg. "Corporal Literacy." *Contact Quarterly* 31, no. 1 (Winter/Spring 2006): 49.

Bull, Richard. "Ithaca." *Contact Quarterly* 20, no. 2 (Summer/Fall 1995): 100–102.

———. "The Joyce of Choreography." Repr. in *Contact Quarterly* 24, no. 1 (Winter/Spring 1999): 23–38.

Butler, Diane, Evangel King, and Kristine Maltrud. "Art Human Nature: An International Gathering of Movement Artists." *Contact Quarterly* 28, no. 2 (Summer/Fall 2003): 47–52.

Campbell, Penny. "Riding the Wild Ephemerid: Glimpses into a Preparation for Dance Performance Improvisation." Master's thesis, Wesleyan University, 2000. Repr. in part in *Contact Quarterly* 29, no. 1 (Winter/Spring 2004): 27–36.

Cardone, Alissa. "Killing the Body-Ego: Dance Research with Min Tanaka at Body Weather Farm, Japan." *Contact Quarterly* 27, no. 1 (Winter/Spring 2002): 15–22.

Clarke, Gill, and Eva Karczag, "What We Use in Our Training and Why." *Contact Quarterly* 32, no. 2 (Summer/Fall 2007): 27–31.

Cohen, Bonnie Bainbridge. *Sensing, Feeling, and Action: The Experiential Anatomy of Body-Mind Centering.* 2nd ed. Northampton, MA: Contact Editions, 2008.

Corbet, David. "Katie Duck: An Interview." *Proximity* 2, no. 4 (1999): http://proximity .slightly.net/v_two/ve4a2.htm.

Dilley, Barbara. "Contemplative Dance Practice." Unpublished manuscript developed at Naropa University, 1997. Repr., 2000. Private collection.

———. "Creative Process and Meditation: Two Streams." *Contact Quarterly* 15, no. 3 (Fall 1990): 40–44.

———. "Two Streams: Many Ways." *Contact Quarterly* 29, no. 2 (Summer/Fall 2005): 33–45.

Dixon, Bill. "Collaboration, 1965–1972: Judith Dunn, Dancer/Choreographer; Bill Dixon, Musician/Composer." *Contact Quarterly* 10, no. 2 (Spring/Summer 1985): 7–12.

Duck, Katie. Interview by *Tangent* magazine, Montreal, Canada. Probably 2002. http:// katieduck.com/Katie%20Ducks%20writing/tangent%20magazin%20montreal.html.

———. "Is Choreography Dance?" *Contact Quarterly* 26, no. 2 (Summer/Fall 2001): 12–14.

Duck, Katie, Garrett List, and Michael Vachter. "Round Table: Talking about Improvisation in Performance." *Contact Quarterly* 24, no. 2 (Summer/Fall 1999): 16–19.

Duck, Katie, and Robert Steijn. "Improvisation Festival Amsterdam 1994–1995." *Contact Quarterly* 25, no. 2 (Summer/Fall 2000): 13–17.

Dunn, Judith. "We Don't Talk about It, We Engage in It." *Eddy*, no. 2 (1974): 10–14.

Dunn, Robert Ellis. "Evaluating Choreography." *Performance Art Journal* 57 (September 1997).

Edelman, Gerald M., and Giulio Tononi. *A Universe of Consciousness: How Matter Becomes Imagination.* New York: Basic, 2000.

Forsythe, William, et al. *Improvisation Technologies: A Tool for the Analytical Dance Eye.* CD-ROM. ZKM Karlsruhe, 1999.

Forti, Simone. "Animate Dancing: A Practice in Dance Improvisation." *Contact Quarterly* 26, no. 2 (Summer/Fall 2001): 32–39.

———. "Animate Dancing: A Practice in Dance Improvisation." In *Taken by Surprise: A Dance Improvisation Reader,* ed. Ann Cooper Albright and David Gere, 53–64. Middletown, CT: Wesleyan University Press, 2003.

———. *Handbook in Motion.* Halifax: Press of the Nova Scotia College of Art and Design; New York: New York University Press, 1974.

———. "The Movement of Attention: An Interview with Daniel Lepkoff." *Movement Research Performance Journal,* no. 29 (Spring 2005): 8–9.

———. "Thoughts on *To Be Continued*: A Sketch of a Dance/Narrative Process." *Contact Quarterly* 19, no. 1 (Winter/Spring 1994): 13–21.

Forti, Simone, et al. *Unbuttoned Sleeves.* Venice, CA: Beyond Baroque, 2006.

Foster, Susan Leigh. *Dances that Describe Themselves: The Improvised Choreography of Richard Bull.* Middletown, CT: Wesleyan University Press, 2002.

———. *Reading Dancing: Bodies and Subjects in Contemporary American Dance*. Berkeley: University of California Press, 1986.

Gable, Cecelia. "Judith Dunn, 1933–1983." *Contact Quarterly* 9, no. 1 (Fall 1983): 52–53.

Galeota-Wozny, Nancy. "Interview with Jennifer Monson on BIRD BRAIN DANCE— A Navigational Dance Project." *Contact Quarterly* 29, no. 2 (Summer/Fall 2005): 12–24.

Gendlin, Eugene T. *Focusing*. New York: Bantam, 1981.

———. "Proposal for an International Group for a First Person Science." *The Focusing Institute*, http://www.focusing.org/gendlin_johnson_iscience.html.

Gere, David. *How to Make Dances in an Epidemic: Tracking Choreography in the Age of AIDS*. Madison: University of Wisconsin Press, 2004.

Gibson, James J. *The Ecological Approach to Visual Perception*. Hillsdale, NJ: Lawrence Erlbaum Associates, 1986.

———. *The Senses Considered as Perceptual Systems*. Boston: Houghton Mifflin, 1966.

Gibson, Jon, et al. "Space Walk: Reflections on Nancy Topf's Spacewalk Improvisation." *Contact Quarterly* 25, no. 2 (Summer/Fall 2000): 42–47.

Godinho de Matos, Ana. *Moving in Space: Suprapto Suryodarmo*. DVD. London, England, 2006.

Goldberg, Marianne. "The Threshold of Visibility: Dana Reitz's *Circumstantial Evidence*." *Contact Quarterly* 18, no. 1 (Winter 1988): 8–9.

Goldberg, Natalie. *Writing Down the Bones: Freeing the Writer Within*. Boston: Shambhala, 1986.

Graham, Martha. *Blood Memory: An Autobiography*. New York: Simon & Schuster, 1991.

Groff, Ed. "Laban Movement Analysis." In *The Illustrated Encyclopedia of Mind-Body Disciplines*, ed. Nancy Allison, 335–38. New York: Rosen, 1999.

Gronda, Helen. "Risking Presence." Interview with Nancy Stark Smith. *Proximity* 6, nos. 3 and 4 (December 2003): 20–31.

Halprin, Anna. *Movement Ritual*. San Francisco: San Francisco Dancers' Workshop, 1979.

———. *Moving toward Life: Five Decades of Transformational Dance*. Hanover, NH: Wesleyan University Press, 1995.

———. "My Experience of Cancer." *Contact Quarterly* 26, no. 1 (Winter/Spring 2001): 50–53.

Hay, Deborah. "A Performance of a Performance: VOILA, a Dance Libretto." *Contact Quarterly* 22, no. 1 (Winter/Spring 1997): 31–37.

———. *Lamb at the Altar: The Story of a Dance*. Durham, NC: Duke University Press, 1994.

———. *Moving through the Universe in Bare Feet: Ten Circle Dances for Everybody*. Athens, OH: Swallow Press, 1975.

———. *My Body, the Buddhist*. Hanover, NH: Wesleyan University Press, 2000.

———. "What if Now Is? The Other Side of O." *Contact Quarterly* 27, no. 1 (Winter/Spring 2002): 34–37.

Hermann, Carmela. "Hearing/Miraculously/Structure: An Apprenticeship with Simone Forti in Logomotion." *Contact Quarterly* 26, no. 1 (Winter/Spring 2001): 15–25.

Houston-Jones, Ishmael, et al. "Cover Artist: Jennifer Monson." *Movement Research Performance Journal*, no. 30 (2006): 15–20.

Johnstone, Keith. *Impro: Improvisation and the Theatre.* New York: Theatre Arts, 1979.

Josa-Jones, Paula. "Delicious Moving." *Contact Quarterly* 11, no. 1 (Winter 1986): 10–15.

Jowitt, Deborah. *Time and the Dancing Image.* Berkeley: University of California Press, 1988.

Kantner, Kristin. "Min Tanaka at Bennington College." *Contact Quarterly* 19, no. 2 (Summer/Fall 1994): 36–38.

Keller, Jennifer, Melinda Buckwalter, and Nancy Stark Smith. "Inter-Views with Nina Martin." *Contact Quarterly* 32, no. 2 (Summer/Fall 2007): 16–17.

Kim, Jiae. "Min Tanaka's Butoh." Interview with Min Tanaka, trans. by Kazue Kobata, *Theme,* no. 7 (2006): www.thememagazine.com/stories/min-tanaka/.

Kirchner, Birgit. "Good Theatre of a Different Kind." *Ballett International* 7, no. 8 (August 1984): 4–9.

Kostelanetz, Richard. *Conversing with Cage.* New York: Routledge, 2002.

Kovarova, Miroslava. "Body of Work: Interview with Daniel Lepkoff." *Contact Quarterly* 27, no. 1 (Winter/Spring 2002): 41–45.

Kraus, Lisa. "At Naropa, 3 Generations: Interviews with Barbara Dilley, Irini Nadel Rockwell, and Lisa Kraus." *Contact Quarterly* 15, no. 3 (Fall 1990): 44–49.

Lepkoff, Daniel, and Steve Paxton. "Between the Lines: Re: Presenting Improvisation. An email volley between Daniel Lepkoff and Steve Paxton." *Contact Quarterly* 29, no. 1 (Winter/Spring 2004): 42–49.

Martin, Nina. "Ensemble Thinking: Compositional Strategies for Group Improvisation." *Contact Quarterly* 32, no. 2 (Summer/Fall 2007): 10–22.

Matt, Pamela. *A Kinesthetic Legacy: The Life and Works of Barbara Clark.* Tempe, AZ: CMT Press, 1993.

McDonagh, Don. *The Rise and Fall of Modern Dance.* Chicago: Chicago Review Press, 1990.

Mohr, Richard. *Gay Ideas: Outing and Other Controversies.* Boston: Beacon: 1992.

Morein, Andrea. "A Practice called 'Road': 'Movement in Meditation' with Suprapto Suryodarmo in Central Java, Indonesia." *Contact Quarterly* 19, no. 1 (Winter/Spring 1994): 29–31.

Morgenroth, Joyce. *Speaking of Dance: Twelve Choreographers on Their Craft.* New York: Routledge, 2004.

Nelson, Lisa. "Before Your Eyes: Seeds of a Dance Practice." *Contact Quarterly* 29, no. 1 (Winter/Spring 2004): 20–26.

———. "The Sensation Is the Image." *Writings on Dance,* no. 14 (Summer 1995/96): 4–16.

Nelson, Lisa, and Daniel Lepkoff. "Improvisation and a Sense of Imagination." *Contact Quarterly* 17, no. 2 (Summer/Fall 1992): 47–50.

Nelson, Lisa, et al., eds. *Fall After Newton.* DVD. East Charleston, VT: Videoda, 1987.

Nelson, Lisa, and Nancy Stark Smith, eds. *Contact Quarterly's Contact Improvisation Sourcebook: Collected Writings and Graphics from* Contact Quarterly Dance Journal, *1975–1992.* Northampton, MA: Contact Editions, 1997.

———, eds. *Contact Quarterly's Contact Improvisation Sourcebook II: Collected Writings and Graphics from* Contact Quarterly Dance Journal, *1993–2007.* Northampton, MA: Contact Editions, 2008.

Novack, Cynthia J. *Sharing the Dance: Contact Improvisation and American Culture.* Madison: University of Wisconsin Press, 1990.

Ohno, Kazuo, and Yoshito Ohno. *Kazuo Ohno's World: From Within and Without.* Middletown, CT: Wesleyan University Press, 2004.

Oida, Yoshi, and Lorna Marshall. *The Invisible Actor.* New York: Routledge, 1997.

Overlie, Mary. "The Six Viewpoints." In *The Training of the American Actor,* ed. Arthur Bartow, 187–221. New York: Theatre Communications Group, 2006.

Oskamp, Jacqueline. "Different Codes Seminar." *Contact Quarterly* 31, no. 1 (Winter/Spring 2006): 38–42.

Paxton, Steve. "Chute Transcript." *Contact Quarterly* 7, no. 3/4 (Spring/Summer 1982): 16–17.

———. "Drafting Interior Techniques." *Contact Quarterly* 18, no. 1 (Winter/Spring 1993): 61–66.

———. "Fall after Newton Transcript." *Contact Quarterly* 13, no. 3 (Fall 1988): 38–39.

———. "The History and Future of Dance Improvisation." *Contact Quarterly* 26, no. 2 (Summer/Fall 2001): 98–101.

———. "Improvisation Is . . ." *Contact Quarterly* 12, no. 2 (Spring/Summer 1987): 15–19.

———. "Letters: Improvisation Issue?" *Contact Quarterly* 12, no. 2 (Spring/Summer 1987): 4.

Peeters, Jeroen. "Dialogues on Blindness: Lisa Nelson, Alexander Baervoets, Andrew L. Harwood, Lin Snelling." *Dance Theatre Journal* 21, no. 1 (2005): 9–16.

———. "Dialogue with Lisa Nelson on Communication with Objects." In *Materials, Dialogues and Observations on Proximity, Walking about Connexive #1: Vera Mantero.* SARMA, http://www.sarma.be/text.asp?id=977.

Pitty, Alice. "Rituals of Chaos: The Movement Work of Suprapto Suryodarmo." *Contemporary Theater Review* 11, no. 2 (2001): 55–68.

Quirynen, Anne, dir. *I Think the Body Likes to Move.* VHS. Brussels, Belgium: Argos, 1990.

Ramsay, Mary, guest ed. "Authentic Movement." Special issue, *Contact Quarterly* 27, no. 2 (Summer/Fall 2002).

Reitz, Dana. "Drawings and Dances." *Contact Quarterly* 33, no. 1 (Winter/Spring 2008): 87.

———. "On the Dispersion of Artists from New York: An American Issue." *Contact Quarterly* 15, no. 2 (Spring/Summer 1990): 9–15.

Rolland, John. *Inside Motion: An Ideokinetic Basis for Movement Education.* Urbana, IL: Rolland String Research Assoc., 1984.

Ruefle, Mary. "On Min Tanaka's *Kimono.*" *Contact Quarterly* 18, no. 1 (Summer/Fall 1994): 61–66.

Sabat, Motria. "Observing Moving: In Workshop with Daniel Lepkoff at the Festival of Interactive Physics." *Contact Quarterly* 27, no. 1 (Winter/Spring 2002): 46–50.

Sgorbati, Susan. "The Emergent Improvisation Project: Embodying Complexity." *Contact Quarterly* 32, no. 1 (Winter/Spring 2007): 40–46.

Shanahan, Molly. *Glance: Molly Shanahan's Eye Cycle.* Chicago: Links Hall, 2005.

Spier, Steven. "Engendering and Composing Movement: William Forsythe and the Ballet Frankfurt." *Journal of Architecture* 3, no. 2 (Summer 1998): 135–46.

Stark Smith, Nancy. "Barbara Dilley Talks about the Contemplative Dance Intensive." *Contact Quarterly* 6, no. 1 (Fall 1980): 18–25.

Stark Smith, Nancy, and David Koteen. *Caught Falling: The Confluence of Contact Improvisation, Nancy Stark Smith, and Other Moving Ideas.* Northampton, MA: Contact Editions, 2008.

Suryodarmo, Suprapto. "Web Art Garden—An Idea." *ACE: Art Culture Environment*, Cheltenham, Gloucester, UK, 1999. Project description for newsletter, private collection.

Suzuki, Dean. Liner notes for *Jon Gibson: In Good Company.* Compact Disc. Point Music, 434 873-2, 1992.

Tanaka, Min. "Quotations: Min Tanaka." Trans. Kazue Kobata. Min Tanaka official website, http://www.min-tanaka.com/wp/?page_id=45.

———. "Tanaka and the Body Weather Laboratory." *Contact Quarterly* 6, nos. 3 & 4 (Spring/Summer 1981): 5–7.

Topf, Nancy. "The Anatomy of Center." Unpublished manuscript, 1997, private collection.

Trungpa Rinpoche, Chögyam. "Dharma Art Letter." In *Visual Dharma Sourcebook I* (1974). Repr. in Barbara Dilley, "Creative Process and Meditation: Two Streams," *Contact Quarterly* 15, no. 3 (Fall 1990): 43.

Tusa, John. "Interview: William Forsythe, Director, Ballet Frankfurt." BBC Radio 3, February 2, 2003, transcript at http://www.ballet.co.uk/magazines.

van der Kolk, Hana. "All at Once: Dancing *The Ridge* in New York City Parks." *Contact Quarterly* 32, no. 1 (Winter/Spring 2007): 19–25.

Vargas, Mike. "Looking at Composition Is Like Painting the Golden Gate Bridge: 86 Aspects of Composition." *Contact Quarterly* 28, no. 2 (Summer/Fall 2003): 28–34.

Vermeersch, Petra. "AboutButoh: In Research for Its Origin and Actual Meaning, an Interview with Min Tanaka." *Contact Quarterly* 27, no. 1 (Winter/Spring 2002): 22–33.

Weschler, Lawrence. *Seeing Is Forgetting the Name of the Thing One Sees: A Life of Contemporary Artist Robert Irwin.* Berkeley: University of California Press, 1982.

White, T. H. *The Once and Future King.* New York: G. P. Putnam's Sons, 1965.

Index